ALL THE WAYS
I Found To
Hurt Myself

Volume Two

Alan Gorsuch

Muddy Puddle Press
Lakewood, Washington

All the Ways I Found To Hurt Myself — Volume Two

Muddy Puddle Press
P O Box 97124
Lakewood, WA 98497

First Edition

ISBN: 0-9679704-7-4 (hardcover)
ISBN: 0-9679704-8-2 (softcover)

Cover design: Sands Costner & Associates, Tacoma, WA
Cover Photo: Jolene Lennon

DEDICATED ...

... to my oldest grandson, Ashton, who at age five has already fed me far more than his fair share of leaky half-truths; and I'm being very kind here. Just last week while I was trying to coerce him into finishing his bowlful of nice steamy rutabagas, he told me he wasn't very hungry because for lunch he had eaten "a whole cow!"

And to Logan, my other grandson, who being only two years old doesn't make a great deal of sense yet; but when he does try to talk, he never quite looks you in the eye, nervously shifts from foot to foot — when he's not leaning too far and falling over — and seems to talk out of the corner of his mouth. He's really cute that way and I'm proud to say that his natural general demeanor appears to also lean — much like his aunt, my youngest daughter, and her three older brothers, towards the more questionable, dodgy foibles to be found so intrinsically and intricately woven into even the finest fibers that make up the fabric of the human family.

Especially my family — which, from what I can tell, contains alotta fiber.

— AJG

CONTENTS

FOREWORD

Volume One in this series of stories about absurd behavior
was, as it turns out, the author's unintentional and somewhat
left-handed apology to the educators and school system that he
so severely mistreated. However, because of his youth, the
"brush" that was necessary with which to paint those early
pictures was rather narrow.

In this, *Volume Two* of *All The Ways I Found To Hurt
Myself*, due to the fact that he is, in most cases in most stories,
a little older, the brush is that much broader — thereby enabling him to annoy, irritate, upset *and* entertain ever-widening segments of the population. In doing so, he is able to
create in his readers the much-needed sense of superiority
required in order to laugh: at someone else and his missteps,
misdeeds, and misdemeanant activities. Stories that certainly
were not at all funny — at the time and to the author — years
later when being recounted to an innocently trapped bystander,
colleague, fellow patient or inmate while simply hoping for a
morsel of sympathy, were met with laughter, open derision,
and further ridicule.

Incredulous remarks, such as: "Do you mean to tell me that you actually caught yourself on fire *three times* in one day?! Har! Har! Har! Your kids are right about you! No wonder they never come to visit; you *are* an idiot. Now, tell me another story. No, wait a minute; I have to pee; hand me my catheter; go wash your hands first."

Alotta things are just flat out much funnier if they happen to someone else. By way of illustration: almost everyone can recall watching someone else fall off the dock or out of a boat into the water. When the author was a kid, *nothing* — NOTH-ING — was more hilarious than watching his buddy accidentally back off the dock or slip on the damp clay of the creek bank and then roll down the hill into the cold water of Mill Creek. More laughter would be spawned if his tackle box spilled — funnier yet if he was to roll through a patch of nettles on the way down. Landing face-first rather than feet-first naturally added bonus points to an already over-the-top humorous situation, sending the author into a royal fit of loud uproarious laughter the likes of which he would pay anything to experience today.

On the other hand, the person who rolled down the muddy bank through stinging nettles while losing half his fishing tackle then fell into the icy water did NOT see it that way. He quite understandably failed to recognize the hilarity of it all — an indication that humor itself is not only elusive, it is a very relative thing.

Alan learned over the years that, although he may not be too clever and didn't, through the telling of many of his stories, warrant any real sympathy, his anecdotes, reconstructed events (of course all names have been changed), and tales of personal woe were enough to distract the listener from watching that damn television for a moment or two. "Your trailer came unhitched *seven* different times and rolled off into the sagebrush and swamps of *seven* different states, yet you *never did* buy a trailer hitch ball the right size? How have you managed to live *this* long? And stop waving that butter knife around like that; you're gonna put somebody's … *owww!*"

As you read *Volume Two*, enjoy your smug superiority, created willfully at the expense of the author. But be careful, because you may quite likely see *yourself* in some of Alan's stories. And if you do, you probably shouldn't tell anybody else, especially your kids. Or your insurance agent.

Two more things: the author wanted me to let you know that as far as he's concerned, if it wasn't for sarcasm, almost nothing would be funny. And lastly, sometimes he writes about himself in the third person — says it's the only way he can "cope."

… ummm … a friend

1

GO GET ALAN

I am compelled to refer to large chunks of my life spent on the threshold of eternity as: The Woollett Chronicles. A good percentage of the scars on my body have one thing in common with each other: most of them were derived from a single source, the Woollett's — Budd, Lonnie, and Danny.

Almost ritualistic in regularity, the Woollett males configured into many a formula, always with similar results: bruised and damaged torso, bent digits, punctured or lacerated epidermis, limp limbs, lumpy frontal and temporal lobes. Always mine.

Whether impalements, contusions, abrasions, explosions, garfs, bites or scorchings, one of the three Woolletts nearly always would be there. Like an antithesis of the three Musketeers, the hue and cry was not "One for all and all for one," it was more like, "Let's go find Alan and try to kill him."

Still, I would somehow quickly forget the previous incident along with the associated pain, and soon reappear as if to say, "I've already mended from that last fall; you guys have any large explosives layin' around?"

For the most part, Lonnie was the most willing and the first to regularly — all in good fun of course — arrange circumstances in an attempt "inadvertently" to end my life. Lonnie's seemingly purposeful attempts were followed by Danny's less deliberate but far more frequent tries. On special occasions Danny colluded with their dad, Budd Woollett who was head of this dynasty of deadliness.

Admittedly, I shared the complicity regarding the many near deaths and periodic mishandlings of my physical future. I was a willing collaborator, cheerfully teaming up with *all* the Woolletts in order to exterminate or, at the very least, regularly disfigure myself. Happily and often, I handed myself over for sacrifice — so that we could all have a little fun.

They would ply me with promises of excitement, a good time and maybe a meal at the spacious Woollett home on the south end of Long Lake. And they were usually generous enough to drop off my abraded, smoldering, blistered, and scabby self back at my place at day's end. That is, if I was conscious and ambulatory to the point of not requiring much help back into my house. Then too, if I had fallen into the rosebushes in the dark — without even Danny or Lonnie there to see it, I would have suffered needless and mundane blood-shed. Under better lighting my plight would have evoked yet more mirth and merriment, in which case, my suffering wouldn't have been wasteful or mundane.

I don't recall ever spending a night in the Woollett house. Sleeping on their dock or down at lake's edge, yes. But inside at night? No. Eileen Woollett, the family matriarch, was smarter than that. Those doors were locked at night. Something about not enough insurance to cover them if I spent the night without military supervision; also how there wouldn't be any food left by the next morning.

Becoming Lonnie's protégé was easy at first. He was four years older, had a car, was charming and charismatic, fast-talking and bloodthirsty. He knew I was not the keenest knife in the drawer. Capitalizing on that, he would haul me off on what he called "quests." Lonnie operated in a similar fashion to my diabolical old bicycle, Sherman, with an insinuation of adventure, laughter, and good cheer.

In fact, Lonnie was aware of my relationship with my, by now, long-gone bike. He was only too aware of my penchant for brinkmanship, with my physical soundness the only item teetering on the brink. But when he said he would buy me a burger at King's drive-in on Capitol Lake in downtown Olympia afterward — if I lived — I said, "Okay!"

The evening before, Danny had phoned Lonnie, asking for his bike to be delivered to Lon Ritchie's house on Tempo Lake near Tenino, where Danny had spent Saturday night with the Ritchie family. Normally Lonnie wouldn't do a damn thing to help his eight-year-younger brother, but this was different. This situation appeared to hold some promise.

"I'll phone Alan," Lonnie said to himself. "He's probably healed sufficiently since that small boat fire by now, and Alan likes to do things on bikes. Heh, heh, heh," he probably added, while twirling his imaginary Snidely Whiplash mustache.

"Danny really needs his ten-speed," bemoaned the out-of-character Lonnie to Alan at seven o'clock on a foggy October Sunday morning.

"What do you care?" I asked, my earlier lessons in cynicism relative to Lonnie's being interested in almost nothing other than himself not easily forgotten. "Since when do you care about Danny or his bike?" Lonnie knew that I was aware that he had run Danny down twice the week before, sending bike and rider screaming into the salal-filled ditch at nearby

Carpenter's Park. "And didn't you *accidentally* back over Danny's bike in your parents' driveway a few days ago?"

"He got a new one." The Woolletts weren't exactly on State aid.

Upon Lonnie's mention of King's Drive-in and a burger, along with the opportunity to escape from Lacey into the thriving metropolis of downtown Olympia, I relented. He had not hinted of the strong possibility that I might lose my life while earning my burger; if he had, I would no doubt have agreed sooner.

Snidely Whiplash pulled into Dudley Doright's driveway about seven-thirty that same morning. Lonnie had a shiny new candy-apple-red Corvair Monza Spyder. As I left the house, my mom demanded to know where I was going, "at this hour on a Sunday?"

"Danny needs help," was my answer.

"They all do," referring to the Woollett males and snorting at her own joke. "Didja change your bandages?" She was alluding to my latest injury.

"It's too late; they've already healed into the wound. They probably won't come loose until the next time I fall into the lake or something."

She squinted and then said through her cigarette smoke, "That should be about two o'clock today, being as how it's October and all," snorteling again.

On the drive over to the Woollett Estate, Lonnie told me why my help was required, explaining that the ten-speed wouldn't fit into his little car — soooo … he was gonna tow me the fifteen foggy miles to Tempo Lake.

"With what?"

"This old telephone cable," dragging out from the woodshed a coil of thick black insulated phone cable that appeared to uncoil to a length of a quarter mile. His usual sadistic smile

4

was enough to satisfy my masochistic cravings, so I followed destructions … I mean, instructions.

"Nothin' to it," he said, a term I eventually learned to be interchangeable with "Your hair's on fire" or "How do we get in contact with your next of kin?"

I held the bike upright by the handlebars while Lonnie hooked us together. "We'll just tie the cable to the front forks, right here, and we'll snug this end up to the car shackle right there, and we're ready to roll," he chortled, bubbling over with carnal anticipation.

I looked through the eight o'clock fog to see if there was blood on the moon. The faint luminary I saw through the lifting fog was not the moon, but the sun. Although it appeared to be dim, I suspected it was a hell of a lot brighter than I was. As it turned out, *my* fog wouldn't lift until later, when we were a mile or so down the road.

"I'll drive ahead real slow to pick up the slack," which he did, stopping about one hundred yards ahead of me. By this time I had mounted the ten-speed and I tried not to notice that a dull fearful awareness was also slowly mounting within myself.

Lonnie was standing next to his shiny red Corvair. Between us, the cable was drooping to the ground from its own weight, otherwise taut between the two tie-off points. Lonnie waited. The red Corvair and Danny's red ten-speed waited. The weighted cable waited. Lonnie climbed in. Slowly he drew the cable tight and I began to roll, just as he had said. Earlier he had also said to be sure to give him instructions regarding our speed — similar to our water-skiing laps around the lake, before the wooden speed craft had caught fire, and before the steering cables had come off, and before the run-about had rammed the dock and sank — thumbs up meant "go faster" and thumbs down, "go slower."

5

I had already told him to go very slow at first so that my brain, as well as my reflexes, along with my fear, could adjust to this new method of travel: travel by tow. Or better said, "travel by twang," by the time the fog would lift, the dust would clear and the grinding of metal would cease.

Lonnie crept slowly along, with me, being as cautious as I could under the circumstances, trailing behind him. I held my grip on the handbrakes to keep the cable taut. When I felt sure Lonnie had me in his mirror completely, I thumbed him up a notch. I could see his sadistic smile glistening in the mirror. I thumbed him up another notch; Dudley Doright didn't want to disappoint Snidely, and Snidely Whiplash was only too happy to oblige. He nudged the gas pedal.

By the time we approached the stop sign near Carpenter's Park and Marvin Road, we were sailing along nicely. We had maintained a respectable twenty to maybe twenty-five mph, with no thumbs down. Confidence was creeping in on me and taking over, like the endemic disease it often proves itself to be among so many otherwise healthy adolescent males. Lonnie deftly curved wide to the right at the stop sign, not stopping; I, of course, soon did the same thing. No traffic, no wobbles, no careening, and no bouncing.

I had earlier assumed the bike would probably come apart, with the front forks diving into asphalt, and me following suit. I thought that's what bikes did. But not so: Danny's bike was a thoroughbred, not a nasty homicidal mongrel like Sherman, my old army bike.

Falsely assuring myself that the whole fifteen miles would go as smoothly as the first mile, I thumbed us up to what seemed to be one-hundred-forty mph. But it was probably closer to thirty-five or forty.

The sleek red Schwinn Arrow I rode behind the shiny red Spyder, was silent as well as swift. I could scarcely hear the skinny tires whirring on the pavement beneath me. However, the confidence I was reveling in would prove to be brief and unwarranted. But for now, all of me had grown sure of my ride. Except for my thumbs.

My thumbs, although embarrassingly short, evidently were trying to prove that they had more sense than I did, because they were, unknowingly to me, maintaining a death grip on the handbrakes. My thumbs had instinctively opposed the other four fingers of each hand; in fact they had essentially opposed the whole idea. My thumbs had been afraid and were squeezing the life out of the handbrakes the entire time. The rest of me was unaware of this, as unaware of the fact that by then I had completely burned them out and was without ANY brakes! In the next few minutes, the new knowledge of brakelessness, and what my chickenshit opposable thumbs had been up to would be made very clear.

Still confident and ignorant of the fact that my spineless thumbs had burnt the handbrakes to a crisp memory, I suddenly remembered the crisp s-curves over the upcoming railroad tracks. Less than a quarter mile ahead were the double tracks — and doubtless death! Marvin Road curved in a serpentine squiggle over the abrupt and very teeth-jarring multiple sets of tracks. Maneuvering at this speed, those tracks would be impossible.

By that time, Lonnie had lost interest in the rear view mirror and was playing with his radio. He appeared as if he was oblivious to the snake that lay over the railroad crossing ahead of us. Snidely Whiplash roared on toward the tracks; Dudley Doright could do little other than holler a lot and extend one arm with a frantic and very fearful thumb down. Dudley's arm and cowardly thumb were moving up and down faster than my mom's Singer sewing machine at full throttle. Dudley kept screaming.

Now, I realize that sweet little Nell is the one who's supposed to do all the screaming for help while tied to the railroad track of an oncoming locomotive. I didn't care about Nell; I cared about Alan. Lonnie's motive was entertainment; by this time, I realized I was loco; I could see the headlines, "Death on the Railroad Tracks; No Train Involved."

Snidely eventually saw the tracks, registered the curves, and remembered the abruptly placed rails and timbers, while at the same time he saw my sewing machine thumb stitching panic into the air. Behind my oscillating arm and hand, he probably also registered the fear plastered all over my face. The obvious panic had spread from my thumbs to my every fiber. Fear had replaced the useless, and usually harmful, confidence I had so briefly entertained.

Finally! Lonnie slammed on the brakes and the Monza Spyder screeched to a standstill. Relieved, I gripped both handbrakes — also to stop. But not only was the red Schwinn Arrow without brakes — the melted brake pads didn't even make noise. Silently and swiftly, the red Arrow flew towards the Spyder's butt.

Realizing now that the brakes were gone and that he was about to perform an awkward and quite unnatural act with a large red metal Spyder, Dudley suddenly remembered his thumb. Again with the erratic stitching motion — thumb UP! Snidley's eyes grew wide and white in the mirror as he saw the red Arrow and the one hundred thirty-pound Dudley Dunderhead streaking towards his new car! Snidely stepped on it, and the Spyder squealed ahead, making, as it did so, a sound similar to Dudley, who hadn't stopped squealing for the last quartermile.

As the Corvair lurches forward, Dudley feels a momentary twinge of reprieve from kissing the Spyder's ass. He stops squealing as the Spyder speeds away. It is then that he sees the phone cable lying limp and idle on the road beside him while he continues forward. He has passed the slack cable — about a hundred feet of it — and now the speeding Spyder is gobbling it up again, the way that only spiders can. Snidley Whiplash is racing toward the s-curves while Dudley is watching the cable snake away from behind and beside him.

Futilely trying once again to thumb-down the wide-eyed driver in front of him, Dudley Dipshit emits a high-pitched final exhalation as the cable that Snidely's Spyder snatched whiplashes into a frenzied activity. When the cable snaps taut again, the bike and rider shoot forth from the previous coasting speed to the new whip-cracking rocket speed, and my ears seem to be left behind, along with what may have been a loud sonic snap — the sound a whip-end makes when breaking the sound barrier. Perhaps it is Dudley's neck, which was now somewhat elongated.

Lonnie immediately realized his whiplash error and attempted to correct it by being, once again, stationary. Whereupon, Alan was once more sizzling straight at the now-stopped Spyder. By the time he connected, Alan and the bike had separated. The red riderless Schwinn went under the Corvair Spyder and its rider went well above and way beyond.

I ended up, over and past the car, beyond the ditch, and up on the hill above the ditch. My pants were torn at the calf from the barbed wire fence. Otherwise not a scratch. The bike, which was only slightly tweaked, actually then did fit into the car. The Monza was undamaged. We laughed; I got my burger. Danny wanted to know what happened to his bike and why it had no brakes. We told him we didn't know.

I told my mom a dog attacked me and tore my pants.

Although Budd Woollett had not witnessed this Spyder-lashing cable twanging, he would beg me to retell him the story. Each time I did so, he laughed so hard the bib on his overalls was wet from his tears by the end of the story. I loved to make Budd laugh.

2

THE WAR MACHINE

W hen Danny Woollett had grown old enough to discover the mystery of fire and the magical properties it held, he may have been about six months old. I didn't know the Woolletts then, but I listened to stories of Danny's early arson career.

At some point in Danny's life, he had apparently set fire to almost everything the family owned. His flaming career was still in full swing when I began spending time around the Woollett home. Fortunately I never was present when the large trees outside, along with his tree fort, other outbuildings, furniture or vehicles in the driveway were sent up in flames. Had I been anywhere in the vicinity, I just know I would have been blamed. That's the way it's always been with me; if there's a fire somewhere, "Alan must be nearby!" I had already dealt with my own issues regarding sudden inexplicable eruptions of flames.

Truthfully, I think that was another reason the Woolletts kept me around — to blame. They acted as if they felt sorry for me, but in reality I was nothing more than their alibi, scapegoat, slow-moving target. Lonnie especially. Lonnie would always point the finger at me; half the time I didn't even know what the infraction was. The food was darn good around there, so I accepted taking the blame.

The year I graduated from high school, I was even blamed, through some abstract reasoning, for Lonnie's nearly getting his girlfriend pregnant; I am still trying to figure out that one. *Her mom* came over to my apartment and explained to me some vague gibberish about how it was somehow all my fault. Not only did I not fully understand the charges nor what she was actually talking about, I told her I wasn't even sure myself about how to do it. But she demanded an apology, which for some inexplicable reason, I amazingly gave her, primarily, I think, to get her off my back. What I really wanted to do was ask her for one of the other daughters that she kept at home so that I could figure this whole thing out for myself, first hand. Give me something to apologize for. Help me clear up the mystery — and possibly my acne. Back then though, except on a superficially social level, for the most part, I kept away from everybody's daughters; I didn't play with fire.

But Danny did. Danny played with fire on a regular basis. Then one day he didn't. His mom had held a book of burning matches under his fingers. He screamed; his fingers blistered. Never again did Danny set any fires. Imagine what would happen today if word got out you barbecued your kid's fingertips; never mind the fact that it instantly cured his pyromania and no doubt saved the lives of the family, neighbors, and pets. Cruel but effective. I wouldn't think her method would work in all cases but as far as fire was concerned, it worked on Danny. After that, Danny moved right on up into explosives.

One summer in particular there seemed to be an abundance of gunpowder at the Woollett place; it appeared to be everywhere we looked. I think Budd might have hijacked a Fort Lewis ordnance truck or something, or maybe he just traded a recent plumbing job for half the firecrackers in Thurston

County; he loved to barter and trade. *"Woollett Plumbing —
Don't fret call Woollett!"* the company name and slogan. Big
firecrackers. Lots of Roman candles. Glorious opportunity.
And, because of Budd's plumbing business, there were also
pipes and metal stuff all over the place. *"Let's make a cannon!"*

We found a pair of old iron-spoke wheels and connected
them to a suitable axle. We had piles of galvanized pipe from
which to select a proportionate barrel. With the barrel connected onto the axle, we then drilled a small hole in the pipe's
end cap. Next, we threaded it on with a large red salute's fuse
sticking out the back end.

What we then had was a cool and crusty old civil-war
vintage-type rolling war-machine. A declaration of a full-scale
all-out martial attack was made on the lake.

Our bastion cannon stood proud, high up on the hillside
plateau overlooking Long Lake, facing the water. We packed
gravel into the business end, lit the fuse and hid. Cannoneer
and fusilier both took cover behind the large trees on the hill.
Fully expecting our cannon to fly apart like most things we
constructed, we cringed, anticipating that shrapnel would rain
down on us. Soon — BOOM!

After the explosion, we looked around the round corners
of our respective tree trunks. Our cannon was fine. From
where we stood, no splits could be seen, and no bulges; but
what about the rocks? Watching the lake below, we saw not a
ripple. Then, after a couple more seconds, we could just barely
see a patch of small splashes way across the lake, over half the
width of the lake itself. Danny and I exchanged wide-eyed
victorious open-mouthed glances. *Superior armaments are in
our quarter! Attack! Attack!*

Continued bombardments of the sturdy and stubborn lake
went on for a couple hours. The lake refused to surrender. We

gradually grew weary in our attempt to conquer this boneheaded lake; besides, how do you take a lake prisoner of war? The logistics were just out of the question. We decided we needed more excitement; we got it by upping the ante. Our next decision was that we wanted to see our cannon roll-and fire at the same time.

Lighting our cannon's fuse and rolling it down the grassy knoll above the lake was our next move; we needed mobile artillery, and escalation of armaments became the order of the day. Sending a loaded cannon with lit fuse charging down the gentle slope was inspiring; anticipating the roar of cannon and projectiles wailing toward an imaginary foe, breathtaking.

What was even more breathtaking was having our own artillery turn on us.

From the very first mobilized attempt of cannonry to when we eventually surrendered to our imaginary enemy, our guns were turned against us. Literally.

Initially our cannon-rolling, fire-at-will, downhill charge looked feasible. However, after advancing ten or twelve rolling feet into its charge, the cannon muzzle fell forward. Whereupon after the mouth of the muzzle dug into a clump of moss, the carriage and wheels somersaulted over. The entire rig then flipped back onto its wheels with the barrel's end facing the other direction — ours. The iron wheels no longer could roll downhill because the fuse end was anchored in the grass and the cannon was taking aim. We breathlessly stared into the hungry muzzle as the mythical foe cried, "Fire!" Danny and I clung to each other. Well, we weren't actually *clinging to each other,* at least not in the resigned expectation of those about to die, as in the final embrace of what might be considered mutual and normal foxhole brotherhood fashion. No, Danny and I each were trying to throw the other into the cannon's blaze to save one's self. Nevertheless, we were mowed down like tender tall grass in the reaper's scythe.

When we were done rubbing the painful purple spots on our bare legs and shins, we reloaded. After discussing what we had done wrong, we concurred; don't barrel the iron hellhorse so hard next time; it loses control and tips forward. And for god's sake, don't stand in that same spot if it does. Find a place out of the line of fire! Again we packed the gravel, lit the fuse, and sent the cannon roaring into battle.

Again we stared into the traitorous mouth of sulfur — more purple blotches on our ranks' flanks.

There we were, out in the open with no trees to hide behind. And no matter where we ran after ignition and mobilization, that cannon would find us. The only things to hide behind on our grassy knoll were each other — and that wasn't even working because we were both too damn skinny. Not once did that blasted cannon not flip over, take aim, and fire crushed gravel at us! Now, this was not a simple case of accident caused by faulty munitions, nor could it be considered friendly fire. Clearly our double-crossing sabotaging heavy artillery had gone over to the other side. Substantial losses and heavy casualties were being sustained by our foot soldiers. Unable to communicate with Intelligence because of a huge understaffing problem at what could be called headquarters — or possible desertion on the part of any intelligence — infantry pressed on, ignorantly, dutifully, and courageously.

Eventually though, some relief was afforded half our ranks. We finally figured out that if we split up after igniting the fuse and nudging the war wagon forward, it could not possibly get us both.

We were right. It thereafter avoided Danny and always — always — swiveled around to fire jagged rocks — only at me. Finally, a cease-fire and retreat were ordered.

The next day, although quite likely we'd've been categorically deemed mentally unfit for active duty, we reappeared to do battle, and this time we agreed to take no chances on the grass and mossy knoll of defeat. Losing every skirmish to a fictitious enemy was demoralizing, so we decided that we should fire across the lake — from the dock's surface. No grass or clumps of moss to cause us lumps.

Just like the day before, although obviously still cut off from all measurable and meaningful intelligence, we lit and rolled the iron war machine into action.

Just like the day before, the barrel fell forward, and the miniature contraption of devastation tipped down, dug into a crack between the dock planks, flipped over and drew a bead on the quivering infantry — and fired.

Just like the day before, heavy casualties were again inflicted on the wavering lines of militia who wished they had not enlisted. But stubbornly they stood their ground, holding firm the small corner of the floating battlefield which they had so bravely earned. Valiantly on they fought, desertion never entering their feeble minds — the courageous but simple fools they were.

Just as the day before, this battle of the dock roared on until nearly dark, when again a cease-fire was called.

Then, just at dusk, when the mosquitoes were coming out to feed on the dead and wounded, we heard the motors of small watercraft fire up. It seemed the raging battle on the dock had attracted several fishermen in small boats. When we had thrown in the towel for the day, they pulled on their little Evinrudes and Johnsons, and moments later, shaking their heads in amazement, admiration — or disbelief — they putted away.

That our cannon was not to be trusted, we agreed; it was indeed a loose cannon. And it had made us look like idiots in front of all the bored fishermen that had witnessed our useless warmongering. A truce was declared on the lake. Full-scale naval warfare was to be next.

The following day we took the Woollett's rowboat out to Unnamed Island — a tiny uninhabited mass of land in the south section of the lake. Thick tall trees cover the small island. Knowing that our double-dealing cannon was out of hand, we agreed to take to the trees, cannon *in* hand. Those fishermen, who had laughed at us over our two-day running battle with our own war machine, were now our foremost enemy.

I vowed not to let that evil tool of destruction out of my grasp. I climbed a tall leafy alder. I loaded up, confident after two days of constant firing, that this was a stalwart mechanical device of desolation and would not burst. I lit the fuse.

Shortly after the initial volley, small circular ripples appeared around the enemy rowboat way out across the silver water. The occupant pulled the cord and chugged off, shaking his fist in defiance — a meaningless empty gesture — while on the run.

Adjusting my perch in the alder, I drew down on another one. Again I held the ultimate weapon in my lap as I balanced across the branches. I packed the gravel, lit the fuse, and adjusted the pitch and elevation.

The cannon discharged its load of rocks — and me — at the same time. The concussion and recoil tipped me off my sniper nest in the tree. I vaguely remember throwing the cannon off my chest as I plummeted earthward, backwards.

My story ends there, as I am unable to write about that which I have no recollection. Apparently I did not die.

A nd kids, a short note on the dangers of Roman candles: If you should ever choose to light Roman candles and chase one another around while spewing fireballs at each other's faces, mind this: never wear a long-sleeve shirt.

Roman candles are constructed to operate *vertically*. If you aim a Roman candle at a target such as a sibling, close friend, or inebriated relative, a *nearly horizontal* position of the candle is required — unless your quarry is up in a tree or on a rooftop, or possibly still airborne from an earlier explosion.

While chasing your opponent, victim, or elderly neighbor down the road and launching periodic colored balls of fire in their direction — be careful. If you had read the warnings on the Roman candle, you would already be aware of the fact that you have ignored them. Chances are that if you are the type of person to point flaming, exploding fire-sticks at others in the first place, you are illiterate. In which case you are excused. It's society's fault for not teaching you how to read. Go to your mailbox and wait for the arrival of your first monthly check. Because of the necessity to thunder the whirling balls of brimstone horizontally, the cardboard cannon in your hand is burning in an irregular fashion; fire is now traveling horizontally inside the cardboard tube — towards the other end — yours.

Possibly the pyro-technicians, or the Romans who apparently invented this tube of glorious hellfire, overlooked the possibility of its inevitable use in this fashion. In which case, the scorch marks you are about to receive are not your fault. Sue the manufacturer. Then go to your mailbox and wait for the arrival of your check.

If you are shirtless, the backfiring brightly-colored great balls of fire will simply bounce off your chest, arm, face and forehead; so the scorching will only be momentary and not too severe. However, if you are wearing a long-sleeve shirt, you will have a lasting and memorable injury to show your children and grandchildren — should society allow you to procreate, which would be quite inadvisable on their part and, to be brutally honest, could border on negligence, leading to yet another check headed your way. The whirling ball of molten pain will be trapped inside your sleeve and travel rapidly up to your armpit, where it will lodge. Hair will never grow in that spot. I suggest you switch hands at this point for the purpose of acquiring matching hairless armpits. There will be fewer questions to answer should you survive into adulthood. Which, by the way, is unlikely.

The shirt manufacturers should have foreseen the possibility of this very situation. They chose to ignore the dangers lurking in their shirts. They are therefore legally culpable and should be more than willing to compensate you for your pain and suffering.

Go sit by your mailbox and wait ….

ALL THE WAYS I FOUND TO HURT MYSELF

3

SLEEPING WITH PUNKS

S leeping with punks is inadvisable. Many the woeful maiden has a sad tale to tell. I too have a sorry short tale. Mine involves a punk and a sleeping bag; I slept with a punk.

If you are expecting to hear a sordid story of the Michael Jackson sleepover variety, you are about to be disappointed. If you are expecting anything of a twisted and sexually deviated variety, you will also be disappointed. If, however, you are expecting to learn of a humorous anecdote from the past life of a healthy red-blooded fifteen-year-old, you're probably going to be likewise disappointed.

Years ago, punks, other than the street vernacular variety, were to be found on nearly every busy intersection immediately prior to and on July Fourth. After that, they disappeared until the next Fourth of July build-up.

Street punks, on the other hand, are presently found on every street corner in America year round. They loiter about, trying to remain on their feet while entangling themselves in their sagging pants draped around their knees. There they wait for the local tattoo parlors to open while busying themselves throwing fast food wrappers in every direction.

Wearing huge clown-like drooping pants with what appears to be a bushel of potatoes dragging them earthward, baseball hats on sideways, and hair six different colors, they surround themselves with discarded McDonald's bags and wrappers, paper drink buckets and French fat scoops — all with the grinning face of Ronald McDonald on them — except for the punks in the clown pants. These punks don't smile like Ronald. They all frown as if they've been cheated out of something, like maybe their brains.

Professional American clowns are all presently unemployed. Who would want to hire an old-fashioned clown when every idiot kid in the neighborhood looks like one? These kids and their asinine phenomenon have put most real clowns out of business. What will professional clowns do to counteract this epidemic idiocy? No doubt they will have to start wearing really tight pants in order to separate themselves from the street bozos.

To get back to the punks of which I speak, the ones from back in olden times — the 1950s — these were the punks that were given out whenever fireworks were purchased. They were thin sticks resembling a corn dog with an eating disorder — only one-fourth-inch thick or so and maybe a foot long. Made of pressed sawdust, they burn slowly, like a teeny-weenie Presto-log. They were used to ignite fireworks. Or hair. Or insects. Or the whole neighborhood.

Lonnie Woollett was a punk too.

Danny and I had decided Lonnie was out of line when he threw our newly constructed downhill soapbox type racer into the lake. Danny had recently set fire to something Lonnie cherished (his bed I think) and although Lonnie had nearly slept through it, he awoke when Budd turned the hose on him through the bedroom window. Danny had cleverly placed a cigarette package wrapper next to Lonnie as he slept so that their father, Budd, would think Lonnie had fallen asleep while smoking in bed. Lonnie never smoked, but Danny usually planted enough evidence around Lonnie that he appeared to secretly smoke about three packs a day.

Evidently Lonnie still harbored some ill will towards his little brother, so he threw the "Hoo-Ha" into the lake. That was the name of our downhill racer, the "Hoo-Ha." It was so named because of our studying the latest issues of MAD Magazine where the term was used in abundance. And I still don't know what it means. Anyway, Lonnie had come home quite late the night before after one of his near impregnancies, and he pitched a fit right after he fell over our little wooden car — the one he subsequently took down to the lake and pitched into the water.

So now he was a punk.

Now we still had our cannon, although it hadn't been pressed into service for some time. It was well maintained, along with all the rest of our munitions depot ordnance. We would lie in wait.

We went out of our way to let Lonnie know that we'd be sleeping down at the lake that particular night. We were quite sure that Lonnie would try to roll a log down the hill to crush us. Or that he would turn the sprinkler on us, or some other dastardly act of defiance and retaliation, such as driving wooden stakes through our hearts while we slept. Once again, I clutched our cannon of questionable allegiance close to my chest; one loose cannon in my sleeping bag was enough. Then I lit one of those punk sticks and determined to stay awake and be ready for his onslaught.

Lonnie's near impregnancies practice could take hours sometimes; I figured anybody who practiced as much as Lonnie did should be much faster at it by now. I thought that he should have been able to streamline it to take less time.

Recently, while writing this, I had a brief discussion with my wife Cheryl over this very topic. Already aware of my thoughts on things that take too long and people who dawdle, she just glared at me. After announcing she was going shopping, she said something that I thought odd. She said the same thing that Mrs. Baughman, my high school composition teacher, had said to me over forty years earlier: "Write about what you know." As the door closed, I heard my wife murmur something about my cannon and how I didn't know anything about fireworks. Then she said some inaudible stuff that ended with "fizzle" and "dud." I doubt if I ever will understand that woman.

My cannon was pointed up the mossy mound. We knew that at any moment Lonnie could begin his nocturnal charge. I kept the slow-burning punk inside my sleeping bag to hide the glowing red tip burning in the ink of night. The cannon was charged and loaded with rocks.

We listened for hours for Lonnie's loud 1958 Volkswagen, "Der Elf." (This was back when many people thought it necessary to name their cars.) Some nights he would come home extremely irritable. He was therefore unpredictable — much like world affairs today, and possibly for all the same reasons.

After burning two or three baby Presto logs away, my head was swimming and my eyeballs felt as if they were two glowing red coals, a condition caused by the noxious and probably toxic fumes. Danny had been snoring for some time when I lit the last punk and burrowed back into my little smokehouse.

We don't know when Lonnie came home. He had forgotten all about us anyhow. In the cold light of morning I discovered the newly burned hole in my sleeping bag; it was about a foot in diameter. I still bear the scar on my belly where I burrowed the little corn dog into my flesh, although I somehow slept through it. The vapors had helped me into a deep sleep. How it is that I didn't hit the cannon's fuse with the lit punk as I slept, I know not. People had always said that I had rocks in my head, but that was the closest I ever came to proving it — by installing them there, myself.

Eventually, Danny woke me up for pancakes. I went into one of the six spacious Woollett bathrooms to wash off the ashes and use some of the Brylcream they kept in the medicine cabinet. That was the morning that I smeared Gleem toothpaste into my hair.

I urge young people everywhere: Do not go to bed with punks – unless you have rocks in your head. And climbing in just to get your rocks off is not a good idea; someone's bound to get burned. Don't lose your head when messing around with a cannon! Don't smoke! And pull your pants up!

4

THE HOO-HA

The Hoo-Ha was one of those projects that Danny and I could have spent more time on in the planning stages. We also should have spent more time in the construction phase.

We spent very little time on the Hoo-Ha itself; we spent a scant amount of time riding it. I'm able to say that mainly because most of the time it was ejecting us into either the hillside or the gravel or toward the lake. It did this mainly because of a loose front axle and the associated poor steering, a separated wheel, broken rear axle or a disintegrating chassis. Any or all of these things would happen, mainly because we never finished whatever we started.

I am using the word "mainly" a lot. I am doing that mainly because of the Mad Magazine writers. *Mainly* was its main word back then. Once you saw the word *mainly* in the written text, you knew the punch line was next. *Mainly* was a favorite word. I don't have a favorite word. I don't have a favorite anything. But if I did have a favorite word, it would probably be "membrane." I like that word. Don't know why. *Membrane.*

We always got distracted and forgot to tighten our nuts. (Now that I'm old and forgetful, it's happening again, and with an ever-increasing regularity.) Halfway down the hill, the Hoo-Ha would fly apart and, as I said, mainly because we hadn't diligently finished wrenching our nuts down. And that was partially due to the fact that we never had a wrench that fit. We had already lost most of Budd's tools in the grass. Soon they would be located by the lawnmower; we knew that. But we couldn't wait for the next time Lonnie mowed the lawn, which could be forever, so we had to make do by cinching up the nuts with a pipe wrench, hammer, or a rock. But it was never a cinch; our nuts would soon jiggle loose and then everything would rattle apart.

We used nails whenever we could. Big nails. We chose nails for our assembly technique after a while because we agreed they left cooler scars — and I have some beauts, nice long ones on my backside hamstring area. They run up and down my leg, three or four inches. Over the years they have appeared to crisscross and mingle with other less nostalgic and less poignant manglings. (Whenever I fall asleep at a lawn or pool party, face down, I awake to find that the neighborhood kids have been playing tic-tac-toe on my backsides.)

Had we cut off the nails, covered them, or even bent them over after driving them up through the seat of our vehicle, there would have been no impalements. And no scars. What would be the point of that? Sometimes we did actually bend them over, but we bent them with the points *facing* us instead of the direction of our ejection.

Seldom did we make the long curve around the edge of the hill all the way to the lake. Usually we were projectiles spit out from the open cockpit of the wooden rattletrap. On a few special occasions, even after we'd crashed into the hillside or sailed over the cliff, we stayed put, connected to the Hoo-Ha by nails in our flesh. There would always be a small flotilla of fishermen in boats gathered out past the dock, watching, while pretending to fish.

After some of the stuff we did together as kids, one would think that decades later, as an adult, Danny would have refused to go on long road trips with me. But that wasn't the case. Danny agreed to participate in some of the most bizarre, nail biting, nut wrenching, cross-country road trips imaginable. Not because he was stupid; Danny was smart. By the time some of our trips were over, he was considerably smarter than when we had left. I think Danny went on those excursions with me because of the opportunity for abstract adventure and a chance to meet people even stranger than we were, as well as to get some cool new scars. Mainly.

My apologies to Alfred E. Neumann.

5

BUDD'S BEANS

These chronicles are not in order; few things are in my life. They are not neatly catalogued and chronologi cally arranged. Some are chronicled in the order of their occurrence, but most others are not. Please do not be alarmed by incongruency or time frame differences. It's just the way it is. I think maybe it's a medical condition I seem to have, and I'm currently seeking the correct corresponding pharmaceuticals for my condition. They have a pill for every- thing. They don't have a name as yet for my condition, but I'm sure they'll have a pill waiting for it once it's achieved medi- cal pedigree by having a Latin-sounding name given to it.

Juxtascramblopia! That's probably a good name for what I've got. Juxtascramblopia, and I think I suffer horribly. Judging from how many drugstores are being built, one on every other block in my area, help is surely on the way. I hope it arrives soon, because now that I'm able to partially diagnose the problem, I'm afraid my condition is growing chronic; I fear I may be fading fast. Everything is a jumble. My mind is scrambled. The harder I think about things, to try to figure out stuff, the worse it gets.

Budd Woollett played a significant part in my teenage life and most of my twenties. It was Budd who first allowed me to integrate myself into their household. He would "let" me work for him.

Budd would "let" me go with him on plumbing jobs. He would "let" me truckle around behind him carrying his 400-pound toolbox. I was the tiny teenage toady who trundled a quarter ton of tools up and down stairs, under houses, to sinks, toilets, pee traps and blown water heaters. I cleaned up after him. I threaded iron pipe; I sweated copper; I pounded oakum and poured hot lead sideways while lying on my back — in the darkness while underneath old houses — to rejoin nasty old cast iron sewer-pipe fittings. I bored holes. And it was my job to keep Budd awake on long drives from job to job. I did all that and more. And for what?

A chickenskin sandwich. He "let" me do all that stuff for a chickenskin sandwich. Once in a while he would give me one of his sweet pickle and onion sandwiches. At the end of the week he'd hand me a few beans in the form of currency.

Primarily, I went with Budd whenever he'd "let" me, just to listen to the thousands of stories he had stored up abundantly from his past. Endless stories. Stories of the old days, the never forgotten Great Depression, and stories from his youth. He told so many stories I just knew after a while that he must be making them up, at least some of them. He had to be. Nobody could have had that many stories. Not in one lifetime. Warehouses full. Storage lockers, silos, steamer trunks, and barnsful of stories. Stories from childhood, young adulthood, old jobs, paper routes, and you name it. It got to the point that all I had to do was randomly point at any old house or building almost anywhere in Thurston County, ask him for a corresponding story and he would begin.

"Oh yeah, that's where old lady Saucepucker lived, back in thirty-eight, I stole one of her chickens and she …."

"How 'bout that house over there, the one with the cords of wood stacked up all over the side yard?"

"The Krinklesworth family used to own that; 'course, they're all gone now. An old lady lives there right now, probl'y in her seventies. I know, 'cause her wood's all rotten — her firewood — about twelve cords of rotten firewood. She's afraid of not having enough, so she's storing it up, not using it. She's afraid of not having enough money to stay warm. Boy, I'm tellin' ya, Alan, the Depression was somethin' yer not likely to forget."

Then he'd go on about how good everybody my age had it and how, when he was young, he was out earning a living for his whole extended family — when he was about eighteen months old. By the time he was five years old, he'd owned his own business for seven years, to hear him talk.

"How 'bout that one there, the old brick one?"

"I was hoping you'd ask me about that one. That's where Randy Puddlesnarf lived, before they hauled him off to jail, something about a goat."

And so it would go. Nearly everywhere we went, I would point and ask. Budd would thumb through his mental Rolodex and serve up an anecdote of some personality, occasion, episode, event or dramatic vignette that would make Herodotus jealous over his ability to record the barest historical detail.

Not gossip. Budd did not gossip. His stories were stories. He spoke ill of no one. I do not recall Budd ever speaking in a derogatory fashion about anyone. Except maybe for his friend, Ed Sorger Sr., who was always borrowing, and forgetting to promptly return, Budd's tools and stuff. No matter how tired

33

he was, or overworked, no matter how much pressure he had to deal with or how worried he was over the many things that bore down on him, he remained cheerful and upbeat. He always had at the ready a funny or curious story about something that he'd seen, done or heard tell, no matter where we went.

The best ones seemed to involve Percy Bean. Budd would get especially upbeat whenever I would point at anything that might trigger a memory involving the Bean Family — specifically, Percy Bean.

The Bean Family owned Olympia Supply Company, a hardware dry goods wholesale store in downtown Olympia. They had done so since the invention of water and had survived rather handily through the Depression. Smart solid business family, Jewish and hardworking.

Budd's upbringing had been similar to mine; he had eaten a lotta beans. Not a lot of money in the family coffers, hence his love for chickenskin sandwiches, although he could afford lobster twice a day by this time. It was easy for me to relate to his childhood, financially speaking.

Unaware at my tender age that many a bigoted person might harbor resentment towards any specific strain of ancestral blood that might course through the veins of whatever branch of humanity's tree — in this case Jewish — I was unaware that racial animosity existed anywhere. Budd and I had something in common, what with his beans and chickenskin sandwiches, and me with my chicken farm naiveté. So, as I said, Budd grew up poor and, as I also said, he resented no one. In fact, when it came to Jewish folks, his reaction was the opposite of resentment; he emulated them. He deeply admired the families that he had watched while growing up during tough times, for their working hard and pulling together, for cleverly levering themselves from, in most cases, poor immigrant status, to become successful business and community leaders. It seemed as though they had set the bar for Budd, who would aspire to his financial independence through his own sheer industriousness. He enjoyed referring to himself as "an honorary Hebrew" and exhibited their mindset, along with a solid work ethic that drove him to succeed through diligence and constant honest labor. Consequently, nobody — *nobody* — could outwork Budd Woollett.

Percy Bean and Budd grew up in the same neighborhood; they went to school together and would part ways at day's end. After school, they'd hang out together for a while before heading off for dinner or chores at their respective homes.

But when they were together, Budd and Percy would trade stuff. Percy's stuff at the beginning of the swap was always better than Budd's: marbles, toys, whatever a kid from a more affluent family might have. Budd would then talk Percy out of his stuff. He'd talk Percy into Budd's stuff. Percy would then head for home with an armload of stuff that Budd had found at the dump, cleaned up or haywired back together. Budd would go home with a new Buddy-L dump truck, or brand new Winchester roller skates. Went on this way for years.

As we negotiated the streets around Olympia's west side, Budd would relate a tale of a toy he had wangled out of Percy Bean, "Right there on that corner, under that lamppost. I shot the street light out, right after I traded him out of his new Daisy Red Rider BB rifle," he'd say proudly, or "Down that alley, that's where I got his …"

Everywhere we went in that area of town, he told a Bean story — how eventually he would "let" Percy Bean help him on his paper route. I have no idea how Budd enticed Percy to do half his paper route for him; I doubt if Percy settled for a chickenskin sandwich. Budd did have winning ways — he was a smooth talker.

Then the day came that Budd had waited for, the day that would pinnacle in his annals of boyhood memory, the day that Budd would forever cherish and bask in the warm glow emanating from his fanning the embers of what seemed to be his fondest recollection.

That was the day Percy Bean showed up with his brand new shiny bicycle, a birthday bike from his Dad. Soon, it became Budd's bicycle. On top of that, if I remember correctly, there was an exchange of some cash. Fifty cents, I think — a day's wages during the Depression. Budd got that too, the fifty cents, I mean.

Evidently, all the other curbside after-school and weekend transactions had gone unnoticed by the bigger Beans. This one got noticed. When Percy pedaled home on Budd's old bike with a box full of whatever it was that Budd had foisted off on him under his arm, they noticed.

After a period of intense interrogation and a subsequent trip to the woodshed, the bigger Beans went to Percy's closet. In his closet, under his bed, and in his drawers were stuffed all the third-rate stuff that Budd had stuffed down Percy's throat. None of Percy's good stuff was anywhere to be seen. All they could see was a closet full of crap.

Back to the woodshed the big Bean dragged the little Bean, where he beat the stuffin' out of him a second time.

This was the all-time most favorite best-ever story for Budd to tell — the stuff dreams were made of — for Budd anyway.

Years later, Budd would choose to avoid doing a large volume of business related to his plumbing occupation through Olympia Supply Company. He felt that somehow

Percy, who ran the place by then, was going to get even with him through the price structuring. Budd would do most of his material expediting through Rosen Supply in Tacoma, owned and operated by another hardworking Jewish family, but one that Budd had not continually pillaged throughout their early years.

Although somewhat out of order chronologically, the time has come to tell the story of how I "let" smooth talking Budd Woollett set me on fire — repeatedly — one Sunday afternoon in October many years ago. Please proceed to the next chapter.

6

CROUCHING TOAD, ROARING DRAGON —
OR
"WHY'S ALAN ON FIRE AGAIN?"

B y the time the following story took place, I had
survived for nearly a full quarter century. For some
reason that I don't remember, I had grown weak in
my resistance to working for free and briefly relapsed back
into association with Budd. Although I knew better, I agreed to
help him and Danny rough-in the plumbing on a new
lakeshore home under construction. By then I had my own
small roofing business, which was dangerous enough, and I
stayed busy trying to keep myself out of my own harm's way.
I had sworn off Budd and his oddball odd jobs. Although
working for Budd had always been entertaining, it was not
lucrative, and I had stopped. Besides, Danny was old enough
and savvy enough by then to help Budd and still fend for
himself at the same time. Danny helped Budd on many jobs,
but he was also getting smarter.

Along came a fall Sunday afternoon job down at Lake St.
Clair — two hours max. Danny and Budd wheedled me into it.
Off we went.

A nice cool country drive later found us at the new structure near the far end of Richeleau Road on the meandering

shoreline of the lake. Budd showed us where the water supply, the waste holes, and the plumbing vents needed to go. As Danny and I laid out the tools and electric extension cords, Budd went to work on his big yellow plumbing truck. The fuel pump on the yellow "Don't fret — Call Woollett" monster utility truck had acted up on the way to the job site. The farther we drove, the worse it became.

"It'sokay—Buddfix," Budd said as he crawled under the hood to disconnect the fuel line.

By the time Danny and I had bored out all the rough-in plumbing holes, preparatory for the copper water pipe, plastic waste and vents, maybe two hours had passed. In that two hours Budd had stayed busy inventing a liquid fuel cell canister capable of caustic carnage, the likes of which Cape Canaveral had not yet conceived. The intention of his gas can invention was to replace the fuel pump and to propel us homeward. It nearly sent us heavenward.

While we'd been drilling, Budd had also been drilling, as well as soldering some makeshift plumbing onto the bottom of a one-gallon handled can. It was a simple enough device. A gravity feed fuel reservoir connected to the top of the carburetor by a … um … an … an … an … Alan! Hood up, Alan on the engine, can in hand. Budd's head was out the driver's window, for navigation. I was the simplest part of this simple device — a full can of gas with a hole in the bottom, a goofy little quarter-inch fitting of some kind, and a simpleton to dribble the gas into the fire-belching orifice of Thor. So there I was — everything my schoolteachers had intimated I was and was destined to remain — a dribbling simpleton.

After the second deafening carburetor backfire, and the corresponding lurching of the truck due to too much gas, then not enough, then too much, then not enough … I was on fire for the first time that day. In fact, it was the first time I had been on fire in weeks.

The truck stopped and I slid over and off the right fender onto the roadside shoulder. Danny had his window rolled up, but I could hear them talking inside the otherwise silent truck cab. I heard Budd first. "Where's Alan?"

"He's over here, and he's on fire," Danny calmly replied.

"What happened?"

"How should I know? I was in here with you. But I'll ask him when the flames die down." Danny climbed out of the truck grinning. "Gonna be a long trip home at this rate," he said as he approached me.

I was still slapping at a smoldering sleeve. Budd came around the front of the big yellow Dodge and asked if I was all right. "I guess so," my reply, as my right eyebrow hairs curled up and dropped off past the vision of the same eye.

"Vent hole! Vent hole!" Budd started hollering, as if he'd just found a huge gold nugget and was shouting the name of some town on the coast of northern California. He was elated to realize he had overlooked the need for a ventilation hole in the top of the can to correlate with the captive liquid leaving the lower leak. Soon a proper hole was installed and I was cajoled back up under the hood. Being Budd's former journeyman toady, I again crouched down on the engine, can in hand, as I had been told. This time the same thing happened.

Only it happened a hell of a lot faster.

Earlier, the line of gas flow had been restricted from flowing freely because it lacked a vent. Now that this was no longer the case, it ran out the bottom of the can like that racehorse that pisses on a flat rock. The big yellow Dodge peeled out and was doing about thirty-five miles an hour — in the first fifteen feet.

When Budd shifted gears, the yellow leviathan with the large open mouth concealing a crouching toad with a leaky gas can lurched. When it lurched, the crouching toad clutching the can of gas then missed pissing into the orifice of the thirsty carburetor, thereby spilling petroleum piss onto the hot engine block, where it hissed and sizzled.

The lurching worsened. Although this clearly wasn't working, I valiantly swung the can back over the guzzling gas-hole, which gulped it down, coughed once, and jumped us forward. On the forward leap, I fell backward, pouring gas all over myself, mostly my boots, especially the one that wasn't caught in the fan blade.

The momentary void during the erratically administered fuel injection caused another lull in the forward direction, which I tried to fill by centering the pecker of Pegasus' piss back over and into the four barrel carburetor. It gulped and coughed, we leaped and lurched, back and forth, over and over. The yellow yawning mouth of leviathan pounded up and down onto my hunkered head and sloping toad-like shoulders.

When finally it backfired a loud belching Vesuvial threat of orange infinity in the form of fire, I'd had enough. I threw the can away into the ditch in a moment when the hood wasn't pounding on my flattening head. But it was too late; my feet had ignited and were deeply involved in flames.

I followed the can out of the gaping volcano's mouth by sliding backwards once again off the right fender, feet apart and afire. This time I clipped the truck's upright turn indicator off the top of the fender with my testicles. The engine died and the yelping yellow yawner coasted to a stop. I was in the ditch, stepping on each foot with the other, jumping about and hoping to extinguish the stubborn flames on each of the blazing leather boots I wore. After I did so, I continued to hop up and down, with both hands clutching the remnants of my aching loins, which had taken a wrong turn on the right signal.

I could hear them again, Budd and Danny inside the truck, safely discussing in a cavalier fashion my whereabouts and condition.

"*Now* where'd he go?"

"He's over here again, on my side. And he's caught himself on fire again. Looks like he needs to pee pretty bad."

"Why does he keep catching on fire?"

"I dunno, Dad, but we can ask him when he stops hopping around, now that the fires on his feet have gone out."

Danny climbed down out of the cab to taunt, "Hey Alan, do you smell bacon?" with the same smartass grin as earlier.

Budd didn't even bother with me on the second flameout. With a sad face, he was busy fiddling with his limp turn signal and inspecting the broad scorch marks underneath the hood from the four-barrel flame-thrower. And he was deep in thought over what had gone wrong.

When I explained to him that my task of evenly administering fuel to the unwilling beast was the gladiatorial equivalent of trying to French kiss a bucking rodeo bull during a severe earthquake, he understood.

Budd climbed into the back of the truck to root around for more clever components to complement his contraptive claptrap. Budd's truck contained over seven million copper, iron and plastic fittings, two and a half million washers, grommets, nipples and doodads. Why in god's name a plumbing truck would have a roll of surgical tubing in it is still a mystery to me. But that's what Budd reappeared with — surgical tubing.

He held it up in the air triumphantly; he was proud. Like a victorious cat with a mouse in its mouth, he proudly pranced back around to the truck's open hood. Budd's truck weighed thirty-four tons and he was always proud when he could emerge with some obscure widget that nobody expected him to have. The triumphant smiling tomcat in bib overalls dropped the roll of rubber surgical tubing at our feet, near my smoking boots, which were making little wheezy sounds in the wet grass like two mangled and dying rodents. I didn't say much. When I did, my voice was high and it hurt to speak.

Quick as a cat, Budd climbed up into the gaping mouth of the Dodge. "Hand me that tubing, now the can." Within only a few minutes, Stage Three of our launch pad was ready for blast off.

He had cleverly hung the can from the roof of the mouth of the beast over the carburetor. Possibly it had been the surgical tubing that had given him the idea for the intravenous feed. I watched as he then connected the tubing to the Portal of Dante by placing the other end of the hose into the carburetor, just under the butterfly. It occurred to me that anything connected to hospital and surgical usage could be a very ominous indication that the worst wasn't over.

I went a few yards into the woods to see if *my* hose had been butterflied. As it turned out, that was a near fatal move — my going into the woods — not because of what I might or might not find in my pants; I should never have taken my eyes off Smokey Stover, the inventive plumber, nor his son, little Smokey.

While I went into the woods for inventory, unknown to me, they had continued to wax inventive. Although I was relieved to learn my services as block jockey were no longer required and that I would be riding inside the truck with what I thought at the time were real people, I was unaware of the new wrinkle in our hose. I was soon to learn of it.

44

Without me under the hood, Budd was now able to see over it. While it was not closed and latched because of the space necessary for the hanging gas can, it was still much lower than before. Its mouth was only half-open, like mine. Budd had hooked a loop of haywire from the grill up and over the Dodge Ram's chrome hood ornament. The ram was cast in a resolute charging position, head down with a determined look in his eye, just like Budd. Budd always drove a Dodge and, in his case, it wasn't just the brand name of the truck; it was an advisory.

Haywire was an ever-present commodity back in those days. Now it's duct tape. Budd always had a roll of haywire in his back pocket. He had asked me to reach in and turn the tiny spigot on the bottom of the can where the tubing was connected. The engine roared and I jumped down and ran around to the passenger door. Danny scooted to the middle and Budd popped the clutch. We launched, and though I hadn't gotten all the way in yet and the door was still open, I didn't fall out — not completely. I hung on, clawed my way inside, and closed the door.

After a couple hundred yards of Budd's speedshifting while trying to match speed and gear to the amount of gas the truck was gobbling, it became obvious we could not keep up. Too much gas. Although it was not slopping and sloshing around as when I was Ram Rider, the result was about to be the same; except that now we were roaring down the curvy road at about fifty miles an hour.

Soon came the inevitable. The overfed four-barrel burbled over with gargling gasoline, backfired twice and hurtled a huge orange ball of fire through the partially open, hinged hood-cowling in front of us. Budd screeched to a halt. He quickly turned off the engine as I bailed out of my door and ran around to the front, unlooped the haywire from the charging ram, opened the hood the rest of the way, and prepared to propel myself toward heroism.

The can hung over the fire, barely off the licking flames. Knowing it was only a matter of time before Budd's truck was toast, I grabbed the can to toss it away. What I was actually about to throw away was my future. With my free hand I unhooked the second haywire, the one from which the can hung; it only took a second. With both hands, I then grabbed the square can to pitch it ditchward. Incredibly however, I was only able to yank the can a few inches, although I had done so with all my strength.

I was to learn later, that while I was in the woods counting my gonads, Smokey and little Smokey had upgraded the can's fastening. Without telling me, they had haywired the can down to *four other points* inside the engine compartment "for stability," they said later — this from two people who had no idea of the true definition of the word. There were only three or four inches of free-play in the wire. Hence, my hearty hurl was hastily hindered, and a very bad thing began to transpire. When my mighty yank was abruptly halted, I *heard* all the wires that I hadn't previously seen, "twang." What I did see, in silhouette framed by the flames only inches behind it, was the can in my hands *without* its now-disconnected rubber hose. From my well-lit perspective, I also saw the stream of seemingly suspended but splattering gasoline speeding — in slow motion — in my direction.

I immediately changed my mind and elected not to be a hero. I decided to drop the can and run, but I evidently took too long to make that decision. And even though it seemed like forever that I stood there holding the can over my head, wanting to wash my hands of the whole thing, it was probably less than a second, but it was long enough for my hands to be awash in gasoline — and fire. My chest, shoulders and sleeves also burst into flames.

By this time it was dusk and Budd didn't need to inquire as to my whereabouts or my condition. It was obvious. I was right there in front of him, running up and down the road, and I was on fire — again. I was easy to spot.

Did I mention that by this time in his life, Danny had become a fireman? Oh yes, Danny was by then a proud member of the Lacey Volunteer Fire Department. Curious, I know, considering his background. But not unusual, I'm told, as oftentimes people with a penchant for pyro become perfect personnel pleased to serve the public in that capacity.

Did I also mention that Budd had, somewhere back in the black bowels of the roaring fire dragon, a fire extinguisher? Well, that's because I didn't know that either, at the time.

Experience had taught me, in similar situations, to pitch myself to the ground and roll around, screaming like a four-year-old in the middle of a temper tantrum. So there I was, frantically flopping about, attempting to roll out the fire that fed on my flaming carcass. At that point, Danny, the skinny volunteer fireman, volunteered to throw his bony self on top of me. About the time he landed on me with his knee in my already quite tender groin, which, other than my head, was about the only part of me that wasn't on fire, I spotted a large pile of wet leaves on the opposite roadside. I wanted so badly to be inside that welcome pile of dank brown autumn leaves. But now I had this giant mosquito humping and flailing away at me. Oddly, it seemed only fitting that in this curious dream-like abstraction, it was the mosquito that was doing all the swatting. Danny slapped me about a-hundred-fifty times in his heroic but futile attempt to smother the flames with his spindly frame. Finally, I pried him off and was able to take a running, flaming dive for the compost pile of rotting leaves. When I dove in, the flames fizzed out.

While Danny had been slapping me nearly to death, Budd suddenly remembered the fire extinguisher that he had buried somewhere in the back of the truck. Quick as a cat, he had climbed in to fetch it. It was mounted by the official factory bracket onto an inside panel. By the time I sat up in my cool pile of leaves amidst my own personal cloud of steam, I began watching the remarkable firefight that was about to begin at the front of the truck. A strange and unforgettable drama started to unfold between me and the flaming stage I faced. Budd had retrieved the red cylinder and was ready to take action on the by now huge fire under the hood of his six-month-old truck.

But Danny was the fireman! So, because of his superior firefighting credentials, he thought he should be the one to extinguish the blaze. Budd didn't agree. It was *his* truck and *his* fire extinguisher. He found it, so he should be the one to do it.

The animated debate went on for some time; not that I could hear them arguing over the loud roaring and hissing of the inferno; I couldn't make out what they were hollering, but I could see very clearly what was happening. They were involved in a lengthy tug-of-war over the fire extinguisher. They were two battling black figures backlit by the blaze, reeling from left to right, then right to left, across the backdrop of flames. I sat there, heaping wet vegetation all over myself, while watching them yank and pull, in a bizarre ballet. I heard a tire blow on the burning Dodge, but the fire dancers raged on; back and forth, forth and back they roiled in front of the open-mouthed roaring Ram. (Insert music from Saber-Dance.)

Eventually, Danny wore out the old man, and then he victoriously turned the fire extinguisher toward the eternal flame. He squeezed the handle-trigger and clouds of white fuzzy foam spewed forth in every direction possible. Up, down, sideways — every direction that is — *except* in the direction of the fire. Soon the can was empty of foam, none of which had landed on the fire. The fire began to die of old age, but no foam of flame-asphyxiation had reached it.

Because Budd had been somewhat in a hurry when he snagged the fire extinguisher from its place in the truck, he had not, in his haste and in the near darkness, read the instructions. He hadn't seen the part about sliding the canister UP and OUT of its mounting bracket. Instead, Budd had torn the extinguisher — screws and all — off the truck's metal panel, with the bracket still attached to the can itself. The spray nozzle on the canister, therefore, faced its still-attached bracket. When Danny pointed the nozzle at the fire, the foam did nothing more than squirt everywhere BUT the fire. The bracket had deflected the fire retardant onto the retarded firemen's hair, faces and feet. At least a few good fluffs of foam had landed on the blackened fenders, but none on the fire.

Darkness began to engulf us as I watched while Budd despondently brushed the misused and misguided foam off the fenders, onto the last few flickers of tired fire. I heard the other front tire expire.

The front half of Budd's new truck had melted away.

My hands blistered, and for a while after that I refused to go anywhere with Budd or Danny.

7

THE FIRST OF MY PERIODIC DROWNINGS...

Most people do not have an opportunity to write about their own death. Twice, I have died by drowning. Oddly, for once, none of the Woolletts were involved in my first drowning. And of course I did not die; but at the time — both times — I sure as hell was convinced of the date of my early expiration. Medically as well as scientifically, by all physical and visible evidence, I most certainly *did* die on the second occasion. But I must explain my first drowning so that you can see how it is woven together with the second drowning by a nearly identical supernatural phenomenon that remains inexplicable — by me or anyone else to whom I've spoken about it — to this day.

The beliefs in, as well as the expectation of, one's own sudden death come naturally when you are six years old. Although a six-year-old has scant information on the subject of death and oblivion, he still has a rudimentary grasp of the subject: *There was a candy bar in my hand; now it's gone. I ate it; it's dead. It isn't a candy bar anymore. I don't want to think about what became of it after its demise.* A six-year-old should not be expected to dwell on the hideous afterlife of a masticated and decimated candy bar. It was a candy bar. Its purpose in life has now been fulfilled. It should just be thankful death came quickly.

I especially have always known death was lurking right around the corner. I was conditioned to expect it at any moment, and that it may arrive from anywhere. My Mom had been threatening to kill me (not that I didn't have it coming) ever since I could maintain a grip on a spatula to defend myself; she appeared to quickly resent my standing up to her, even though I may have only been a few months old.

Still, all the spatulas in the world cannot save a floundering, panicked, and thrashing six-year-old who has allowed himself to become adrift, then swallowed by the lazy current of the Deschutes River.

My older half-sister Lo-Ann lived in the apartment next door to my mom and me. Lo-Ann lived with our grandparents, Jenny and John Aarde. I was always proud of my grandparents because of the two A's in their last name. Theirs was therefore the very first name in the local Tumwater-Olympia phone book. I didn't have the same last name, but I was proud nevertheless. We all were.

We were likewise proud of my seventeen-year-old sister. She was a natural platinum blonde, not that I had a clue what that was, and she was pretty. Occasionally she took me swimming. Maybe she took me only once. Although I cannot say for sure how many swimfests we went on, one in particular is seared into my memory. No one else's — just mine.

To this day I remain unsure whether or not buttercups have a scent. I do not know if they smell as sweet and moist as my recollection dictates; I have lived in the quiet fear they may not. Because I stay passively afraid of the simple fact that the cluster of buttercups growing under the trestle that day were possibly odorless, or even worse, offensive to the nose, I have chosen the path of an ignorant sentimentalist — at least in this case, the case of the buttercups. In over fifty years I have never bent down to smell a buttercup. I have always worried they may not smell as wonderful as I want my six-year-old memory to remind me.

When my sister led me down Tumwater hill to swim in the public swimming area of the winding Deschutes River, it must have been July or August. It was hot. Scorching hot, the kind of hot that shimmers the air between viewer and the viewed — wavering quicksilver puddles of mirage on asphalt hot.

Leaving the torch of the midday summer sun and entering the chasm of cool under the expansive trestle near the river bend, but not yet at the swim spot, there lay a new world. New to me. How it could be so hot outside, yet so cool under the old wood overpass, was beyond me. When my eyes became accustomed to the relative dark — compared to the sizzling white heat yellow sunlight outside — I could see that it was *nearly as yellow* under the wide and lengthy canopied shadow of the old wooden trestle — at least much of the dark wet slippery earth floor that stayed perpetually enveloped in cool shadow was. Large, thick patches of bright yellow buttercups grew in every untrod corner under the creosoted timber cavern above us. And it was quiet.

But most remarkable to me that day was the odor. The odors. I had never smelled creosote before, but I knew instinctively that particular odor emanated from the giant black timbers, beams and pilings above and around us. Maybe I had sniffed at a piling upon nearing the dank cavern; I don't remember. Still, I was easily able to distinguish the creosote smell from the ultra-feminine bouquet of flora that grew wherever I looked. I can now say that part of the ambrosia came from the nettles, as well as young fiddlehead fern, and from the rich smell of the sweet black earth of the trail down to the river. The narrow dark earthen trail, wet in spots from lack of sunshine and from frequent footsteps, included crushed greenery that had been flattened into the path in patches.

But the buttercups stole the show. Just as I had never before sampled the heavy sweet damp aroma of all the mingled greens, along with the black acrid smell of creosote, I had never seen buttercups before. Or, if I had, certainly not in such abundance as this. Because the thousands of bright canary blossoms growing in shadows overpowered my visual sense, I concluded the nectar that hung in the air belonged to them. I was six. That's how conclusions are drawn when you're six. It was a glorious aroma, it was a glorious sight; the two were one … and still are. That was a moment, however brief, that I have clutched as tightly as the last fifty-some years would allow, without wilting in my grip the tender blooms that I have kept forever fragrant in my memory and its secret rooms.

If buttercups do not smell of crushed green, women's breasts, newly dampened earth on a hot day, and the inside of my grandmother's purse — please, never tell me.

The flat wide riverbank sloped gradually down to the easy-flowing water. The river's current could barely be perceived at that spot where everyone swam. Across the river, up on top of yet another trestle, the railway trestle, were creatures — large, loud, hairy, scary creatures. Those creatures were the real reason my sister was there — to be noticed by the loud, hairy, scary things in swim trunks that were jumping off the trestle into the river. They were trying to kill themselves in order to be noticed by my sister and others like her that occupied the sloping sands and pea gravel on our side. Both camps pretended not to notice the other. Each was just as bad at not noticing as the other. This I noticed right away, and I made a mental note not to participate in such asinine behavior should I ever be expected to do so. But, I had a river to … swim.

In one of the less vigilant moments on my sister's part, one of the moments when she wasn't doing a very good job "not noticing" one particular flexing brute, I tiptoed out to deeper water. I'm sure I had been instructed not to. I assume I had been told to stay in a certain shallow area — worthless words spoken in rote by an older sister to six-year-old ears half filled with wax, sand and the sounds of bigger kids frolicking in the deeper water — water that ever so gradually became higher than me as the river bottom sloped stealthily away from the touch of my tiptoes.

Soon, I felt the gentle current nudging me softly towards the center of the river. As my ears filled with water, I sprung slightly on my straining tiptoes in order to keep my nostrils and bugled lips above the surface, all the while silently bouncing into ever-deeper water, aided by the palm of the river's open hand softly pushing me from behind.

Before long, I was unable to stretch my trumpeted lips and well-watered nostrils at regular intervals. I was beginning to lose track of when to drink and when to inhale. Only occasionally did I find the bottom, enough to push upward, skyward, towards the beautiful blue — and the air and all the noise of life and the living: the rowdy baritone brutes, the laughing older girls, the screaming moms and squealing kids, rushing traffic on nearby Highway 99, buzzing insects, and birds in flight; I may even have heard buttercups blooming in the creosote shadows behind me.

The water's gentle push changed into a downward pull. The river had closed its open palm on me and now began to grip its fingers around my legs as if I were a fresh bouquet of handpicked wildflowers being thrust into the cold water of a narrow vase. Down I went again.

As life began slipping away and I silently thrashed about underwater, only rarely breaking the surface to crane my neck towards the sky, something very odd happened. Each and every time I touched bottom — which was seldom at that point — and was able to propel myself to the surface for a choking gasp, I saw an image in the sky — a clear glass tumbler full of water! It hung perfectly still in front of my view of the great blue sky above. When I re-submerged a second later, it stayed up there, hanging flat against the sky. When I bobbed up again a few seconds later for what I was sure would by my last gurgling breath, there it still hung, right in front of me. Each time: a tapered tumbler, wider slightly at the top. No pattern in the glass. The water inside the glass was still and clear, one-half inch or so below the rim.

No bright lights for me. Just a glass of water! As if I didn't have enough already.

While I had given up any hope of surviving my first time swimming and was, for all purposes, unconscious at that point, evidently my limbs were still active.

Apparently the water had carried my underwater floundering small carcass slightly around the bend of the river. One of my flailing arms whacked something solid. Weakly, I opened my eyes underwater. It was the hairy back of a trestle brute! He was standing upright on the river bottom, his upper chest, shoulders and head above water. He was facing a river nymph — not my sister — but a similar one, and they were talking. He was explaining to her the fallacious reasoning behind her needless and bothersome retention of maidenhood, and he skillfully and rationally was imparting to her the simple virtues of breaking the silly chains of adolescence, something about how he was willing to set her free from the pointless bondage of all burdensome virginal Victorian thinking. She was listening. She was willing to be reasonable. She appeared to be growing weary from the chafing weight of her tiresome and senseless heavy burden.

As I drifted by, I clawed furiously at the trestle brute's back with both hands. My fingernails were filling up with hair and, as I sank to the bottom, I vaguely remember my fingertips finding the waistband of his trunks. I took those with me to the bottom — at least the back end of his swimsuit came down with me towards the boulders of the river bottom. The front of his garment appeared to be snagged on something. My life was fading away and the last thing I would ever see was a trestle brute's hairy ass!

While he had not felt my fingernails carving notches in his now hairless back, the smooth-talking brute noticed, finally, something other than the nymph who had his undivided attention. And though he hadn't even noticed the back end of his trunks slide down, he evidently began to grow aware of something yanking on his snag.

He reached around behind him, grabbed me by one arm and, with his other hand, clutched my trunks. Then he threw me up onto the gravelly grassy bank. Turning back to Victoria, the smiling river nymph, he resumed the lengthy pontification of his preferred principles revolving around pleasure and promiscuousness. She continued to listen politely while I gurgled, gasped, choked and flopped around in the weeds and river rocks like a spawning salmon.

Not one person — not one — had noticed the little six-year-old drowning trestle troll flailing about in the water. I learned then that when you die, you die alone.

The buttercups that I feared I would never see again welcomed me on the return home. My sister, who thought I had made far too much of a fuss over them the first time, had no patience for my ravings on the way back. But the blossoms seemed even more beautiful than before. And everything smelled even thicker and sweeter than earlier. That evening I noticed the sunset and its fuschia illumination of Mount Rainier. I noticed many previously insignificant things for a while after my first drowning.

I neither complained about my sunburn that night, nor about the rutabagas that my mom, as always, had put in the stew.

Nobody has ever wanted to hear about my glass of water.

I love the smell of creosote.

8

"It's the Water"

Having carried with me into my later childhood, and miraculously my adulthood as well, not one but two images related to my initial drowning, I maintain a healthy respect for swift or deep water.

Neither of the two images include the hairy butt of an amorous river Neptune, even though he had saved my life; I managed to blur that image into the murky obscurity of my silted memory for the sake of my own mental health.

The glass of clear water hanging in mid-air as I drowned is, of course, one image.

A second image has also stayed with me for years — the scene of what … might … have … been. I can still call to mind, when thinking about how close I came, the remains of a dead little boy somewhere downriver. Buried in the rich earth of river's edge. Stuck among rocks and weeds. Years of sediment washing up over the bones, covering them in black river silt and matted leaves, small broken branches, bits of river flotsam with periwinkles among them. Half of the half-grown skull is exposed and lies above the muck; the other side is concealed by the riverbank at water's edge. One mud-filled eye socket stares down into eternity; the other dark eye catches glimpses of sun and flickers of blue sky through the few small specks of light that filter through the ferns, nettles, maple leaves and tree limbs that hang just inches over the long-forgotten — only yards from the pathway along the river; but not one person has ever noticed.

The remains of one all-but-completely-buried hand is slightly higher up the ebony edge of riverbank. The thumb and first fingers lie partly protruding from the constantly soggy soil. The hand appears to be reaching up into the leafy foliage on the bank for a handhold — a tree root possibly, or some other means of extraction that failed. The river had won. The rest of the dead little boy was part of the river now, and part of the sediment that holds him in place, possibly forever. And the little boy's rest would probably never be disturbed.

If, however, someone should ever crawl down to the river through the thickly shadowed verdant bower, they would notice. They would no doubt notice the small half-skull with algae on it, the dark circle of an open eye socket with the crawdaddy that lives inside the nearly submerged and buried cranium.

"It looked just like the other rocks — at first," they would say. "Then I saw the crawdaddy disappear into it."

And then they would notice the bones of the small hand; just barely beyond the empty hand, only a couple inches up out of its reach, there would be growing a small cluster of buttercups.

"I came down to pick those yellow flowers," they would say. "That's when I first saw the crawdaddy."

In this, my eerie vision of what — almost — was, the buttercups remain unclaimed, unspoiled.

In 1896 Jacob Schmitt began Capitol Brewing Company, later to be named Olympia Brewing Company. At this writing, seven days have passed since the last whistle blew at the Tumwater brewery, the whistle that had told me in my youth when it was eight a.m., when it was noon, and when it was four-thirty p.m. They say that the Olympia Brewery in Tumwater, Washington has closed forever. The large old brewery situated on the overlook to the Deschutes River was the economic center-pole in Tumwater for nearly a century.

If you ever have occasion to pick up an out-of-production Olympia Beer product container, look closely at the label or logo. You will notice an image of the old original brick brewhouse situated at the base of thundering Tumwater Falls. And at the top of the cascading waterfall you should see trees, on the left-hand side, hanging over the crest of the falls. And if you cannot discern one, then imagine if you will, a horizontally jutting tree limb — a large sturdy outgrowth of a hefty old hardwood growing high above the crest of falling water and higher still over the boiling white cauldron of churning liquid at the cascade's base. The distance from the tree limb to the cold kinetic chaos below was around sixty or seventy feet — not exactly Niagara, I realize. Still, only the stout-hearted or the Pilsener-preferring lager-lappers would consider a leap — except for those too young to drink and too dumb not to know any better than to plunge seventy feet into the frothy brew. Not everyone has survived this descent. There are very large boulders at the bottom of Tumwater Falls. This jump — or dive if you are especially daring, or drunk — could easily be your last. And it is therefore highly inadvisable, unless you recently have had some very, very bad news from your doctor.

I was in the middle group. I was one who didn't know better. After my first near-drowning, when I said I had acquired a healthy respect for swift or deep water, I didn't intend to imply I *avoided* either. I was *drawn* to swift *and* deep water. I had come to respect the fact that one can lose their life inside a very brief period of time spent below its surface. So I had taught myself, by the age of eleven or so, to practically live underwater. I was able to hold my breath and swim underwater great distances well before I learned to survive on the water's surface. That's the kind of respect I absorbed from my first trip while drifting, submerged, downriver in the Deschutes at a point that was about five hundred yards upriver from the Tumwater cataracts. Somewhere in between is where I've always envisioned the little dead boy to be, steeping into eternity — while no one notices.

As years went by, I believe security at Tumwater Falls tightened and it seemed that fewer of the lagered-up limb-leapers were allowed to plunge into the liquid refreshment at the bottom of the falls. In my case, there never was an incident whenever I made my plummets into the thundering froth; I must have avoided security, if there was any at all. I don't think they had yet initiated a program of security personnel for the purpose of protecting us from ourselves. That may have begun in the early '70s. LSD and other drugs most likely were a contributing factor. I heard a couple stories of falls-jumpers who were too stoned to swim once they were in the water, so they sank like stones — hence, I think, the advent of security personnel. Stoned people landing on stone was probably another solid reason.

If there was security back in those days, I apparently avoided them. I was also able to avoid the rocks.

Although I was scared spitless on my first jump once I was out on the limb — a quite natural and common scenario for me — I felt as if I was obligated to make the splat ... I mean, plunge … to the rocks, rather the *water* below. I was nearly twenty-years-old by that time and, being a transplanted back-to-Tumwater tenant, I felt I owed it to the community. The "community" at that moment was comprised of two drunken soldiers in uniform, an old geezer with a sketchpad, and a pretty, dark-haired young lady of my age, avoiding her pic-nicking family who were up in the grassy area. The girl was doing her best not to notice me up on the limb.

So now I *had to* jump. I didn't want to, but I had to. If I didn't, she would never not notice me again. Because I had studied the exact spot in the noisy suds where the experienced survivors had entered, I went for it.

Half expecting to hit the concealed granite that I knew for a fact lay under the thick rolling foam and have my hips permanently pushed up around my ears, I didn't enjoy the ride down. I was however somewhat comforted by a fleeting fantasy of the pretty dark-haired girl clutching my hand to her firm perky breast while begging me not to die as she pro-claimed her everlasting gratitude for my display of fearless-ness while distracting her from her boring family with their potato salad which she hates because of the onions. But, I still was wishing I had not jumped, and I wasn't prepared for what happened next.

We all know what it feels like to jump into water. It's a solid flexible mass of wet. It presses on all of your flesh as you enter. Instantly it's everywhere, engulfing you, and imme-diately you are moving in slow motion. As soon as you enter, it breaks your fall. And normally the world underwater is relatively quiet.

Not that day!

It wasn't water. It was a loud shaving-cream-cotton-candy-and-whipped-cream cloud. As I continued to descend, even *after* I landed on the huge wet haystack of thunderous nimbus, I drifted down in a rolling white wetness until I feared I would never stop. And the noise! I lost all sense of direction.

Boiling around in the roaring white, I thought after a while that I was doomed to become something similar to one of those tiny balls trapped inside a cheap whistle that you can see rolling around if you look cross-eyed down your nose while blowing. Eventually though, the cataract released its hold on me and I drifted softly up out of my loud cloud into the placid flat beginnings of Capitol Lake. Once again, I was proud.

After a couple more ear-splitting baptisms into the pounding white fuzz, I discovered the cave behind the falls and the joys it held — which was ... discovering the cave behind the falls.

Later, I walked up the trail alongside the river to the parking lot, where I noticed that the pretty dark-haired girl who had wanted my hands on her breasts was long gone, as was the old geezer with the sketchpad. One upright weaving soldier was peeing on his shiny black shoes, while the other soldier slept, face down, in the blackberry bushes nearby. None of the small audience had even bothered to congratulate or thank me for letting them watch me sample immortality through public displays of indestructibility and reckless abandoned acts of fearlessness.

As I neared my car, I noted the geographical changes that had occurred from when I had visited the river my first time. The Olympia Brewery had, back in the late '50s I believe, altered the course of the river. Interesting what you are capable of if enough beer is consumed — something about how they wanted the railroad tracks on the other side of the river, so they just moved everything around until they liked it. They rearranged the river, the railroad tracks, and the trestles, until it all took on the appearance that it has now.

The old creosote trestle canopy that nurtured my shaded acres of buttercups had originally been very close to the spot where I was then climbing into my car. It had, by that time, all become a tourist park with large asphalt parking lots. The narrow nettled trail that provided my indoctrination to creosote smell and cottonwood shade isn't even so much as a memory to most people anymore; I speak of those that may have had the privilege of partaking of the buttercup, creosote, and squished-plants-into-river-soil ambrosia that once graced that small place in space. And the river had been pushed around so that even the bend had been relocated. And no swimming.

I don't know when the brewery's whistle first blew. I know it has blown all my life — until last week. I, for one, will always miss the heady smell of brewing hops and malt that once filled the air of Tumwater Valley. I'll miss the loud whistle that was so familiar to me during the times I lived on Tumwater Hill — except for when I was sleeping. But mostly, I'll think of them, and will especially miss them, only while driving past the old brewery on Interstate 5, curving around on the Capitol Lake Interchange. That's when I normally glance over at the original brick brew house and to the falls behind it — just to see if they're still there.

9

BICYCLE BOB

This is the story of a boat.

I always thought I wanted to ride a unicycle. Up on the crest of Olympia's Eastside Hill, on Fourth Avenue and only a couple blocks from where I would later own my first small antique store, was an establishment named Bob's Bikes and Boats.

I had seen, along with his other sidewalk inventory, a couple of crisp shiny new unicycles out front. I stopped in for a tire kicking. I'd never been on a unicycle before and my track record with bicycles was not exactly stellar. Although I never expected to participate in the Tour de France, I considered myself coordinated enough to pedal off into the rainbow on anything with wheels and pedals — as long as the wheels stayed on, as well as the chain, handlebars and seat. (I'm remembering Sherman, my murderous bicycle.)

Unicycles don't have chains to come off or devour my leg, I figured. *They don't have handlebars to pierce my flesh. They don't have front wheels to separate from the forks, causing my front teeth to fang into the sidewalk, asphalt, or any slow-moving creature crossing my path.*

Unicycles, I tabulated, were therefore half as dangerous as bicycles, since they have only half the parts; consequently, they should also be twice as easy to master! *How come I never thought of this before?*

I had grandiose pictures in my head of me doing festive tricks in the downtown Olympia pet parade. I could see myself pedaling circles around a buxom baton twirler during the Lakefair celebrations, or maybe just tootling down the road with both hands free — the filthy fingernail of one hand picking at an elbow scab, while picking my nose with the other hand. Right then and there I decided I wanted a unicycle! *Maybe I should learn how to juggle.*

Bob, the bike guy — and a boat guy too, but at that moment he was a bike guy — would be only too happy to help me pick out a spiffy new unibike.

"You know …" he began, instructively, as I centered myself over the black saddle — and then his phone rang. Some guy on the other end wanted to talk about oars. So Bob now became a boat guy. I thought maybe I should practice a bit while Bob talked on the telephone to some moron who couldn't handle his oars — or maybe they were talking about whores … I didn't know. All I knew was that I wanted a unicycle and I had no time to waste. If I was ever going to join the circus and get paid for acting stupid, I needed to learn to ride my unibike.

Putting all my weight on the top pedal and lifting my other foot off the floor to place it on the opposing pedal, I thrust forward with the top pedal. This was about to be the third time in my life that my head nearly became disconnected from my thorax because of some spoked-wheel skinny-tired demonic device called a *cycle*. The first time was when I was a child and my bike tire blew up in my face; the second time was when I was a teenager, whiplashed to the back of a car. And now this time.

My unicycle and my body (at least from the shoulders down) had suddenly gone cycling without me; that is to say, without my head. The cycling device, along with everything below my neck shot forth across Boat Bob's shining linoleum tile floor, leaving my immediately very overweight and about-to-be-exploded-onto-the-floor head hanging in space. I felt my Adam's apple stretching taut as my lower body pulled with a mighty force on my slendering neck. Suddenly I felt like I had the neck of a turkey with the head of a donkey.

Boat Bob quickly decided to be Bike Bob; I heard the phone receiver bounce on the linoleum. Bob was no longer in conversation about things nautical or naughty. Bicycle Bob was now concerned with his bikes and melon-heads bonking their donkey brains out on his showroom floor.

In the minuscule amount of time it took for my neck to stretch and my head to momentarily bobble about in space while the unicycle and the headless rider propelled forward, I made two snap decisions. I decided I didn't want a unicycle, and I decided I had better snap my large heavy head forward or there was gonna be a fine mess all over Bike 'n' Boat Bob's immaculate linoleum tile.

Remember, I only stopped in for a tire kicking. In one split second, it had become abundantly clear that I was headed for a serious split-headed ass-kicking.

Somehow, in the fractional moment that was left before I impacted onto highly polished linoleum, I tucked my head forward, thereby avoiding any permanent damage to Bob's nice floor. I was able to accomplish this forward tuck with the aid of my diaphragm.

As soon as the whip had cracked, so to speak, and when

the rest of me had made its sudden departure forward on the evil device, I instinctively activated my diaphragm muscles. This was done in the form of second nature; it had become a conditioned response from many earlier experiences in self-preservation … I screamed.

Thus, the back of my donkey head was saved by my instinctive deeply diaphramic scream. Instantly, I had let out a shrieking EEEYYYY! Which was followed, when my back slammed onto the floor, by a loud, HAAWWW! Only it was all connected together, into one long sound: EEEYYYY-HAAWWW! Not unlike the bray of an unwilling beast of burden that has been placed in a situation that it finds to be unacceptable and distasteful at the moment. My noisy collision with the floor knocked all the wind out of my lungs.

I made no other sound, at least none that emitted from my vocal chords. I was making floppy-scratching noises on Bob's Mop 'N' Glo shiny floor, but nothing vocal. I watched the unicycle sail off across the room into a nicely arranged cluster of new bikes, all of them nonchalantly leaning in the same direction, confidently stable, each on its own individual kickstand; it was, up until then, an impressive display. Bob watched, horrified, helpless, and in dismay, as his display dominoed into a loud disarray. I continued to claw at my own reflection in the floor.

Bob slowly turned away from the endless crashing metallic destruction to look down at me. I turned to look up — for assistance, mercy, forgiveness, or possibly, a tracheotomy. His cold eyes met mine. In his I could see the cool dispassionate look of one who had made the decision to put out of its misery the life of a large useless farm animal. Not for food, but … well, in my case, I guess out of utter disgust. He went to get his gun, or the police, or worse yet, his calculator.

That was the day I bought my boat.

I didn't breathe properly for some time after that. For a day or so I had to hold my head up while eating by gripping my hair. My rubberized neck wouldn't allow my mandible to function unless I elevated the larger portion of my leaden head off my chest. I had to hold onto my hair, with one hand suspending my head, or else my donkey bobble would swivel over to one side and all the food would fall out. Today, whenever I see an antique bisque doll that is badly sprung and seriously in need of restringing, I am reminded of that sorry incident at Bob's — and how I made an ass of myself.

Actually it was a kayak, the boat I bought. It was a rubberized canvas inflatable two-person kayak. Bob suggested I buy something soft and squishy "for everyone's sake." Then he went on about how he thought I needed to wear this stupid-looking orange-padded safety helmet at all times, even when asleep in bed.

When I was leaving Bob's with my new rubber boat and my new rubberneck, I heard a voice from the floor. I saw Bob's beige phone receiver still hanging by the curly cord, down to its own reflection in the tile. So the guy on the phone was actually talking to himself! I heard him saying something about warlocks ... or oarlocks ... or something.

Soon after I got my head on straight, I took my new twelve-foot kayak to Tumwater Falls Park. And that was the day I forgot, in my exuberance over new boat ownership, about the middle falls in the Deschute River — the falls just below the Falls Terrace Restaurant.

My friend, Bill, and I took the kayak for a spin. Watching Bill disappear from in front of me, along with the front half of my new boat (the half he was in) was electrifying. Following him over the forgotten-about falls was heart stopping.

Hard shell kayaks don't bend in the middle; inflatable ones do. My face slammed into the back of Bill's head at the bottom when the kayak bent the other way. His half had straightened out while I was in my half, still pointed straight down. Then we were both flat on the water's churning surface again as the kayak filled with water from the falls above us. We were stuck there for a little while at the base of the small dynamo, thrashing about in white water going nowhere. Our paddles floated down river into "little dead boy" land.

All the people in the restaurant were pointing and laughing.

I told you this was the story of a boat.

10

EXTRA! EXTRA!

My confidence (which should be spelled N-E-M-E-S-I-S in my case) began to grow to hazardous proportions. I got to the point of feeling cocky around swift water. My confidence had slowly mutated into overconfidence, an indication that I was soon to be, as always, slapped back to reality (should I be allowed to survive the slapping).

But it wasn't completely my fault. I had help in the miscalculations of my ability around white water.

Word was getting around about some idiot who repeatedly attempted to drown himself by jumping off tree limbs into the lower Deschutes Falls and going over the smaller falls in bending boats — feats that were far from remarkable. I knew that, even then. Those exploits, mediocre or not, were possibly complemented by some of the other things I could occasionally be found doing on dry land — traveling seventy-miles per hour on roller skates, for instance, while hanging onto Danny Woollett's '58 Chevy. When people see you going past on roller skates at seventy while holding onto a Chevy bumper or door handle, they talk. Word spreads.

At some point, word had reached the ears of some public

relations advertising consultants for the Olympia Brewery. Instead of my being sought out for prosecution for raising hell in the Tumwater Falls Park, they wanted a "falls" guy. They wanted to pay me to go over the falls in a barrel!

The advertising angle was for the brewery itself. Although I never spoke directly with any staff, a representative of the ad guys approached me. They wanted to film a real life idiot in a barrel — Niagara fashion — for a television commercial. Coincidentally, because of my new over-cocky outlook regarding swift and tall water, I already had made half-sincere inquiries into the cost of a rubber barrel for just such an opportunity. So I was already ripe. Overripe. Over-cocky *and* overconfident *and* ready to plunge over the top, wedged inside a flattened barrel between boulders and *over with* at the bottom, which was what I most likely would have been, had that little vignette played out as planned. I'm alive today only because those ad guys were such cheap bastards.

Negotiating the fall would have no doubt killed me. Negotiating the terms saved me. I was willing to take the plunge for a thousand dollars. But the barrel's cost was around twenty-five hundred (I had already checked into it). Because my terms included final ownership of the barrel, negotiations broke down and I never heard from them again.

Still, those guys nearly killed me anyhow, because they had injected me with a fatal dose of perceived indestructibility. They had jacked up my overconfidence level to a new euphoric high watermark that would not recede until the drought of the following summer.

The Olympia Beer people, the two girls we had with us, and Danny Woollett. Those are the principle figures of accountability in my next drowning. It feels good to be able to write this and list all the other people to blame. All those years

I suffered as an only child, with not one person anywhere to point at to take the fall. My early life as solitary perpetrator had been cruel, but a whole spectacular universe of blame-shifting had opened up for me. Surely, I thought, full-fledged manhood must be right around the corner.

I have already noted the reason it was the beer people's fault. It was also Danny's fault just because he encouraged me by agreeing to participate. Finally, it was the girls' fault because they were girls and were therefore required to witness periodic and random acts of bravado on the part of us who were careening around the corner towards manhood. Add to that the fact they told us we were idiots and had begged us *not* to do it. That's how girls have always worked it. That's how they egg us dumb guys into doing stuff we might not have done otherwise. (You women should think about that when you want things done around the house.)

It was also the fault of the people at the Crystal Mountain Ski Resort — and the weather.

Back in those days, Christmas Day and New Year's Day were two of the best opportunities for downhill skiing because hardly anybody went; over the years, the opposite has developed. The four of us left early in the morning for a full day on the sparsely populated slopes. It was drizzling rain when we left. After an hour's drive we reached the ski area; it was closed. Because of the unusually warm rain reaching above six thousand feet, the slopes were ruined for the day.

We turned around and made the two mile descent from Crystal Village back down to the highway, which runs congruently with the meandering White River. White River was more active that day than at most other times due to those same warm rains falling at higher-than-usual elevations. The normally small stream became quite engorged and energetic for the month of December. A warm heavy rainfall quickly melts the snow pack, thus contributing even more water into all the rivulets, streams and, eventually, rivers. That high up, near the source, the White River at the end of December normally isn't too much more than a respectable stream — until the annual spring meltdown … and that particular Christmas Day.

If you ever visit Crystal Mountain in winter, be sure to look west across the valley and the river to the tall escarpment on the far side. From Crystal Mountain cutoff road and most other vantage points along the lower highway, you should easily be able to see an incredible arrangement of ice dangling from the cliff's crest. Icicles. To be precise, one-hundred-fifty-to maybe two-hundred-foot-long icicles when conditions are right.

Unable to ski that day, we decided it was our job — Danny's and mine — to hike the mile or so over to the other side of the valley and jar some gargantuan icicles loose. We thought it would be cool to be nearly killed by big pointy frozen sabers of silence that hung steadfastly in their winter solace. The girls sat frigidly and also in silence, shaking their heads somberly as we slipped and slid down the steep slope in sloppy snow to the White River's winding edge.

Throughout my life, I have suffered intermittent fits of sporadic intelligence. It comes and goes and normally isn't anything to be alarmed about. If I feel a sudden spasmodic attack of intelligence coming on, I am usually able to avert a full scale, full-blown episode of clear thought by quickly doing something absurd, thereby breaking the chain of synapses from firing in any particular order that may otherwise have resulted in something other people — onlookers for example — might have considered rational and reasonable thinking. My attacks are never too severe, and seldom do I remain ensnared in the convulsive throes of reason for long. I have always managed to free myself, usually in just a matter of moments.

That particular day, I was completely and utterly free of anything that could, even by the loosest of all possible descriptions, be described as rational thought.

I had made up my uncluttered mind to wade my way across the White River (which I later learned was at flood stage) and I was fully clothed in soaking wet apparel. Once on the other side of the torrent, I could stumble through the frozen jungle and maybe then disembowel myself with a jagged ice slab the size of Idaho.

Danny's exact words were, "Okay, you go first. If you live, I'll think about it."

Unfettered by reason and now spurred on by Danny's warm-hearted encouragement, along with his solemn promise to join me on the other side, I stepped into the river. My clothes were already soaked from the slippery trek down through heavy wet snow and underbrush. So temperature was not an issue. What *was* an issue was the river's speed.

Although not at a wide spot, the pinch in the river's waist that I had picked to cross was deepening faster than I had anticipated; I had watched the surface currents' speed and had prepared myself based on what I saw. Accepting the fact that the water appeared to be rolling along at a gentle, but indeed perceptible clip, I concluded it was manageable. I could lean into the current slightly while aided with the rigid staff that I had selected from the driftwood lying about and which helped me hold a three-point stance. Correctly, as I hoped, I was able to maneuver in this manner, nearly to mid-point across.

But it was quickly getting deeper. Under the water's visible surface, it was also moving increasingly faster. Visually, the situation I had waded into had been misleading. The river was unexpectedly fast; I was half-assed. The river was now halfway up my ass. And yes, it was cold!

I had selected a crossing point in the river that afforded me an option, should I need it. Across the torrent, and only a few feet from where I was, lay my safety option — a large broken-off log in the water, perpendicular from the opposite shore. It stuck out about one-third of the river's width across the surface. The harder and faster current was white in places, and now I could see the turbulence that I hadn't paid much attention to earlier, just in front of the two-foot diameter log. Behind it and on the downriver side, the water's surface was smooth and flat after being ironed down by the rigid timber.

Cleverly, I had picked this spot in case of just such a scenario; I had reasoned that I could abandon my three-point shuffle across the current if I had to, and dive for the log. Although I hadn't wanted to take this option and wasn't looking forward to it, I had planned for it — if need be.

When first I had entered the water, the noise of the rushing river seemed to have an unusual and unfamiliar drone about it. The farther in I waded, the louder and more ominous it sounded, more percussive than any water I had ever encountered. The low drone had been so unrecognizable to any earlier frame of reference I held regarding water, that I originally had disregarded it.

Before too long, however, I was able to isolate the sound — both in my far distant memory of having spent hours underwater and from the aid of the odd pain I was experiencing on my ankles and shins. I was finally able to discern the cause of the sound; it was the clacking of thousands of rocks being whacked into one another. The low resonating clatter of rolling stones underwater multiplied into a mountainous sound. Some stones now were large enough and rolling along the river bottom fast enough that my ankles, feet and lower legs were beginning to turn into cube steak; I decided to dive for my option before a large boulder took me bowling. I dropped my staff and lunged for my log. The current caught my back and quickly slammed me into it, as planned, although a little more firmly than I had hoped. The river was deeper there, as expected, and it was even faster there, also as I anticipated.

What I had not expected was the sheer power the river now held on my back. My cheek was pressed onto the gnarled bark of the mountain log as if we were long-lost lovers. The water roared onto my back like the steel blade of a full-throttled logger's bulldozer. It soon became obvious I did not have the strength to move along the log onto shore as I had planned. My chest, face, and arms seemed to be part of the log. Because of the water's roaring turbulence, it had become very loud at that spot where I had grown so attached to my timber. At this point, breathing was not a problem; leaving was the problem.

I know fear *should* have been a variable in the equation at this point. But it wasn't. Keep in mind I had done everything up to that point on purpose. Everything up until my being pinned to timber had gone roughly according to plan. Now, factor in my perceived invincibility in situations such as these along with the fact that I was once *almost* a television stunt man for a major beer manufacturer. Oh, and one more thing: Danny and I at this juncture in our lives were both licensed Red Cross Lifeguards; and we all know that lifeguards don't drown — that *would* be absurd! So up until that point I still had no fear.

Now I had a decision to make. Did I want to starve/freeze to death there on the turbulent side of my log where the water was full-fast? Or did I want to dive under while holding onto the log and reappear on the other side, in the breakwater where it was half-fast? Once again I made the typically half-assed move.

This too went according to calculations — all except for the breathing part. Although I went under the log, hung on, and bobbed up on the other side as planned, it was time to become very, very afraid. The anticipated and hoped-for breakwater was evidently only a few inches thick and just barely on the surface. I expected to be able to breathe on that side; my expectations in that regard soon failed, along with my air supply. My confident bravado was immediately replaced with instant panic.

The roaring river that had crushed me onto the log on the upriver side now boiled up and over my stomach and chest, shooting a white flume into the air over my head. Oxygen was no longer an option. I clung to the log with all my strength and, though I was strong in those years, I was still unable to go hand-over-hand down the log to shore. It took everything I had in both arms just to hang on, which wasn't about to last much longer. No matter which way I turned my head, my face was buried in a churning whitewater rooster tail. I saw flashes of Danny on the other shore; I could only catch glimpses of him and he seemed to be gesticulating wildly and hollering like hell, but I could not hear him.

I heard nothing other than the roar of water and the thunder of thousands of river rocks below and around me, migrating towards Puget Sound, fifty miles away. Maybe I also heard the call of eternity roaring up from the depths; I didn't know. Still clutching my long lost log, I felt I was losing consciousness. Before I did, and in between choking gasps and an occasional peek of the gray sky above me, it happened.

Just as I had seen, when succumbing to the river's pull when I was a child of six or so, an image appear — an apparition of a glass of water — I witnessed again the inexplicable.

As I fought for consciousness, daylight, and the odd thimbleful of air mixed with all the white froth I was inhaling, I had another opportunity for a trip into the twilight zone — alone.

It was as if I were watching a movie, one of those familiar scenes mostly viewed in older films, but often a scene segue in contemporary flicks as well. Suddenly the headline of a newspaper article materialized from nowhere. Whenever I caught a glimpse of gray sky, a saved newspaper article seemingly clipped from the front page appeared. Each time when my vision wasn't awash with the pounding river curling over my face, there it hung, flat and suspended in mid-air.

The article, slightly yellowed, showed what appeared to be some degree of age and oxidation. It was headlined: ONE LIFEGUARD WATCHES ANOTHER LIFEGUARD DROWN IN WHITE RIVER. The body of the article was, of course indiscernible to me, since I had little time to read newspaper accounts, new or old, about any events, current or otherwise — including those that might pertain to my own death. I did recognize in the first sentence, however, the words in a smaller font, but all caps: CHRISTMAS DAY. They led into the sensational story — sensational to me, anyway.

The future old news — covering a non-event — was becoming, rapidly in the grip of the river's surging rampage, a current event at that precise moment in space and time. It reported the location, date and lifeguard credentials of him who was about to drown — two columns wide at the top and about eight column-inches long on the first left-hand column. It was half that length on the second column. I have no idea what paper it had been, or was going to be, clipped from. Not big news on the grand scale, I guessed it to be a local newspaper: the *Daily Olympian* maybe, or the *Tacoma News Tribune*.

And then it was over. I have no memory of losing my grip on the water log. One cannot survive for long without air and I just couldn't stay awake long enough to finish reading my article. The lights went out and I was behind in my reading. I had held onto the fallen timber, one arm over it, one arm around it from underneath, inhaling the liquefied snow and the freshly fallen rain in its endless water cycle towards the ocean and back again until I fell into darkness. Falling rain in any form has always made me drowsy.

What I had also fallen into before slumber was the grasp of panic. Panic — I knew it then but had forgotten — is your worst enemy in a clutch situation. I'd had many minor scrapes underwater when I was younger, but had taught myself not to panic. This time I panicked. I knew better than to clutch the log and drink the river, but my suddenly overwhelming fear had a stronger grip than I did. Danny, otherwise helpless in that situation, had been screaming at me to let go, to swim *with* the current.

Never fight the river — the river will win. Become part of the river's ceaseless flow by swimming or floating with it; go with the flow while you still have breath and a heartbeat.

I hadn't done that. I had fought the raging torrent. I lost. I fell into panic and then I fell asleep — a deep and peaceful sleep.

I have always been one of those people able to take a nap anywhere and at any time. Also, I'm one of those cranky people who does not wish to be disturbed when napping or endeavoring to get a good night's rest. I am grumpy if you disturb my slumber, especially when it's not time to awaken.

Someone was interrupting my cozy-warm Saturday morning sleep-in. Some obnoxious fool was continually droning into my ear a constant and irritating moan. *If they don't shut the hell up, I'm gonna kill 'em!* I opened my eyes to find the

offender and put him out of his pathetic moaning misery —
and mine.

*Where in the hell am I? Wait a second! That's me moan-
ing! Where am I and why in God's name am I moaning like
that? Holy Christ, my stomach is splitting! I'm lying on my
back in cold water and my stomach is going to burst. I'm
freezing. I thought I was at home in bed asleep; this is a
dream! Wake up! Make it stop! I'm cold and it hurts. I hurt all
over! My stomach is breaking and I've been hit all over my
body by a thousand hammer blows! Why is this happening to
me? Why can't I wake up?*

That's when I knew I was awake. I was awake and I
wished I wasn't. Unlike a nightmare you are so glad to escape
from by suddenly awakening, I awakened *into* my nightmare
and *now* I wished I had stayed asleep.

I began to comprehend through the pain, the noise, the
cold and my semi-consciousness, why I was there. How I got
there is still a mystery. I was there because I had challenged
the river — somewhere upriver, I remembered — and by the
look and feel of me, it must have been about ten miles upriver.
I struggled to sit up and take stock. My stomach was stretched
and it hurt like hell; I had drunk half the river while unconscious. I looked at my clothes; they were in shreds. My heavy
wool turtleneck sweater had about a hundred holes in it and I
had some corresponding holes in me.

I knew then that I had no business being alive. I had
obviously bounced along the river bottom, dead by all accounts, newspaper or otherwise. I had been poked and snagged
by every root and broken branch my dead corpse could collide
with on the river bottom. I had scores of bruises from being
shattered by both rolling and stationary boulders. And for how
long? I had no idea. About a week, I figured.

Suddenly I saw Danny crash through the brush on the
other side at the water's edge. He was searching for my body

in the water. He was trying to catch a flash of color from the burnt orange sweater that I wore. He was pale; resignation was the true color on his face. Danny looked up and had not expected to see me sitting in the shallow water on a sandbar on the other side of the torrent. He looked shocked, and elated at the same time, to see me alive. He had caught up with me on foot and he appeared tickled pink to see me, although I was on the wrong side of the river. Still, I was on this side of the Great Divide. As miserable as I was, I remember being happy to see him also.

I began to moan less about my lot in life. I was no longer annoyed and grumpy about my morning wake-up call, so to speak. By then I had weighed the alternative and had concluded that sleeping in that day would have caused me to miss a lot of appointments.

No longer interested in slabs of ice, since hypothermia was setting in, and since I was becoming one myself, I needed to focus on the river I had to re-cross. The next crossing wasn't as elective as the first time. I wasn't going to see the New Year, or tomorrow, or tomorrow's newspaper if my next crossing was as ugly as the earlier one. However, I had no choice but to cross back over to the other side.

Once I managed my roly-poly sloshing carcass, wearing a 200-pound holey orange sweater which was now grossly misshapen, I moved as fast as I could muster, which was not too fast. Although my thick sweater contributed to my awkward lumbering condition because it hung down below my knees and the sleeves nearly touched the ground, it did help retain body heat.

Finally, I found a split in the river and in the narrowest spot of the worst of the two forks was another short jutting deadhead log, this time on my side. From that point, even in my condition, I could leap to a standing hardwood, which offered a horizontal limb for a simple overhead monkey-bar maneuver.

Skier, Olympic water champ, underwater explorer, innovative fashion modifier, ice climber and now gymnast — all in one day. In fact, all before breakfast! I stayed busy back then: full-time job just trying to maintain a pulse.

Naturally, when I made my two-step Hollywood-style Burt Lancaster-type running leap onto my sturdy limb it snapped off, right at the trunk. The frozen brittle limb made a loud crack and I hit the roaring cascade, feet first, running. I took a deep breath before I hit, anticipating another deep sleep after consuming the other half of the alpine torrent and then rotting away somewhere halfway down the river's route to the sea, but I was surprised. I was happy to learn that the frigid froth wasn't as deep in this spot as I had expected. Maybe five feet deep, enough to cancel all my appointments for life, as well as any future newspaper subscriptions, but shallow enough to afford a momentary upthrust once my shoes felt the river rock bottom. My momentum was enough to carry me close enough to the far shore so that I was able to grab branches and pull myself to the bank.

But when I had first hit the water, I was handed yet another surprise in icy river criss-crossings. When my hypothermic head went below the melted glacial artery of ice water for the second time that day, I was delivered a new shock. As if by two sledge hammers, one on each temporal lobe, I received simultaneously the hardest, most painful head blows of my life. My body temperature had already lowered to some point of concern due to my earlier arctic baptism. My *second* submersion nearly flash-froze all the tiny capillaries, veins, and arterial blood supply to and in what was my evidently otherwise empty head.

My feet had instantly found bottom and I shot up out of the water like a hooked marlin desperately trying to shake off a Florida fisherman! I had one hand over each of my temples and was bellowing loud enough to cause a serious North Cascade avalanche or trigger a giant icicle cascade. *This*, I was convinced, *is true pain*! I made it out of the river and, with Danny's help, on up the hill.

I had dry clothes in the car. The girls had waited there and were not impressed. Danny told me I was stupid. I agreed with Danny. I checked the papers the next day to see if I had died. Evidently I hadn't. Or, if I had, they didn't consider it newsworthy enough to print.

Here is a curious side note: the brand name of my big burly burnt orange wool sweater was "Brolly Male." I have never forgotten the name. Why is that? I can't tell you the name of any other article of clothing I ever owned in my entire life, or own now, except maybe Levi jeans. And I can still see that saved newspaper clipping hanging against the flat gray sky.

The remarkable and otherworldly abstraction of foreseeing a never-written newspaper account of an event that never was, is beyond my comprehension nearly four decades later. It was my second of such similar apparitonal experiences, and among the many things beyond my ability to comprehend. However, the real mystery still lies unexplained, the tangible physical mystery of *how*.

How does an unconscious person, drifting on or near the river's bottom, eventually end up *with clear lungs* on land? I have never heard of such an experience. People are always going under in the rivers around here, with the Olympic Mountain range on one side and the Cascades farther inland.

We have lots of rivers, and many bodies are never recovered. The ones that surface, are usually found sometime later, much later in some cases.

But a person washing up from the depths and deposited *on his back* no less, on a shallow sandbar? If I had washed up face down, that newspaper article would indeed have been printed. I have no doubt that I would have continued to consume water lying face down in the river until there was no breath — and no pulse.

If the river had not rejected me by somehow rolling me up onto the bar onto my back, spitting me out, as if from the belly of a big fish, someone today would have an old faded-to-yellow news clipping. It would be tucked away by now and forgotten in a drawer, possibly inserted and ignored in a boring old book or scrapbook — a two-column news item, a note from long ago about someone hardly anybody can recall. Except maybe Danny.

11

SKI LESSONS

W hile geographically close to the subject of the
Crystal Mountain Ski area — and Danny
Woollett — it seems appropriate to disclose events
related to my first experience on the slopes. This story pre-
dates my escapade in which I spent Christmas Day under the
surface of the White River by about eight months. I am able to
pinpoint the time because I know it was the previous ski
season, but late. And that under the instructorship of Danny
Woollett, it took me a fair matter of time to heal from my very
first official ski lesson.

Danny learned to ski early in life because his family's
income could afford him the opportunities: high school ski
club and what not. I was still somewhere by the roadside
beating my bicycle while he was up on the slopes. Danny soon
became a monitor in ski patrol and I was still in the ditch
being monitored from a distance by the State Patrol.

Because I didn't know what I was getting myself into, I
begged Danny for a ski lesson to the point that he caved in and
agreed. The terms were simple enough: I pay for his lift ticket;
he'll teach me to ski. Eventually I scrounged the money

together for two lift tickets and ski equipment rental; Danny, of course, already had all his own Zen Buddhist ski trappings of some special pedigree that only he and others like him understood. Whenever a cluster of the privileged Zen-head skiing masters gathered, they started to speak a dialect that I clearly would never learn.

After nearly two hours fighting with the acerbic smart-ass punks downstairs at the ski rental facility, I was ready to stomp up to where Danny had said to meet. Of all the service personnel jobs in the world, I doubt if there is another to parallel the likes of "ski rental outfit guys," or whatever they're called — the most smarmy, loudmouthed, sniggering class of peckerheads I have ever met. As they go about ver-bally abusing the rental victims while snatching things from them (like their rental cards, their dignity and their shoes), they make insider comments to each other in ski language. They shove ski gear in your face while hollering obscenities at other rental thugs on the other side of the room. Radios blare from their Walkman headphones; they chew gum, mouths open; they scream at you because you got in the wrong line; they thrust the wrong-size ski boots at you while sneezing in your face, then spit their gum at you for correcting them.

Shaking his head and mumbling foul language to himself, my rental guy pointed at the door. "GO THERE" he finally hollered, eyes wide and nose rings clattering. Ski rental thugs were, I think, the first ones around here to get scores of tattoos and multiple body piercings.

"Why, what's in there?" I sheepishly asked. "The gas chambers?"

He took my new sneakers around the corner and began urinating in them. While doing so, he turned his head in my direction and yelled, "That's the door to go outside — to the CHAIRLIFT!"

The most mean-spirited and socially retarded, obnoxious and self-centered reprobates I've ever met seemed to qualify for these positions. So I applied. Right then and there.

They very politely turned me down, of course. They patiently explained to me how, because I had never skied before, I just wouldn't work out. "Get a few lessons under your belt and come back. Oh, and sorry about your shoes." His hand was on my shoulder as he held open the door for me.

"Atsokay," I said. "I do it myself all the time."

Danny already had made several runs with his other friend and fellow skier, Wyatt. When I caught sight of them ahead of me waiting for the chairlift, they both had apple-red cheeks and looked as if they had just graduated from the Campbell Soup Ski College.

After getting one ski boot attached to its corresponding ski, I attempted to attach the second one. Several near misses later, I clicked the second boot into its binding. But now the first one disconnected; I had gained nothing; my glass had half-spilled. I focused again on the first boot and binding. When it finally went CLICK, the other boot escaped bondage. So it went, with me repeating my first-time-on-the-slope virginal indoctrination of ritualistic embarrassment over and over until the people behind me waiting for the chair reached clear down the mountain to the gas station at Greenwater. Then, all of a sudden, another CLICK, and I was ready.

The Campbell Soup kids had made six more runs while I snapped my bindings. I was already worn out and all sweaty. But as I stood up, I felt as if I looked like a skier. Danny showed me how to board the chairlift alongside him. The lift curved around and scooped us up, and he pretended not to notice when the bar support hit me in the forehead because I had turned my head to the wrong direction. He also looked off when, halfway up, one of my gloves fell from my lap into the snow far below us as our chair vibrated us upward to some scary pinnacle of doom I had only heard stories about.

But when one of my two candy bars slipped from my grasp and silently sailed south towards the sloping snowfield, he noticed. He grabbed the other one and stuffed it into his mouth, chuckling, "You dropped 'chers, so this one's mine." There was no point arguing; it was gone.

"So!" Danny yelled, turning in the chair toward me, peanuts stuck in his startling yellow teeth; not yellow due to candy residue, yellowed in comparison to the world of pure white in which we dangled. "Ready to ski?"

During the last couple hundred miles, just before the chairlift was to drop us down onto a ramp of some sort, I asked Danny what that other thing was that we had passed, way, way down at the bottom.

"Oh, that was the rope tow — bunny tow, we call it."

"What's it for?" I knew the term sounded familiar, but had never listened in much on ski jargon.

"Little tiny kids. Special Ed people. Old people. Blind people and chickenshits," he said solemnly. "You wouldn't want to learn on that thing. More work than it's worth. Besides, if you want any lessons from me, you need to be where I am. Right? Did you see me down there with those wimps? No, you didn't. That's because I'm up here with you, where the actual skiing is done. Now get ready to get off the chair and follow me around to the side."

Our skis gently connected with the ramp and I rose from the chair in unison with my very own personal ski instructor. We curved around to the left and it dawned on me, I was skiing! Yes, I could do this; I knew I was a natural! Apparently, traveling sixty and seventy miles an hour on my roller skates had built up equilibrium or something, so that I could ski like a Swiss yodeler my first time out. Boy, was I proud!

On the flat spot just below the chair, where everyone had stopped to put on gloves, lipstick, hats, sunglasses, ski straps, sunscreen, scarves, ski wax, fingernail polish and Preparation H, Danny also stopped. I kept going.

I might have stopped if I had been instructed how. But I kept right on going. Danny's voice was mingling away into the distant background behind me, along with all the other stationary voices I was passing. Talking blurs. None knew that I had no ability to stop and, up till then, none had been in my path. I had brushed, slightly, one or two talking blurs as I slid silently past without incident. There had been two loud clicks when I ran over the back of one guy's new red skis. He said something — I didn't know what — my hands were full.

It was still nearly flat at this jumping off point, but I wasn't slowing down much. Then I saw her. I knew she was beautiful, even though she had her back to me. She had to be beautiful with a rear-end like that. She was bent down from the waist in those tight black stretch ski pants, the kind they wore in the '60s, the ones that caused guys, even those living in Kansas, to take up skiing. As I said, my hands were full. In a moment, they would be even more so.

Unable to stop, steer, or slow down, I thought I might as well enjoy the scenery for the remainder of the trip. So I focused on the lovely swaying shape directly ahead of me. She continued to apply toenail polish or play "This Little Piggy" with her feet, or whatever she had bent over to do. I had no control whatsoever of my two skis by then, but somehow, instinctively, at the last moment I was able to separate my feet.

One of my skis went to the right of her, the other to the left. My momentum picked her up in a what I thought was very satisfying fashion and now both of us were coasting straight ahead. Unfortunately, she didn't stay in her original position for long. My full hands were on her hips, while ski

93

poles, hers and mine, stuck out in every direction. She was screeching and cursing at me.

When we eventually fell over into the snow, I tried to get a good look at her. All I could see was fangs and fingernails. She was hitting me with her gloves, her ski poles and her hands. Most of the onlookers assumed we knew each other and that I had done it on purpose. They all smiled and shook their heads, as if this was some kind of foreplay — horseplay — between us. So I played along by laughing and cooing, "Honey ... stop."

By the time she was done beating me, Danny showed up. "Making friends already, huh?" He still had peanuts stuck between his teeth. "Okay, let's hit the slopes!" was the next thing out of his mouth, except for a partial peanut.

To which I countered, "Wait, what about my lesson?"

"This *is* your lesson."

By then, we had scooted up to the edge of the pinnacle's small plateau. All the people that had finished applying lip-stick and whatnot were crunching past us, one by one. They came to the edge of the cliff and shoved themselves over, weaving back and forth until the tiny dot that each became disappeared. A shapely figure clothed in black whizzed past, cursing.

"I don't know how to ski! You haven't taught me a damn thing! How am I supposed to get down there without killing myself?" I began to tremble. "Show me *something*." I begged.

"Okay, let me show you where the lodge is. Down there, to the left. See it?" He aimed with his ski pole.

"That infinitesimal gray speck?"

"No, that's the parking lot. Up a little ... there ... that's it. So here's your lesson. Shove off from here and head for there. If you live to reach the lodge alive, you must know how to ski or you couldn't possibly have made it that far. At which point the lesson will be over."

I told Danny I didn't want to shove off. I told Danny I wanted to shove my skis up ….

"Quitcherbellyakin!" he interrupted. Then he was gone. I watched as my peanut-riddled, Campbell Soup-cheeked personal ski instructor of Zen zigzagged from view. The familiar phrase, "If you live …" was still ringing in my frozen ears.

A constant stream of confident skiers were coming up from behind, pausing momentarily, and then hurling themselves like lemmings over the precipice. I asked one lemming how long we had to wait until spring. He ignored me and threw himself into the chasm to become part of the stinking, vile pile of rotting flesh that must surely be somewhere below. There was no doubt in my mind that most of these lemmings must certainly die on this cliff. Knowing I would only be one more bloated corpse when the snow melted, I made up my mind to stay put, wait for the spring thaw. I would then march victoriously past all the Zen dead lemmings that had so carelessly thrown their lives away.

I searched my pockets for more candy bars. If I was going to stay put until spring in order to walk down and jeer at dead lemmings, I needed food. Danny had eaten my last one, that damn Danny! I vowed to kill him if I survived. Not until I again heard the familiar female voice behind me, the sexy voice of that shapely bending one who I had caused to squeal with delight when I had earlier swept her off her feet, did I decide I'd better shove off after all.

But first I asked for her phone number. It quickly became crystal clear to me that not only was she not going to render to me her phone number but, if I was to stick around, the chances were good I would be rendered my second thrashing at her hand. As she approached, cursing as usual, to administer what I hoped would be my final beating of the day, I tossed myself off. At the moment I lunged over the crest of death, I heard a ski pole make a swishing miss near the nape of my neck, nearly causing a nasty nick.

She reminds me way too much of my mom anyhow, I told myself.

There I was, shushing! Mostly I was screaming. I was also picking up speed. My goal was to find Danny and severely punish him before the mountain, or the mountain witch (who I could still hear hurling curses and casting spells after me) killed me first. But here I was — skiing!

Unable to turn or slow myself, much less stop, I shot straight down the three hundred-mile long cliff to where Danny hinted I could pick up my diploma … if I lived. I knew if I fell over, I would surely die. At the speed I was traveling, I would come apart, like those cars in the movies, when they sail off over a cliff and crash — fenders, doors, bumpers, bolts, nuts, teeth, ashtrays and gearshift knobs scattered all over the mountainside. I clocked myself unofficially at six hundred eighty-four miles an hour. I heard a stationary blur say, "Wow, look at that … a speed skier!" as I passed. So I stopped screaming and tried to act like I was doing this on purpose, as if I actually was in control.

There is a remote possibility I might have been able to pull that one off — the one about looking as if I was doing that downhill speed record attempt on purpose — if not for the hideous carnage I caused in the lift line at the bottom. I don't know how many people I took out, but there seemed to be a lot fewer skiers on the hill for the rest of the day … at least wherever I went.

Because Danny had said so, I actually believed that I could ski! I made several more of those straight-down-the-mountain, straight-out-of-the-barrel-of-a-Winchester shots. I tried to pick a different spot to crash and burn each time, so as not to attract too much attention to one landing site and thereby maim too many rubberneckers and innocent spectators, in case a crowd gathered in anticipation of the next spectacle.

The rest of the ski day passed without incident. Except for one time when the chairlift knocked me down and I grabbed it from underneath. The lift operator was messing around with some pouty blonde babe and was not paying attention to the lift. His back was to the chair departure area, his concentration in the direction of lifting her spirits — or her sweater. Anyway, by the time Juliet noticed and alerted Romeo, who then stopped the chairlift, I was halfway up the slope, hanging onto the seat of the chair from the bottom. Then he got all annoyed, like it was my fault.

I did receive another beating that day at Crystal Mountain. It was a beauty and took weeks to heal. It did not happen while actually skiing however. Nor was it administered by the mountain witch with the great assets and the colorful vocabulary of a logger with Turret's Syndrome. (I still have absolutely no idea what she looked like; I never actually saw her face.) Nope! My thrashing was completely self-inflicted.

At the end of the ski day, the three of us met — Danny, Wyatt and me — near the lodge cafeteria. Everyone's skis and poles were stuck in the snow, pointed up, and there were my rental skis, right next to all the other Zen ski stuff owned by handsome and muscular guys named Biff and Bruce, Todd and Mark, Lars and Sven. I had survived! And my scratched-up rental skis were there to be counted. My skis looked as if they shared with me the pride I felt. Danny and Wyatt needed to pee.

The ski rental office where I had earlier applied for work was at the bottom of a long, steep flight of wooden stairs that had four thousand six hundred twenty-nine steps — not counting the top landing. To show my gratitude for my ski lesson, I offered to take Danny's skis and poles to the car after I turned in my stuff at the Dale Carnegie ski rental office.

I slung all six skis onto my right shoulder. I tucked all six poles under my left armpit. I put one foot on the icy top landing and then flew into space. I slipped and fell, head over heels, clattering down each and every single ice-block of a stair step. The skis beat me, slapped me, and whacked me all the way to the bottom. The poles entangled me, tripped me, poked me and were bent all to hell.

The trip was loud. It was long. It was painful. And the end of it drew applause. Although it did elicit some concern from a few strangers, it drew laughter from Danny. After all, we were friends and he knew I was indestructible. Wyatt was sad that he had missed the whole thing while peeing, but said he heard it and had assumed it was a small avalanche.

Lying motionless at the bottom landing, hoping for a priest to administer Last Rites, I heard faintly the shrill cackling of a hysterical female, laughing as if satisfied and victorious, from somewhere farther below, out in the vast parking lot.

I had broken nothing, other than a few ice-covered three-by-twelve-inch wooden stair treads. Still, I had colorful sore knots all over me for weeks. I took no more lessons from Danny — not in skiing. I was to learn, however, many other lessons while in Danny's company. And vice versa.

12

SOLIDARITY OF THE ELDERLY

W hen I was a kid I used to have to pretend to listen
to all the cookie-cutter complaints from the
previous generations. *Codgers*, we called them,
quietly though, and only when among other kids.

On and on they would drawl, about how rough they'd had
it when they were our age. How they all had to work twenty-
two-and-a-half hours a day — when they were twelve. They
had to hike fifteen miles to school through blizzards and
snakes, and then they had to hurry home after school to milk
all the cattle.

I only stuck around for those grim fairy tales in case some
candy, or maybe coin, would materialize as my reward for not
interrupting or falling asleep. I would pedal my bike to the
next old codger's house, strike up a conversation, and then
have to listen to exactly the same damn story!

It was clear that somehow, they had all gotten together at
some point before I was born to get all their stories straight.
Although at first, it may not have appeared that every one of
the previous generations even knew one another, they must
have, or maybe they all had just memorized the same handbook, "The Handy Handbook of Hardships."

The Great Depression, the pestilence, diseases, dust storms, wars, hunger, famine! On and on it went — the endless suffering, no television, the movies weren't in color, some older movies didn't even have sound! Tribulation was everywhere. The four horsemen of the Apocalypse had not only shown up early; apparently they had stayed. And they must have started a horse ranch. They bred, and spread their misery to every conceivable corner of Elderland. I'd be drowning in pity for the lost generations, the ones before mine. I'd be emotionally wrung out. Then I'd have to depart for a nap. Satisfied that he had worn me out, the old codger would close the door to his house and go lie down for *his* nap.

Surprisingly, almost every single one of those painful and pathetic purges from the past by any given geriatric (which was anyone over thirty-five) had started out innocuously enough. Each conversation had begun with a far-away wistful look and some phrase of introduction such as: "In the good old days …." Then after a forty-minute dissertation on the abject horrors of antiquity, it would conclude with "Yep, those *were* the good old days." As if they hadn't even been listening to their own story! Then they would act like they were sad and all because those days of misery and deprivation were behind them. What the hell did these people want out of life anyway? Half the time I couldn't tell if they were happy they had lived as long as they had or if they were just annoyed, inconvenienced for living *too* long.

So I asked one once. I asked Gramma Lennon. She was eighty-five and I think it was her birthday. She wasn't my grandmother; she was grandmother to my cousins, but we all called her "Gramma Lennon" when she was present. When she wasn't, the term was "Old Lady Lennon." Not me though; I had been taught to respect the elderly. I referred to her as "mean old bat." Which always drew a chuckle from *my* Gramma Jenny, who never did like Old Lady Lennon in the first place.

Patrick, my cousin, and I were out in the yard during Gramma Lennon's party. It was a sunny day with Mount Rainier in full view when Patrick and I began a six-year-old's philosophical dialogue. It didn't last long. Soon we were in a fistfight over who or what was the oldest: Mount Rainier, Gramma Lennon, or God?

We decided to go in and have Old … I mean … Gramma Lennon settle it. Except by the time we went into the house to ask her, we had forgotten what the exact question was in its original form. I still had a bare outline in my head of the subject matter as I looked at Patrick. He had absolutely no idea why we had left our cake outside to come into the house. He just looked at me and shrugged his shoulders, so it was up to me.

"Gramma Lennon …" I began, "… if you're eighty-five, aren't you afraid you're gonna die pretty soon?" The room drew very quiet and I could hear the black marble clock with Westminster chimes harmoniously gonging away on the mantle in the other room — the catalog of death, life, and time, the ever present mantle clock, a requirement for being old.

"Listen boys, once you live to be as old as I am, *you don't give a damn,* one way or the other!" Then she threw her head back and laughed loudly.

"Can God pick up Mount Rainier?"

"Getouddahere!" she yelled, stomping one foot on the kitchen linoleum.

My whole life I have maintained an admiration of the image of that eighty-five-year-old woman tossing her head back and laughing at death. Could you do that? I might say I can do that, but I'd know I was lying. Could she have done that when she was thirty-five or forty-five? Maybe, but I doubt it. I think her being Irish may have helped. From everything I've heard, and the small amount I have read, the Irish seem genetically predisposed to dealing with misery, death and stew. I just know that if I had ever once tossed my head back and laughed heartily at the subject of death, I would have been struck dead on the spot.

So, Gramma Lennon was another one of the previous but still breathing generations of oldsters I would periodically probe about the meaning of life. It seemed to be unanimous; everything about the present irritated them, nothing about the future appealed to them, and everything in the distant past seemed a painful melancholy stew of distasteful maudlin memories simmering in a thick sauce of banal morosity — *their good old days,* they called them. As usual, I could make no sense of it.

I was mainly bothered by the continuity of the whole thing; I secretly suspected another large-scale plot. The universally aged had evidently devised a way to suppress the thundering hordes of effusive youth they saw charging towards them. Worse yet, it appeared to them as though we were all poised to trample underfoot and thereby obliterate any memory of their good old days while we relentlessly ran amok. Not only were their flowerbeds no longer safe from our continual insipid stomping; we now were encroaching on their squalid, but sacred, past.

Eventually I figured it out.

Guilt. They had all, in concert somehow, agreed on a way to hold us at bay. They were manipulating us by making us feel guilty — guilty because we were lazy, guilty because we played after school instead of coming home to milk every damn farm animal in sight. Guilty if we napped on the lawn instead of baling hay. Guilty if we didn't eat everything on our plate. Guilty because we didn't have to pull stumps, drain swamps, or build fences during our school vacations. We were made to feel guilty if we didn't clean our rooms, guilty because we had no "respect" for our clothes, and that back in the old days, how they didn't have rooms or clothes.

We were made to feel guilty over electric toasters, comic books, TV, transportation, telephones, toys, electricity, store-bought clothes (especially shoes), spare time, and particularly money. Gum, candy and soda pop — that was a category of its own. Back then all they'd ever had was tree bark and chicken fat or whatever … and how "they had felt mighty grateful to get *that,* once every two years or so."

In fact, gratitude itself was another issue. They had had nothing, yet they had been, as kids, dutifully grateful all the time. We evidently had everything, yet we were grateful for nothing. So right there was another thing about which to feel guilty — our shameful ingratitude. There we were, trampling all over their pansies and nasturtiums, and their precious memories of misery and malnourishment. Not once did we ever think to thank them. We were up to our necks in guilt and ingratitude.

Then the '60s came along and saved us.

Guilt was abolished. We were emancipated from ingratitude. In fact, ingratitude was *required* in order to graduate into the '70s, where it was also required. (Come to think of it, to the best of my knowledge, it still remains a non-elective requisite.) The shackles of guilt were thrown off like yesterday's dirty tie-dye t-shirt and kicked under the bed. The '60s had arrived bearing a blanket-sized free get-out-of-guilt card. Hippies were everywhere, and not only were they now in people's flowerbeds, they were picking the flowers and wearing them! They flouted any respect for their clothes, especially bras — which regularly gave me two good reasons to extend towards them my hearty gratitude for the clever fashion innovations of those times.

The 1960s self-taught a whole generation to laugh at life, death, and everything in between. They even came up with a band called the Grateful Dead.

Old Lady Lennon never did die. She's still out there somewhere, head back, laughing hoarsely as she sneaks up behind some poor ungrateful little kid who's stealing the hydrangeas out of her flower garden to sell them to the neighbor lady, who drinks a lot, so that he can buy some candy, which will ruin his appetite for dinner ... which then will elicit another series of worn-out sayings, thinner than the knees of an ancient hippie's old jeans, that will include: "Back in my day ...," "Hungry people in ...," "When I was a kid ...," "You don't know how good you've got it ..., "... kids of your own," and, "where on earth did you find your grampa's smelly old tie dye t-shirt?"

13

ASK ANOTHER OLD LADY

T wo days after writing the previous story, the following took place: I returned home from a county-sponsored softball game, where I play in the over-fifty-five league — that's age, not IQ. The Viagra league, I call it, a term that no one but myself seems to consider clever. We lost 5–4. I was last up and last out. Bases loaded, I took an outside pitch, which normally is my pitch, and hit a wussy dribbler right off the end of the bat to second base. Game over.

I picked up my stuff and slunk off and away from the thick silence that followed. I felt like an aged and recently fingered war criminal.

It wasn't my best game, although not my worst either. But, for that game I have an excuse. I'd had a vasectomy one week before. I know — most guys sixty years of age are not lining up for that particular procedure; I'm aware of that. It's just the way some things work out, at least in my life. Chronological disarray. *Chron-illogical*, if you prefer.

But my point is this: after fathering five kids, due to my own formative young adulthood having been molded by the social mores of the '60s and participating in the rampant experimental breeding induced thereby, I have been, once again, indirectly victimized. Because after being forced into a situation where society actually expected me to feed and clothe all five of those kids — which I did — I feel I have paid for my crimes. But now, here I am, recuperating from the big-V, years later. This is exactly like being tried and punished for the same crime twice. And it's certainly not helping my swing; I'll probably bat like this forever — nothing but wussy dribblers that don't even clear the mound.

(The foregoing had nothing whatsoever to do with what I intended to say. But thank you for letting me vent. You seem to have an understanding, if not kind, face. I didn't mean to go on like that.)

So, after returning home from the softball meltdown, I found my wife was not at home. My young and lovely wife was out shopping. Saving me money. My wife saves me more money annually while shopping than most people even earn. She probably saved me two or three hundred dollars while I was at the ballgame; she has therefore revealed to me a new source of wealth. Anyway, I limped down to our neighborhood corner restaurant, Ravenous, for a cold one and a table outside.

That hot July Tuesday appeared to be a slow evening inside the restaurant. There were only three diners in the small corner establishment — one couple and an elderly lady eating alone. I noticed the elderly diner only because of how nicely she was dressed, and also that, as I watched her eat for only a moment or two while my beer was being poured, she never looked up. She remained intensely focused on her food or her evening out or her relative solitude. She seemed to be a hearty eater for her small size and her frail appearance. As she concentrated on her plate and the food in front of her, her head remained bowed while she chewed and readied the next bite.

One couldn't help but notice more scalp than hair on her carefully coiffed-but-thinning hairdo. When I caught a glimpse of her face, she appeared to wear a slight smile, although I couldn't have said for sure.

I was dirty, uncomfortable, overheated, sore, and irritated with my last at-bat. So when I exited the hot restaurant, it felt soothing to sit with my cleats off and feet up, outside in the early evening air. It had become somewhat cooler by now and also quite thirsty out. I sat alone under the café's solitary green canvas umbrella with my cold beer, alfresco.

By the time my second cold brew arrived, the sun had barely slipped behind all the buildings on the uphill western slope of Tacoma's hillside, and it had become even cooler, or maybe it was just the beer. Soon, I heard the soft rattle of the rubber wheels on her walker. Out the corner of my left eye, as I faced the upside of the Ninth Avenue hill, I saw her slight form moving quite slowly.

I did what we all do. I allowed my thoughts to overcome her time-infirm and fragile presence as she crossed from my left stage corner view to center stage, just in front of me. I allowed her, in her old and frail silent smallness, to be as invisible as she seemed in the sight of others, to expect to be.

That's when I noticed again what I thought had been the tiny smile on the corner of her thinly lipsticked mouth, as her passing form monopolized my view. My dirty stocking feet were propped up on the metal railing of the café's sidewalk verandah. Up until my registration of the narrow hint of her smile, or merely my perception of its presence, she was, and would have remained, as invisible as society contracts in these situations.

The infirm, the misshapen, the aged, and the disenfran-chised, for the most part, seem to agree to not expect to be acknowledged — at least not completely. Just as we who are more fortunate seem to agree not to completely notice them. And I speak in the voice of over-generalization, I know.

The players accept their respective roles and, in subdued awkwardness, pass each other on small stages everywhere, usually in silence. Except for the weather. Commenting on the weather would head the very short list of topics up for discussion. The weather once noted, the players usually exit the stage.

The unwritten contractual agreement appears to be mutual in its content. Those with not much time left or those who have suffered the unkindnesses of time agree with the firm and fortunate in their unspoken paradigm. Mostly, they silently agree not to be bothered, by not acknowledging and seldom speaking to one another as they brush past each other on the stage of daily life.

While I was deciding not to be a silent actor this particular time and was searching for something to say other than on the subject of meteorology, she looked down at me and spoke first. That took me a bit by surprise when she did so, as she seemed almost too frail to speak; but then on the other hand, I thought, she was a good eater. When she spoke, her head was again lowered, as it had been when she dined. I was slouched back and down in my café chair, so I was in the same visual proximity her plate had been earlier. Her vision was focused now in concentration of me, over my dirty stocking feet. In stopping, she became framed by my extended and open legs. Although not seeming to notice the incongruity of our appearances (she must have), I was uncomfortably aware, but not enough to lower my feet. Peering into the cheap seats she graciously said, "You just can't ask for a more beautiful evening than this, can you?"

"No, this is perfect." When I realized my reply was something less than profound, I upped the ante a little. "… if we could just learn to appreciate evenings like this one." Now I immediately felt foolish, as if I was attempting to lecture an elderly lady on life's values, something I knew I had no business doing.

That's when her focus truly zeroed in on what the stage of life had set before her, the face in the footlights betwixt the filthy feet. She looked at me as if I had thrown a head of cabbage at her, then she slowly said, "That … is … RIGHT! If we would only LEARN!" Turning away as her walker was again pressed into service with the weight of her small frame and the spindly wrists that steered it, she added over her shoulder, "You look like you know how to appreciate times like this. You enjoy your cold beer now." She had gone only a few feet towards the exit, my stage right, and was preparing to rattle on up the sidewalk, when I spoke again, "Won't you sit and have a cold one with me, or a glass of wine?"

"No, thank you for asking, I need to be going." And she completed her exit, softly shuffling, accompanied by the quiet wobbly rattle of plastic and rubber wheels on the still-hot concrete sidewalk.

"Okay then … the next time," I called as I studied the colorful floral and vine embroidery that patterned the back of her black silk dinner jacket. I noticed the white lace on her cuffs and the round red earring on her right ear, the ear I could see from where I sat. She had indeed dressed for dinner.

While the detail of her embroidery faded in the next minute or so, I made a very crass observation — if not comment — under my breath, as if I had a drunken buddy sitting with me that might be listening for just such a crude remark between two grimy thugs. I silently muttered, "I wonder if she's aware of the fact that she'll be fertilizer within the next couple years … at most?"

As soon as I said it, or maybe just thought it, I was sorry I had. Although there was nobody anywhere nearby, I wished I hadn't thought it, or said it. Yet it *is* a fair question. She must surely think about it. Hell, I'm sixty and I think about it all the time. So she's aware the dwindling sands of time are grinding away her days. How could she not be? Especially after her comment regarding appreciation of fine evenings and, in her favor, of fine dining as well. I wondered if she had eaten dessert.

She had already demonstrated to me through her comment that the time left to her was valuable when she politely turned me down as I asked her to sit for a drink. Each time I took a swallow and put my glass down in the next few minutes I turned my head and looked up the long, otherwise empty sidewalk, in order to monitor her progress. Somewhere near the middle of the block, which is actually a full block away because this particular block is over two blocks long, she stopped.

Some fool kid had the boom-box in his car turned to an obnoxious decibel and he too was making his way up the long block, spoiling my evening air with his "rapcrap." She appeared not only to have stopped but was then turning, as if to see where all the noise was coming from, to see who was spoiling the lovely evening that we had, by mutual agreement, contracted to appreciate and enjoy together, although separately.

When the fool kid blared past her and her head did not follow, I knew that wasn't why she had stopped. I watched as she then began shuffling back toward my direction. I had my doubts that she had changed her mind about my offer. But by the time she was within casual speaking range, I pretended I had no doubt that she'd indeed had a change of heart about that drink. "I knew you would change your mind — let me get you a chair."

"No, no, no, thank you. It's just that I went up the wrong street. I'm supposed to be on Saint Helens Street, not Broadway." Before I could say anything or offer assistance she added some verbal ice to my beer as she crossed in front of me for the second time. "It doesn't really matter where I am anyway, young man. All I'm doing is arguing with time."

Aware of what I thought she meant, as if she had been reading my mind, I ignored my thoughts and asked stupidly, "Who's winning?" As soon as the words were out of my mouth I wanted to hit myself over the head with one of my dirty baseball cleats. She stopped again and looked once more downward at me. She now appeared as if someone had served her a plate of stale sponge cake; nevertheless, with all the focused attention she had earlier lavished on her meal and my earlier response regarding the weather, she answered; "Time, I'm afraid, is winning. Time *always* wins." And with a quiet *you-silly-boy*-sounding chuckle she made her way into the crosswalk and rattled softly away.

I'm sure she lives up Saint Helens Street in the nicely restored vintage apartment building, The Kensington. I made a vow to go visit her, maybe take her to dinner. But at least go talk to her.

But I know I won't.

14

Dopes

When the 1960s came around, large-scale adjustments were made in many people's habits. Some familiar habits and previously widely accepted social mores were discarded, while other new ones were formed and adopted. Many people sought "enlightenment" (a word seldom heard today) while curiously large numbers of people seemed to lose all ability to speak fluently or rationally. Still others began fervently learning small-container gardening skills. All of these groups, and many variations thereof, mysteriously became voluntary-mandatory owners of used Volkswagens, primarily vans and buses.

Philosophical adjustments were occurring with mind-blowing frequency. Most of the noteworthy adjustments seemed to take place later in any day with the aid of the cheapest beer available, along with the interactive support of whatever exotic vegetation was then growing in plant containers on the windowsill, or behind the garage.

The habits of early rising, going to work on a regular basis, conversing with any degree of clarity, and the purchase of new clothing were the first to go. The Victorian, overblown and evidently downright questionable, virtues of monogamy and apparently even worse, sexual abstinence, were quickly dispatched into the yellowed pages of history, figuratively speaking. The actual yellow pages of the phone book were often to be rolled up and smoked later, when all the Zig-Zag papers were gone.

Some people further distracted themselves by diving from rooftops and windows, onto the sidewalk and into empty swimming pools, usually during one of their moments of being *highly enlightened.*

Old family traditions and religions were exchanged for Far Eastern and Indian religious practices, along with the newly popular residential experimentation known as *communal* living.

Open marriage, abstinence from employment, pursuance of mystical religious enchantment, swimming naked, and the apparent requisite ownership of beat-up old Volkswagens led to these dramatic and specific new adjustments: a conspicuous upswing in venereal disease, embarrassing and repeated supplication to severely judgmental parents for money, arrest and prosecution, curious rashes along with occasional snake bites, and frequent opportunities for catching colds while standing for hours in the pouring rain or in the ditch while hitchhiking home. Usually all in that order and sometimes all in the same day.

The abandonment of brassieres led later to Cooper's droop and earlier, because of one thing leading to another, unnecessary childbirth. The absence of a job resulted in too much spare time which therefore caused more unnecessary childbirth. Profound chemically-induced religious experiences in the middle of the night led to moral confusion and the "miracle" of unexplained children. Skinny-dipping led to painful-but-even sunburn on top of the curious rashes and yet more unneeded children. Hitchhiking and being subsequently ignored by motorists because of the hitchhiker's accompaniment of at least two large stinky wet dogs led to even more unexpected children, conceived during the long hours spent in the ditch — the children, not the dogs. Well, okay, sometimes the dogs also.

Miraculously, many people survived the '60s. We have proof, although it's been left up to only a few to record that proof; the vast majority of people who made it through the 1960s seem to have very little recollection of actually being there. History has recorded their presence, however, through the multitude of self-help books authored by a relatively small number of people from Connecticut and California. Also there has been a remarkably accurate oral accounting of the times by those who went up into the hills of California and Oregon and later established the world's finest Pinot Noir vineyards. Still others, after completing extensive rehabilitation for substance abuse, opened clinics of their own. A great many of these survivors raised children with names like Autumn, Brook, Spring, Blossom, Summer, Meadow, Winter, Rain, Gravel, and Ditch. I know of at least one person named, "Behind Larry's Market."

The constant drone of the continuously repeated mantra echoed throughout the land. All over North America the same exhausted chant was heard: "Volkswagens are dependable — and they get really good gas mileage." Nearly a full decade passed before one of the greatest icon boondoggles of the twentieth century was exposed: Volkswagens were *undependable — nearly worthless pieces of crap* that broke down every other day! The only reason they got good gas mileage was because they were always being towed somewhere for repairs.

Half of the odometer readings on any given VW were racked up while under tow. Reality became the iconoclasm for what nearly became Hitler's second takeover of the free world.

I am able to speak with some degree of authority on the subject of "Hitler's Revenge," as they eventually came to be known; I owned several of them. Back then, the mentality of most of us VW owners was, "They must be good cars; if they weren't, why would I own so many of them?" Although I am a slow learner, I do eventually learn from my mistakes — at least on the subject of Volkswagens I did. Which brings me to my point … drugs.

I have gone duck hunting only once in my life, and the guy I went hunting with shot me. I have operated a motorcycle only once in my life, and that was when I hit the "Lacey Lanes" bowling alley brick wall (I'll have to tell you about it someday). So, when the issue of drugs came around, in my case the decision was simple: *don't tempt fate,* I told myself. I was fully cognizant of my track record when it came to recreational thrill seeking; therefore it was easy for me to decline drugs. I figured my distorted perception of what I thought was reality was already as cloudy and misconstrued as it needed to be. So I had no reason to press my luck. My mom had referred to me as a dope most of my life, especially during my teen years. I had stumbled through all twelve years of my schooling in some kind of a naturally induced apparent stupor; I once had all the report cards to prove it. If my past record with guns and motorcycles was any indication of what the outcome no doubt would be, had I dabbled with the mind-expanding, chemically-altered, enlightenment-experiments of the day, I'd be dead now.

With my luck, I would have choked to death on my first and only Quaalude; I would have set myself on fire with my first joint, or I would have blown out my aorta and had an aneurysm during my very first hit of acid.

Consequently, I have never once ever taken even one puff of pot, or if I did, I'm sure I never exhaled. (I'm sorry … I never *inhaled.*) I also never took acid; I never took pills; I almost never even used aspirin; everything scared the hell outta me — with the eventual exception of beer.

But many of my friends were brave, adventurous and experimental. Many of my friends are dead and gone.

15

"PHONE ME"

I look in the mirror now and I can't believe what I see. Suddenly I've been vaulted into old age. I don't feel any different now than when I was fifteen; I felt like crap then too — no, I'm only kidding about that part. I felt great when I was a kid, except, of course, for when I was in school. Or at home fighting with my mom, or recuperating from my last injury. Or diving into the bushes whenever a car went by because I was avoiding the authorities, and anyone else, over my latest social or legal infraction — and that's not even true either; I thoroughly enjoyed that last part.

I don't feel as if I have changed at all. Except for my wrinkled flesh. In years past I was consistently accused of being much younger than I actually was. That was several decades ago. My face is so wrinkled now that whenever people inquire about my ancestry, I tell them that my dad was a registered pedigree Sharpia. Inside I feel the same, but everything around me sure as hell has changed. Every facet of life seems to have taken on many new wrinkles.

Telephones for example. The accumulated changes in telephones over the last few years add up to more new wrinkles than those on my eyelids — one of which I stepped on just yesterday, by the way. They aren't even telephones anymore; they appear to be devices snatched from the page of a 1960's *Omni Science Fiction* magazine. Although I'm not aware of what their total capabilities are, I know it's something diabolical. I'm pretty sure all the cell phone satellite waves, or whatever they are, are contributing to global warming and the melting of ice in the polar bear's nightcaps. And they are probably causing tennis elbow and cauliflower ears all over the world.

I don't own a cell phone; therefore, I have no friends. I do not have a social life. Because no one ever calls me, I am not only able to pay attention to traffic when on the roads, I am also able, while driving, to defensively observe and consequently swerve, brake, accelerate, scream obscenities and gesture at all the morons who *do* have friends on the phone. Accordingly, I have much more free time to study these idiots as well; and as I further observe them, since I don't have a life of my own, I have been able to conclude and catalog the following: they don't have lives either.

For example, by far the most often repeated phrase into the transmitter of a wireless, telephonic, electronic, cellutonic, satelletic globally messaging, ego massaging, life interrupting, I'm–so–damn–important phone is: "Where are *you* – now?"

The entire consortium of cell phone owner's underlying reason for joining up with each other and the gaggled global constituency of gabbling garblers, is nothing other than to track one another's exact location at that moment.

Why didn't they all just keep their old phone lines? Back in the old days, you knew *exactly* where the person was that you had just called. They were at home, or at work, at the number you just dialed. Back then nobody phoned someone else and asked the stupid question, "Where are you?"

I recently saw four twenty-somethings sitting together at a nice Tacoma waterfront restaurant. All four were on their respective cell phones. Each was in deep communication with some chattering and conversational clever clatch counterpart from another quarter of the globe (probably, I figured, less than a hundred feet away). While their food got cold, each of the four astutely were able not only to locate their respective quarry with the aid of their global positioning system device, two of them simultaneously realized they were talking to each other; I have observed that many of these particular conversations usually finish — especially if the person doing the parroting is a female blonde — with "Oo–Moy-Gawd!"

After all the important people on the planet that this dynamic quarto had set out to corner, into whatever quarter each of their missing quarry whose whereabouts had previously been called into question had been located, their GPD's were laid next to their bread plates. And it was silent. The silence was noticeable. It soon became painfully clear that none of the four was capable of interaction by carrying on a real live conversation with another person. I can only assume this was because each of them knew where the others were; they were seated across from them. Therefore, there was nothing left to talk about. Everybody was accounted for.

Soon, however, their phones started beeping, tootling, ringing and whistling. Another wave of hapless sojourners had evidently either lost their way or were in a chronic, phonic fear that each of these four were out there *somewhere*, floundering about, lost and bobbing around in the sounding sea of cells, needing to be found. So they were phoning to fix that. After all, it had been five minutes since their last phone fix, for crying out loud.

Whenever I hear a pay-phone ringing, I answer it. I assume it's for me because I'm the last person on the planet not to have a personal wireless telecommunication global positioning electronic satellite gadget and I figure somebody's calling me to tell me I'm lost. But alas, it's never for me. It's almost always for a crack dealer named Garth.

I never dive into the bushes anymore, although I do spend a fair amount of time there. At my age, I just *fall* over into the bushes. Usually I have to remain there until someone comes along who isn't on their phone. And if no one comes by to help me out, it's just as well. If I stay put, at least I know where I am; with my saggy eyelids and wrinkled flesh all stretched out and snagged on thorns and brambles.

If Garth gets to me before I can untangle myself, he usually kicks me free.

One week after writing this little litany on our society's addiction to cell phones, my wife and I were "T-boned" on First Avenue in downtown Seattle, having just left a very relaxing brunchtime aboard the KPLU-sponsored "Argosy Jazz Cruise" around Elliott Bay.

Naturally, the woman was *on her cell phone when she ran the red light* at Spring Street. And when she got out of her car, she was *still* talking into her phone.

Cheryl's jaw and head had shattered the driver's window on our car. We spent the rest of the day at Harborview Hospital, and Cheryl now has a permanently injured disc (or two) in her back.

As we drove away from the scene in an ambulance, I watched as the very patient Seattle police officer handed the irate lady her ticket — yes folks, running a red light is *still a crime* in some places — and she indignantly snatched the notice of infraction from the officer's hand, all the while yammering into her damned phone.

16

WWW.ALANDONTKNOW.COM

Then there's the Internet. I am smiling roadkill, lying peacefully in the ditch alongside the "information highway" — if they still call it that. I'm so technologically free that I am *proud* of it; I wear my Internet ignorance like a badge. I enjoy a soft warm fuzzy feeling realizing that, once again, I know less than the average second grader.

I like to think of it as freedom. It's very much like when I was a schoolboy. In fact, there is an eerie, nearly identical analogy to be found in the comparison. Back when I was in grade school, once I had made up my mind to skip learning how to diagram sentences for example, I felt a new sense of freedom — or maybe, *empowerment*, is a better word, popular in the '90s. I was also quite adept at avoiding long division and fractions. The list goes on. I was then able to sit back and watch all the other little lemmings bending their brains around common denominators and dangling marsupials.

I was able, in my self-emancipation from studiousness, to pursue much more meaningful and satisfying endeavors. The instant self-gratification that I have always chosen to pursue was usually fresh, available, and close at hand through my newly afforded free time. Sitting in the back of the class with one hand cupped under my armpit, flapping my arm to make farty sounds, was one of the best ways to express my self-gratitude for emancipation at my own hands. These particular activities also seemed to relax the rest of the class and helped them to study. Many of them studied hard while I helped them think, and they grew up to become state workers. Today many of them are sitting at their desks in Olympia, eating potato chips, donuts and the ever-present daily birthday cake. There, they get to sit around all day making *actual* farty sounds which they get paid for, while playing video poker on the computer. And I helped. Although I'm not interested in taking credit for the extra weight they have gained, nor the fact all their eyes have gone bad, nor for their carpal-tunnel hands, I feel that I assisted them attain their positions.

My hands, however, have never touched a keyboard. I have never fondled a floppy. Never have I manhandled an electronic mouse. I think this whole Internet thing is a sinister abomination, and I quickly avert my eyes whenever a computer screen is activated in my presence. I don't want to be sucked into the techno-netherworld of needless knowledge no one ever knew was necessary until a bunch of eggshaped knotheads invented the whole nasty distraction. Although I find it unlikely, I hear Al Gore might be to blame. Creepy, how similar his name is to mine.

I believe the entire cyber-snare is a huge Satanic cult, and the whole world has gone over to the dark side. All they do is sit around, getting fattened up for sacrifice while encrypting coded messages to and from other cult members, all cleaving to the *Great Cloven One*; although none of them appear to be aware of it.

They sit for hours, knuckling away at the keyboard, plastic

rodent in hand, nibbling away at necropolyptic tidbits of needless knowledge, gleaned from the virtual undead. Not knowing that as they vegetate in their catatonic trance, the information incubus is draining them of their vitality, their time, their health, and their ability to see their toes. Worshipping at the altars of flickering frames of infinite information in front of them, they interface (and in some cases, so I've heard, intercourse) with necropolatian images and letters of encryption from androgynous sources in cyberland. They are logged onto the abysmal *great beyond,* and are dying from information obesity.

Well, they're never gonna get me. I don't have time for any of this timesaving, life enhancing nonsense. I was dragged, kicking and screaming, into this twenty-first century anyway. I liked it the way it was back in the middle of the last century. Those were good days — back in the good old days of my youth, when everything was slower, more personable and meaningful, far less stressful and less trivialized by too much useless information.

Avoiding all this information and most of the timesaving devices available today affords me much more opportunity for naps, relaxation and quality time spent alone. I prefer slow food (unless I'm in a hurry), passive thought, talking to myself, listening to myself, working, as well as playing, with myself, and watching all the other body pods ripen for the great apocalyptic harvest of UNIVAC.

I don't wanna know anything about any of the other stuff. I'm not interested in all the androidinal hyper-technology they can stuff into a laptop, lapdog, Laplander or lapdance. I shall remain a non-participant, unless I happen to be in the room when some downloading or upcropping of educational nudity should materialize. Although that has never happened yet, I

125

am willing to admit the possibility of some future modification in my otherwise flawless opinion regarding all of the bleary-eyed info-clustering presently taking place.

Unfortunately, my hands are slightly arthritic now and they don't allow me to cup them correctly under my armpits for the effect I once enjoyed, not to mention the glee it also brought to others in the room. But, at least I didn't wear out my hands — nor my eyes either for that matter — on a keyboard and a computer screen. My eyesight is not too good; I admit that; and my grip is failing as well. But at least I've worn everything out the old fashioned way.

www.alandontknow.com

17

APPLE ANNIE'S PANTIES

My employment with the Department of Natural Resources tree farm in Tumwater was seasonal. I was only in their employ during the cold, wet, and nasty winter, late fall, and early spring months. I was forced to take the late spring and summer months off. Not the worst thing to happen to a nineteen- or twenty-year-old, but back in the old days, mind you, you had to argue with those stingy bastards down at the unemployment office for your weekly handout.

They actually placed me in the awkward situation of having no choice but to lie to them when asked if I had been actively seeking employment the previous week. They didn't appreciate answers like: "I was too sunburned" or "I couldn't look for work because I went hiking on the Olympic Peninsula and got lost in the mountains." They tried to deny my unemployment benefits one time, a whopping twenty-six dollars a week, because I inadvertently blurted out that I couldn't work "because of all the blisters on my fingertips from playing pinball machines." This was another clear example of how people just *do not* want to hear the truth. Although during this brief period in my life I was attempting to break free from the bondage of falsehood, I was forced to revert to telling them the lies they needed to hear.

After waiting forty-five minutes in the line for my turn to grovel for my money, the small man who had been sired by a ferret, glared at me over his little ferret nose and eyeglasses. "What makes you think you can come into a State Office Building without a shirt on?" asked the little ferret man.

"It's August. It's hot. I was swimming in Capitol Lake." Which back then was right across the street. "This is my appointed day to plead for my unemployment benefits. You're just mad 'cause you hafta work on such a nice day and I don't."

"Go put your shirt on." So I had to leave their office, cross the street, shake the wet Cheetos and corn chips off my shirt, put it on and get back in line again — where I waited another forty-five minutes to crawl up to the ferret's window a second time. "That's more like it," he said. "Have you been actively looking for employment in the last seven days?"

"Ooh, Yassuh!" I says, "Why ah looked down dattaway, an ah don't see noo job. So ah looks up dattaway, an' ah still don't see noo job. 'Den ah looks ober dissaway an' ah *still* ain't got noooo job." Not only did Mr. Ferret not appreciate my *Amos n' Andy* routine, he told me I wouldn't be receiving any benefits in the mail that week. "How about next week?" I asked anxiously.

"Keep your shirt on. NEXT."

In order to conserve what meager financial resources I had, I moved from Tumwater back to the Lacey area for two reasons: I needed to be closer to the pinball machines I was so hopelessly addicted to, the ones at the Lacey Lanes Bowling Alley. *And* I had found a small apartment on Hicks Lake.

I moved into a teeny little studio apartment right next to the old Sunrise Resort, where my fulltime summer employment, back when I was twelve and thirteen, had been dredging up old soda bottles from the lake bottom. My new apartment was off to the side, but still connected to my landlady's house — Mrs. Ann Maynard.

Mrs. Maynard's occupation, at least a good part of the time, also involved bottles. But she only dredged the bottoms of the bottles themselves. Seldom was there enough room in our shared garbage can for my garbage, as the can was brimmed with hard liquor bottles whenever I tried to stuff my trash in. She claimed that she held a lot of bridge parties at her place, although I don't recall seeing any bridge people coming or going. Maybe she was just visited by imaginary card players; I cannot say.

I am fully qualified to comment on her bridge*work* however. I can say for a certainty that her false teeth did not fit, at least not correctly. I know about this stuff because my mom's false teeth didn't fit perfectly either. I remember vividly, when I was around five, while my mom was chasing me with a stick and hollering real loud, her false teeth came flying out of her mouth. They nearly got me and I would otherwise have been traumatized by the episode, but mom started laughing. So I was off the hook; I gently slid them back toward her with my trembling foot.

Anyway, Mrs. Maynard's teeth held my interest because they seemed to have a mind of their own. I sometimes would even initiate a conversation with her, just to observe the curious ongoing tug-of-war between a woman and her teeth.

The first thing I noticed was the continual clicking. At first, I couldn't figure out where it was coming from. As she spoke, it sounded as though a tiny train was arriving from nowhere into the vicinity of our conversation. Actually, it sounded as if the tiny train was tap-dancing its way up to the platform. I have no recollection about any of the conversations themselves. I couldn't have reiterated one word that she uttered; I was incapable of retaining any of the information, advice, opinions, or secrets she was imparting. I wasn't purposefully impolite; I was completely distracted by the invisible tap-dancing train just about to arrive. I kept my eyes on the opening of the tunnel, her mouth, and after a brief wait I could see, ever so slowly, her false teeth working their way past her lips and out of her mouth. She just kept right on talking. She may have been pontificating to me the one true cure for cancer. Or the answers to world strife. Or, even more importantly, how to make fluorescent light fixtures stop buzzing. I wasn't listening. Occasionally I envisioned itsy-bitsy horses clip-clopping around inside her mouth.

I was transfixed by her teeth, both uppers *and* lowers, that together were slowly peeling back her lips, and extruding themselves. As she spoke, her lips stretched wider as more teeth began showing. Slowly they were escaping the oral cavity they were supposed to adhere to. Accompanied by all the small clicks and clacks inside the ancient orifice, the aged orator continued the awkward oration until, just when I knew the teeth were going to fall out and chase me around the yard, she'd suck them back in!

SSSSUMMPP! One quick powerful sucking noise, ending in a sloshy thump! And the wandering tap dancing white horses had been reigned back in. Then she would continue talking; in fact, she had never stopped. It would begin again with the ever-widening mouth, exposing slowly more cuspids, bicuspids and soon all the way back to molars, until the inevitable invisible yank from within suctioned the entire meander-

ing menacing misfit denizens of dentistry back into their
slurping socket.

When I didn't have any quarters to feed the pinball machines at the bowling alley and I guess when I was pathetically
desperate for entertainment, Mrs. Maynard's mouth must have
sufficed. I'm able to say that now, because of the clear impres-
sion I carry in my memory from watching her deal with her
dental work. I'm quite certain that if I'd had any money at all,
I wouldn't have found myself hanging around conversing with
her.

My landlady did, definitely, very nearly traumatize me for
life on one occasion, and it had nothing to do with her teeth.
One sunny afternoon, when I actually had a job and was
returning to my apartment after work, a terrible thing happened.

Mrs. Maynard was in the yard planning her next imaginary
bridge tournament when I walked up onto my small porch, a
couple steps from the walkway and lawn, which was where
she stood talking to me. I made the mistake of conversing with
her on this particular day out of polite neighborliness. I still
wish I hadn't. Just this one time I wish I had excused myself,
unlocked my door and gone in, but I didn't. I stood there and
listened, keys in hand. Soon it would be too late.

She was shaped like an apple, my landlady, an apple with
knobby poles for legs. On this particular day, Apple Annie
wore a short mumu type dress. As she stood there on the lawn
talking to me, I watched in subdued terror as her larger-than-
my-vocabulary panties slowly slid down and clung to her
knobby knees. I nearly fainted.

Obviously unaware that her elastic waistband had resigned, she kept on clicketty-clacking her dentures and sucking them back into her head while I fumbled with my keys.

Possibly all the rattling of her teeth is what had vibrated her panties down in the first place. Maybe, I silently hoped, if I remained stuck there long enough, the vibrations might cause them to reverberate themselves back up to where they belonged, like a hula-hoop. Well, I for one wasn't going to stick around to see if there was any chance that they might vibrate back up the stick legs. Unfortunately though, I did seem to be stuck on the porch, since my hands were then shaking and the key just wouldn't work.

I smiled and pretended to be interested in whatever she was clippety-clopping about when Apple Annie's rattlings apparently loosened her blossoming bloomer's grip from around the knobby knees and stick legs to the point that now her panties vibrated all the way down to her ankles! I knew from her continuing chatter, that she was still oblivious to the fact that her underwear was escaping, being as how she was still knee-deep in non-stop singular conversation while at the same time contending with her contentious dentures. I also knew that sooner or later, she was bound to notice.

What I knew for sure was that I did not want to be there when she bent down and wriggled them back up to wherever they came from. *But wait! What if …? No … it's not possible … is it? So help me god, if she is somehow able to suction those bloomers back up, like she does her teeth … I'm just gonna have to kill her!*

At the same moment that I mentally selected a soft area of the yard to roll her body into a nice deep grave, my door unlocked. Up till then, she still hadn't noticed her undergarment billowing about her feet. This was also about the same time she decided to go for a walk. As I dove into my small apartment, I heard her underpants — *TWANG!* — as she took her first stride.

I locked my door and closed the curtains. I turned up my old radio real loud. I clutched my pillow to my chest and rocked myself back and forth on my bed until I passed out. I lost my job because I didn't leave the house for four days. When I did, I came and went under the cover of darkness. Because of that, I couldn't make any supplication for unemployment benefits. I nearly starved to death — not that I had much of an appetite for a while — all because of my landlady's bloomin' underwear.

18

UNEXPLAINED PHENOMENA

A fter living on Hick's Lake in Thurston County for a year, early the following summer I scored a cabin, just across the road and down Holmes Island Road on the shore of nearby Long Lake, the same lake where the Woollett's lived. I was now living on the north section; whereas they lived on the south. My humble cabin was situated right on the water just two or three houses from the very small Holmes Island bridge, comfortably nestled among fir trees and dogwood. I eagerly looked forward to an endless summer. A gnarly, twisted old madrona grew sleepy-hollow-style between my porch and the nearby water. This time, I even had my very own small dock. I was in lakeshore heaven.

Then came winter.

When I was young and habitually unobservant, changes in the seasons somehow seemed to occur quite suddenly and without prior notification; these abrupt changes would always catch me unaware and ill prepared. Now that I am old and unable to make meaningful calculations regarding my own whereabouts in time and space, it's happening again.

Somehow, almost overnight, I was shocked to find it was the middle of winter. We were also in the middle of a very severe and out-of-character-for-the-Pacific-Northwest cold snap. I had been plunged headlong and unexpectedly into the arctic throes of frozen pipes and winter snows; there was now a block of ice where, only a few days before it seemed, the lake had been. I had a sneezing runny nose and painful frigid toes. Quickly deducing that summer must be over, I removed my swim trunks and hunkered down for whatever the Yukon had in store for me.

Now admittedly, I had never been a brilliant student while in school. However, I seldom missed any school days, was never truant and, believe it or not, I did assimilate, although mostly quite by accident, some of the information they were trying to inculcate into our heads. I steadfastly fought against worthwhile knowledge in any form quite valiantly, but was outnumbered, outmaneuvered and outsmarted. They were clever and they tricked me into learning far more than I had wanted or intended to. Although I learned and retained much less than my colleagues, it was still considerably more than I would have liked.

So now it's twenty degrees below freezing and I'm at work at the state tree farm. I'm indoors, finally, baling bundles of evergreens for reforesting our northwest foothills. I am at the end of a line of ten or twelve women sorting and culling seedlings, where I run the bagging and steel strap-baling contraption. (I will seriously hurt myself and require surgical embroidery while mishandling the baling strap on a future date.) The seedling sorters discuss the weather outside, along with their future vacation plans.

At this point one of the seated female seedling sorters said matter-of-fact like, "Just think, if we lived in Australia or Argentina we'd be enjoying summer vacation right now."

They all sighed wistfully and groaned in agreement. I stopped ratcheting the strapper and looked at the sorter who had said something about summer. "Why did you say that?" I asked, as it had made no sense to me.

"What?"

"That thing you said about summer."

"That it's summer in Australia right now?"

"Yeah?"

"Because it is."

"Is what?"

"They're having their summer while we have winter, and vice-versa. The seasons are reversed; everybody knows that."

"Just Australia?" I knew she was lying, but I'd heard the Aussies were an odd lot.

"Noo," in the patient tone of, *you-re-getting-silly-again,* "anybody living in the Southern Hemisphere. It's summer below the equator."

Others nodded in agreement as the conveyor belt began dropping small bunches of sorted seedlings onto my shoes; these were the seedlings I was supposed to be strapping. I stood straight and still, squinting, while sorting through synapses that were suddenly short-circuiting.

"What in the *hell* are you talking about? Summer here and winter there? That is the most *stupid* thing I've ever heard in my life, except for maybe being told to diagram sentences."

I heard one of the gals up the line mutter, "Here we go again."

Right off the bat I knew they were obviously all in on it. These women had tricked and teased me by talking way over my head many times. The term "workplace harassment" hadn't been invented yet, I don't think; it seemed to appear around the same time as the invention of pantyhose. (Now *there* is a form of harassment and frustration, if there ever was one.) Neither would I have understood nor had I ever heard of the words "innuendo" or "entendre," so these women had had

137

their way with me many times. But it would probably be another twenty years in the future before I'd realize I had most likely been legally violated.

I heard another gal up the line, "See, I told you he has no idea what's going on, *down under*." Half of them pretended not to laugh. The other half didn't pretend; they just laughed.

"Keep your minds on your pinuses girls," said Ada, the line boss, smirking. *Pinus Strobus* — white pine — was what we were processing. I had already heard many variations of that play on words, and *even I* got those.

"I know summer's summer and winter's winter, no matter where you are." I wasn't going to cave in to this balderdash, not yet anyway.

"Alan, do you mean this is the first time you've ever heard of this?" interrogated Ada, with a slight smile.

"Well … yah … but that doesn't mean I'm falling for it."

"You're not falling for anything; it's a simple fact," Ada further reasoned. I could hear sniggering up and down the line. Little trees were piling up around me. "But you are falling behind," as she pointed sternly at the floor.

I have never been a distant stranger to bewilderment. Bewilderment has been my life-long companion. In fact, I have always been able to rely on bewilderment as a confidant, long after all of my real, as well as imaginary friends have turned on me. That day, I was beyond bewildered. My brain was bound to break if I further burdened it with this abstract aberration, so I withdrew from the lopsided debate and started strapping. Already aware of what must be an acute shortage of neurons in my head, I knew that I needed to salvage what few misfiring synapses I retained, those that hadn't yet shorted out. I needed to think.

Did I somehow sleep through this turvy-topsy geographical trivia wizardry while at school? Had they waited until I was sent to serve time in the principal's office to talk about this? In what grade had they dredged up from the depths this unlikely drivel and fed it to everyone except me? I was deeply disturbed; so after I caught up with the overload of twisted seedlings, I delved back into my overload of twisted information.

"So if I'm standing on the equator, one foot on each side, you people are telling me my left foot is in *summer* while my right one is in *winter*?"

"Yeah … like it would matter. You're on the equator — where it's *always* summer!"

As they chuckled away, I asked them another question in the form of a logical probe. "So, if the equatorial line of demarcation runs through a city, for instance, all the calendars hanging on everyone's wall say *December 20th, first day of WINTER,* in this half of town, while all the calendars on the other side of town say *December 20th, first day of SUMMER?*" Every single woman — and the married ones too, come to think of it — stopped sorting and with a faraway puzzled look on each face, remained silent.

"Whatabuncha horsepucky," I concluded out loud.

When I stopped for my evening meal at Larry's Market on the way home to my frozen lake and pipes, I would make some inquiries; I'd get to the bottom of this upside-down nonsense. I'd find out if the women at work were scrambling my brain for fun, or if I had accidentally slept through something of actual interest while in school.

My first stop inside Larry's Market on Sleater-Kinney road was always the candy bins. I never stole any. I never bought any either. But I sure as hell sampled a lot. I could cram more chocolate peanut clusters into my jowls than a skinny squirrel at a nut farm in November. After purchasing the needed nourishment for my next lunch or two, along with my nightly candy bars (dinner) I asked the clerk a question.

After quizzing him about the summer-winter, inside-out, black-is-white nonsense, he leaned back against the cash register. With his arms crossed, he answered in a scholarly fashion, "Yes that's right. And not only that, the whirlpool in a sink or a toilet swirls in the opposite direction from one hemisphere to the next."

I coughed up a peanut. *So now he's in on it! Those women know I stop here every night for sustenance; they must have phoned him and clued him in on how to further pith my belea-guered brain into formless, useless mush.* Then, he asked *me* a question.

"Are we gonna have to start weighing you when you come in the door, and again when you leave?" I wiped my mouth, knowing I must have left some telltale chocolate smeared all over my face. I swished saliva around my front teeth in an attempt to dislodge any more accusatory peanut fragments.

My turn: "I'm supposed to believe the toilets and sinks swirl one direction where we are, and the other way in Uru-guay?" As I made small swirling gestures with my finger I saw him notice the melted chocolate between my forefinger and stubby thumb.

"Absolutely," resolutely.

"So what do the sinks and toilets on the equator do? Do they fall straight down?" He suddenly wore the same expres-sion all the tree ladies had, earlier in the day when confronted with my logic. I left.

I laid off the latitudinal and longitudinal logistics for a long time. While at work with the women weaving together the teeny weenie trees of our future wilderness, I kept my conversational platitudes to simple stuff, stuff I understood. In other words, I didn't talk a lot for some time. And when they embarked on some topic I knew nothing about, I didn't ask any questions. My mom may have been right after all, back when she said, "Ignorance is Bliss."

Note: In my research for this story, I flushed the downstairs toilet in our Sanford & Son Antique shop three times. Each time, the swirl went counter-clockwise.

I flushed the shop's upstairs toilet three times. Each time it went clockwise.

Then I went into our apartment in the back of our antique shop. My wife Cheryl and I flushed our toilet three times, which upset our cat, Peanut. Each time the water went straight down. (I am not lying!)

Conclusion: My downstairs is in the southern hemisphere; the upstairs is in the northern hemisphere; and our apartment lies smack dab on the equator. Outside our window on the backside of the building, at the very moment I write this, it's raining cats and dogs; therefore it's winter; at the same time, outside our front window it's sunny.

I want a candy bar.

19

PERILS OF THE KLONDIKE

If I had been around for the Yukon Gold Rush in 1898 and ventured north to Alaska, I no doubt would have been the first to wander off the trail and perish. My aptitude for survival in a winter wilderness of that magnitude would have been slim. I proved that to myself over one winter while living alone; alone — except for my cat and the hallucinatory visitors I entertained during a very brief period of attempted self-medication — in my frozen cabin on Long Lake.

My cat and I were also plagued by actual claim-jumpers. I'll get to that shortly.

One mistake I made was not waiting until spring to bathe. I knew better, but I needed a bath, because it was the weekend. I had to get cleaned up so that I could roam around downtown Olympia and be ignored by girls. My plumbing had been frozen solid for a week or so, and I had made the decision to hammer a hole in the lake for an arctic lathering.

Pounding on a large spike with a boulder while atop the surface of a local lake wasn't foreign to me. Nor was bludgeoning a stick of dynamite with a big chunk of granite! Nor swimming in the Pacific Ocean during a blizzard while living in Kalaloch! I had done all these things and many others; boring a hole through eight inches of ice should be a piece of cake.

Basically, I was correct for once, except the icing on my cake was quite hard. Bit by bit, blow-by-blow, I chipped a two-foot diameter hole in Long Lake. It only took about an hour; and I didn't mash even one finger. But I think I annoyed most of the lake dwellers to the point of homicide. Not to mention the fact that every fish in the lake was now deaf.

Have you ever slammed a large boulder down onto the frozen ice cap of a pond or lake? It makes an indescribable sound. The shrill peal of the impact resounds across the floating cap of frozen water completely to the far shore. If you do decide to experiment with cracking the ice you are standing on (not that I can imagine your being that dumb), I have one piece of advice — don't do it in the middle of the night. Not if your neighbors have firearms. Sound travels in the frozen north. Birdshot travels faster than sound. These are things you need to know if you expect to survive the white wilderness.

However, I did wear a hole in the lake and I took my bath. I did not linger long in Long Lake; a luxurious bath I did not take. (Incidentally, I just remembered Linger Longer Resort, an older and, even then, nearly defunct camp at the far end of the south section of Long Lake — land's sake! The things one remembers.)

So I was set for the weekend. Somehow I had cajoled my old school buddy, Bob Richards, into frolicking with me at one point during the weekend. I don't recall what we had been doing recreationally, but he was dropping me off back at my frozen homestead. I didn't own a vehicle of my own at that point.

In my somewhat usual method of thanks, I thought I'd quickly form and launch a friendly snowball into the cab of his

144

'58 Chevy pickup, in the near vicinity of his head. However Bob was used to this type of display of thankfulness since he had received many similar companionship awards from me. Although I'm not proud of it, back when we were in high school, I once layered a dissected frog skin into his peanut butter sandwich. We shared lunch period right after my biology class. Why he still associated with me is still a mystery; he should have killed me on the spot; everyone in the lunchroom had told him so. Except for me, I had asked him not to, out of friendship, and said that I was sorry.

When I wheeled around to throw the snowball at him through the open passenger door, he was already reaching over to close it. He had expected some form of "thanks for the ride" such as this and evidently had seen me bend down for a double scoop of snow. The door was closing as I prepared to release the arctic fastball. I knew I had to act quickly, so I did. By the time the door slammed shut, I had, with lightening speed, ejected the ice wad from my grip, and my fingers were fully extended. Because he was stretched across the seat with his head down, the wad of soft white ice whacked him harmlessly on the top of his head.

At that precise split second, a wad of lightening-white-hot pain shot up my arm and nearly blew off the top of *my* head. The middle finger of my right hand had become clamped in the jaws of his now-closed-and-latched doorjamb! As Bob wiped snow from his hair and face, I watched through my tears and the locked door's window as he showed me the healthy middle finger of his right hand, while the middle finger of my right hand still lingered tightly in his doorjamb.

In that one regretful split instant, I had become very sorry I had thrown the silly snowball, especially since I could feel my digit growing more unhealthy and painful by the moment. Admittedly, I have over the years placed my middle finger into some curious as well as questionable places and situations, but — to this very day — this seems the worst place it's ever been.

Right off the bat when I had released the ball, I immediately decided I didn't want my finger where it was for long, and I said so. The reason Robert reckoned my finger should linger longer than I liked was simple; he thought I was jumping for joy because I had nailed him with my sliding fastball; he naturally assumed I was only howling in loud celebration over my perfect pitch. He didn't know that I was connected to his Chevy by a flattened piece of meat that I still thought I needed. Bob left for home.

Halfway up my driveway with me running alongside, he finally made the connection. Although the look on his face told me that he briefly thought about ignoring all the loud squealing and wailing of my high-pitched pleadings while my legs frantically matched the acceleration of his speed, he stopped. When Bob finally opened the door, unlatching my very unhealthy, unhappy, purpled patch of pain, I heard him say, smiling, "Forget something?" The instant the doorjamb opened, affording my finger a welcome release, I dropped to my knees and jammed my open hand into the snow for relief. Bob closed the truck door and left for home a second time.

That was when I began my self-medication.

After spending a considerable amount of time thrashing around in the snow and howling at the cold gray sky like an injured timber wolf with its paw slammed in the steel jaws of an evil trap, I lumbered into my cabin to forage for my bottle of aspirin. The cat dove for cover under my bed as I cursed and hollered in typical Alaskan fashion.

After locating my only pharmaceuticals and then filling a large bowl with snow, I piled my blankets on the floor next to my small oil-burning heater. I dug in for what would be a long and memorable night.

Nobody told me aspirin had caffeine in it.

Not only did I not drink coffee, I almost never took aspirin. As it turned out, I ingested enough caffeine-laden aspirin in that one night to last a lifetime. The first four seemed to have some effect, but not enough. So I took four more.

With my throbbing plum-colored fingernail and my hand immersed in ice water, I drifted into sleep while watching the flickering flame inside my oily "Siegler" stove. Soon the caffeine kicked in and I jerked awake. I took another aspirin and a slurp of ice water. My assumption was that if I ate enough aspirin I would stay asleep and not have to face my pain. Every half-hour however, I'd get yanked awake by a fitful dream and be forced back into the heart of throb-land. Another aspirin.

Eventually my herky-jerky naps were reduced to five minutes each. I'd be asleep for five minutes — if you could call it sleep — then awake for five minutes. *Exactly* five minutes, each time. I know because as soon as I would jerk awake, I'd glare at my small and, that night anyway, extremely loud alarm clock. During those in-and-out five minutes in one world and five minutes in some other, I met people. Odd people. Although I have no actual specific memory of those twisted people or the creatures they brought with them, I remember the effect the encounters had on me.

I couldn't tell after a while which world was which. My small purple appendage seemed to throb in both five-minute worlds. Soon my new friends were more than happy to sit with me, wrapped up in my blankets next to the stove. And sometimes they went under the bed to be with my cat, who seemed to grow larger every ten minutes. Occasionally my cat was purple and also appeared to throb.

By sunrise the pain in my finger had lessened somewhat. I hadn't gotten any of the names of my new friends, nor had I wanted to. My cat stayed under the bed for two days. And I had another reason not to go near drugs — even if it *was* 1965. Furthermore, I was unable to play the pinball machines at the Lacey Lanes Bowling Alley, due to my oversized dark purple digit. They nearly went bankrupt due to a loss of revenue, and it was all Bob's fault. He had set all these things into motion when he hurt me by slamming his door on me.

Eventually, after a mild case of gangrene and a welcome change in the weather, I was able to shower whenever I wanted. And I had several choices of locations — as long as it was *under* my cabin. The pipes had thawed and split and there was water squirting every which way under my floor. The cat didn't like all the hissing sounds the house was making and moved back under the bed.

I spent most of my time and energy trying to grow a new fingernail. After the original one had rotted off, I found I had a curious curly pink-ribboned fingernail underneath the old one. The new one looked like that hard sticky ribbon peppermint candy my grandmother always had in a candy dish. The candy no one was allowed to eat. Not that anyone ever wanted to.

Eventually spring arrived and my cat came out from under the bed. This is when we were beset by claim-jumpers.

Whenever I left the cabin, which was always unlocked, local kids would sneak in and eat all my candy and whatnot. Actually, my cabin door didn't have a lock. In fact, I don't think it had a doorknob. There had been a rope and a stick that somehow hooked onto another stick or something; it was far too dramatic in its attempt to be woodsy, far too Alaskan for my taste. Plus I couldn't figure out how to operate it, so I had thrown it away.

My door therefore was always open, or at least unlatched. After some time, even the most stupid of the local kid-thugs figured out my door was perpetually unlocked and fed there whenever I left. My cat had an identical problem.

Sometimes when I came home from work or from roaming around and being ignored by girls, I would return to find my cat had crapped all over my pillow. After three or four of these incidents I knew why.

My small, possibly malnourished and already slightly dysfunctional kitty had been repeatedly bullied by a giant interloping tomcat.

I came home one afternoon, to find the door flung wide open and the meanest, mangiest, most abominable rancid-assed tomcat on the planet in my cabin. He had my kitty cornered — as usual, I concluded — on top of my bed and on my pillow. I came in abruptly, to see that my damn cat was splattering my pillow, also as usual. This was apparently his defense mechanism, sort of a "you just better get out of here right this minute, or I'll crap all over our only pillow!" At which point I guess Godzilla catmonster would leave, because my skanky cat never had any marks on him; I had just assumed he had bathroom issues.

When I barged in and scared the shit out of all three of us, Gargantua, the giant wild-eyed wolverine cat creature, almost broke my knee running into me on his way out the door. I thought he was gonna get me, and I came quite close to having incontinent problems of my own.

Not long afterward, my cat was the first to pack up and break camp. I was soon to follow. Not everyone is cut out for life on the frontier.

20

I Don't Smell Anything

As I peer back into the misty haze of my youth, I'm able to conclude that given more opportunity and had I applied myself, maybe I could have been a hippie. Although inadcquate in many areas, I excelled in others. My short hair and clean-cut appearance would have immediately disqualified me, true. But my lack of respect for authority, ability to sleep anywhere, get naked at the slightest provocation, and materially survive on the periphery of society would have otherwise given me nearly all the credentials necessary.

Living for almost a year in a plastic Visqueen tent could also have been included on the résumé.

I lived in the bushes. Not *the* bush, as in Alaskan or Australian-wilderness-bush phraseology. I moved into the *bushes* — sticker bushes and hazelnut, along with a dogwood tree, all of which were very close to the spot where my dad had dug huge holes to bury chicken parts by the bucketsful, back when I was a child. I was to take up residence over an ancient chicken burial ground.

Not wanting to waste my money on rent any longer, my folks had agreed to let me wrap plastic sheeting around a couple trees and over dogwood branches to squat, in typical hippie method. I was then also able to sneak in and burglarize their refrigerator occasionally. Living in this manner translated into more money for the pinball machines! It was then that I began to cast periodic glances at the bowling alley billiards tables as well. Before long I would find another "nega-source" to cause my meager income to evaporate.

Similar to my experience while living on Long Lake in my cabin, my compatibility with the pleasant summery months living outside in my plastic tent was remarkably exhilarating and noteworthy, in the summer-fun-loving sense. By fall I was unprepared for a seemingly overnight climate reversal, which once again hurled me unexpectedly into the throes of winter; it began to take its toll. I was cold. I wanted to migrate to a warmer climate.

By mid-November I had gathered enough information to know I would never be able to take a bus to Australia and enjoy their upside-down summer. I just couldn't raise enough money. So I invested all my saved-up Australia bus money into kerosene lamps and lots of kerosene.

I actually used a small kerosene tin lantern to warm up my clothes before donning them. I also used the same lantern to preheat the interior of my sleeping bag. Over a period of weeks my clear plastic Visqueen tent took on a shimmering ebony-coal coloration. At least on the inside. So did my lungs. So did my clothes. So did my sleeping bag. Some of my teeth already were that color, so I don't think there was any noticeable change there.

The annoying odor of urine, which had mysteriously surrounded the area outside my tent and had mildly bothered me all summer, appeared to dissipate by this time however. The continual Pacific Northwest winter rains, along with the thick smoldering fumes from my lamps had evidently either washed away or cloaked the heavy ammonia smell around my camp perimeter.

Finally, whenever I went into town, girls were beginning to notice me. In fact, lots of people were — for the first time — taking notice of me. Because my olfactory senses had apparently burned out, or at the very least were dulled from kerosene inhalation, I thought I smelled fine. Evidently other people thought otherwise. Most people with lit cigarettes thought they had better extinguish them immediately whenever I was nearby, otherwise everyone in the immediate vicinity could be extinguished. I, a nonsmoker, assumed they were just being polite. In reality, it was just the opposite. Most people, especially the girls, were significantly ruder towards me than usual; of course, why was still unclear to me. *They don't know me well enough not to like me already.* And so, I would optimistically hang around and sidle up to people for a little longer than what they deemed appropriate, especially the pretty ones that appeared to be close to my age. I'd sidle; they'd split.

After being completely cold-shouldered by what few girls I encountered, and also being subsequently ditched by the homeless wino at the downtown Olympia Greyhound Bus Terminal lunch counter, I gave up and boarded my bus for home. The bus driver took my ticket with his right hand, made a stinky-face, and then opened the driver's window with his left hand. That's when I realized that for a change it wasn't *me* that was so offensive to everyone; it was my *clothing!* Judging from all the scrunched up noses I had seen, I probably smelled like the sooty old chimney of my ancient cabin's oil-burning stove when I lived on the frozen tundra of Long Lake. I tried to explain it to the driver. "It's not me that smells funny … " I began.

"Well it's not me either, kid. I hope you don't smoke, because you'll go up in flames if you light one up. What'd you do, fall into a vat of kerosene?"

"No. *I* smell fine, but I think my clothes might smell kinda funny. That's because I put my kerosene lantern inside them to warm them up; I live inside a big plastic bag-type-deal and my pants get real cold."

"Uh-huh." He was watching my every move, every gesture.

"It's only my clothing; if I was naked I wouldn't smell this way."

"I don't know what you're driving at kid, but we have to head out, and you're not taking your clothes off on my bus. Is that clear?"

"… Okay," as if I wanted to get naked on his stupid bus anyway. Although now that I look back on some of my bus trips, had I been naked, I would have enjoyed them a lot more; especially my after school activity detention bus rides with Liz Jones and her friend Carol, on the bus of lust.

He carefully eyed the plastic shopping bag I carried, containing my new socks and underwear, and then he asked, "You don't plan on putting that plastic sack over anybody's head do you? Yours or mine — right?"

We each managed a weak smile as I turned and went down the aisle to where I chose a seat near the middle of the otherwise empty bus. I could see him in the mirror, watching me. I flapped my shopping bag around, pretending to inspect my new underwear. I knew I was making him nervous and he was monitoring my movements the same way the Thurston County cops kept their collective eye on all the hippies that were multiplying like jackrabbits thereabouts. As always, I enjoyed unnerving anyone who represented authority, The Establishment, the hippies were calling them.

Deep down I knew. I knew I could never qualify to be a real hippie. Not that I wanted to, but even if I did, I just didn't have what it took. No matter how antisocial I was, no matter how bad I smelled, and even if I did live in a plastic sack in the sticker bushes, and even if I had let my hair grow, I still wouldn't have been able to cut it as a hippie.

Who ever heard of a *real* hippie taking a Greyhound bus into downtown Olympia, going into J C Penney and squandering money on new underwear?

21

LOAVES OF BREAD I HAVE KNOWN

B elieve it or not, I have two separate stories — each centering around a loaf of bread. I'm aware that most people who live to be eighty or more don't even have one story that revolves around a loaf of bread — not counting people who may have served a life term for stealing one. Does that mean my life is more notable, or less so, because of it? I don't know, but my guess is that anyone who has gone through what I have just for a sandwich, has suffered enough at least to be allowed to tell their story.

My first loaf story took place when I lived the life of a young and underfed bachelor in Mrs. Maynard's rental apartment on Hicks Lake. I was broke and on foot. One summer night my friend Jim Richards (no relation to Bob Richards) and I walked home after the doors closed at the Lacey Lanes Bowling Alley and after we had been forced to vacate their overheated pinball machines. It was around midnight.

Jim Moore, the bowling alley manager, had yelled at us for molesting the machines, particularly the "21" flipper machine. Over the months that we had shoveled mountains of quarters into the gaping mouths of the insatiable contraptions, we had learned a couple tricks, the primary one being to lift the front legs of the "21" machine off the ground and put each leg on top of the tips of our shoes. We had to curl our toes up in our shoes in order to provide space for the round medallion foot of each leg. The playing field was thus leveled somewhat in our favor. In this fashion not only were we able to rack up a higher score and win more games; a welcome surprise lay in store! Occasionally, the shiny steel ball would get stuck in one of the scoring mechanisms, whereupon the capacitor relays would begin racking up jillions of points! And games! Kachunk! Kachunk! Kachunk!

The best part of that arrangement was twofold: the blisters on my thumbs caused from inserting countless quarters into the cursed machines could heal, and I could now *sell* all my extra games to some other kid who wandered by — at a slight discount of course. The downside was likewise twofold: I had permanent circular indentations the size of a fifty cent piece in the toes of each new loafer; and we occasionally got caught by Jim Moore, whereupon he'd immediately throw us out.

While attempting to rack up more games so we could sell them and then buy something to eat, either on our way home or the following day, we were indeed caught and subsequently punished by Mr. Moore. He kicked us out and angrily clicked off our game credits. We were already hungry by the time we walked the length of Shady Lane Road to where it joined Carpenter Road. Soon we were at my apartment, peering into an empty refrigerator, empty except for a jar of mayonnaise. So we went to bed hungry.

The next morning (noon) I awakened before Jim and started rooting around in my cupboards for sustenance. Eventually I scrounged up a previously hidden can of tuna fish. Having barely enough coinage to purchase a loaf of Wonder

Bread, I struck out alone, for Alverson's corner store over a mile away.

Believing it was up to me, because Jim was my guest and I his host, I, who had slept on the floor while Jim snored away in my bed, tramped off into the heat of the day, hoping to return soon with a fresh loaf of fluffy white bread. I vowed silently to show Jim a morsel of old-fashioned hospitality, even though I was of most humble means.

Eventually, I stumbled weakly up the concrete steps and into the small store and, although my strength was rapidly fading, made my meager purchase. With blurring vision, I turned anemically to face the return trip. Spurred on by cheerful and rewarding imaginary images of Jim's smiling face when he would awaken to freshly made tuna fish sandwiches, I force-marched myself into one step after another; of course, I was also naturally driven by my own gnawing hunger.

As I trudged towards home, I repeatedly went over in my head the Wonder Bread TV commercials, how Wonder Bread builds strong bodies — eight ways! Niacin! Riboflavin! ... and six others. (A few years later, Wonder Bread was building bodies twelve ways! I haven't kept track, but I s'pose by now they're up to around seventy or eighty ways.) Knowing the precious nourishment we both needed was safely cradled in the brown paper bag under my arm and that soon my body, as well as my friend Jim's, would be strengthened with tuna, mayonnaise and "eight-ways" Wonder Bread, I steered my starved and shaky legs into step after wobbly step.

With mouth watering, body wringing wet with perspiration, and hands quivering with anticipation, I opened my apartment door and went inside. My only outside door opened from the tiny porch into my small kitchenette where I flopped my soft fluffy loaf of life. Then I saw it — sitting in the sink

— a bowl with a fork in it, and traces of drying and darkening fish fibers along with the transparent blotches of mayo on the edge of the bowl and partway up the shank of the dirty fork. Two houseflies were dancing on the rim of the bowl.

The voice from the loafer living the soft life in the other room, who was flopped in front of my TV said, "Hey, I been wondrin' where you went. I found a can of tuna, so I ate it. Where the hell you been anyways?"

Now, I had a wonderful fifty-cent loaf of nice, fresh but useless bread, and I began wondering if maybe I should put a nice fresh indentation in "wonder-boy," my useless new loafer.

My other loaf-of-bread-story takes place just across Carpenter Road and begins in my small cabin on Long Lake, where I moved after residing for a year on Hicks Lake.

It was a crisp, clear, fall afternoon, nearing dusk. I was once again without a vehicle of my own and I was, of course, hungry. I can't remember what I had in my cabin to put on the bread I didn't have, but I'd guess it was peanut-butter and jam. The closest loaf of bread was in a straight line, directly across the lake to where the "Pioneer Park Resort" people operated a small store.

Earlier that summer, I had scored a rickety old rowboat mired in the tall weeds, cattails, bulrushes and lily pads of a small lagoon in the northernmost section of the lake. This small lagoon had once been the log pond for the long-gone Union Mills Sawmill. And, it was the same millpond and just about at the same place that my friend, Tom, had shot me, back in the eighth grade. In fact, this may even have been the same rowboat! The brick sawmill, collapsed and overgrown with vines, brush and saplings, had been quite active back in the first part of the century when there had been massive logging operations of the local old growth. Back then, Long Lake and Hicks Lake were still connected by a narrow and shallow canal. Just before the uphill curve, just below the Thurston County Fairgrounds on Carpenter Road, you can still discern the old filled-in canal — if you use your imagination.

Anyway, my salvaged and quite flexible old rowboat had some serious separation problems between the planks. The boat itself had about as much play in the ribs as my childhood bike had in its chain. I threw in a coffee can and shoved off, knowing the store closed at six and that sometimes they ran out of stuff. I decided if they were out of Wonder Bread, I'd buy hot dog or hamburger buns for my peanut-butter and jam — almost the same thing anyhow, and they never seemed to run out of those.

As I had known it would, my boat was leaking profusely through the seams, especially right at the water line. Periodically I stopped rowing and bailed furiously for a few minutes. When I was able to reduce the water level inside and the curvature of my red two-pound Folgers coffee can no longer cooperated in the bilgy corners of my decrepit watercraft, I'd quit. I'd drop the can and grab the oars to resume rowing.

After rowing and bailing, bailing and rowing for several hundred yards, I was well past the halfway point across the lake. Just after I finished bailing and as I picked up the oar handles — right before I began rowing — I noticed one particular log in the chained-together half-ring of logs surrounding the perimeter of the then empty swimming area of Pioneer Park Resort. Maybe thirty long logs in a half-circle were chained together, end-to-end, in the water. They were there to form a barrier to keep motorboats from dicing up swimmers. They also interfered with my straight-line-shortest-distance-between-two-points approach to future sandwichland.

From where I had been bailing out my bilgewater I also saw signs of closing time. I knew then that I had no time left to go around the log flotilla. *I'll hafta row like hell and skim smoothly over that one log that's almost completely submerged.* Knowing that if anybody was watching, they were bound to be impressed when I darted across the nearly sunken old log and up to the near shore close to the closing store, I began rowing extra hard.

I anticipated the weight of my boat being enough to push the waterlogged old trunk down just enough to allow me to continue over the back of it. I was wrong. I anticipated that I had enough *momentum* to help carry me over the waterlog as well. Well, I was wrong about that too.

As the bottom of my sad old craft ground quickly to a halt at mid-ship, it seemed to exhale as if exhausted from a long journey, widening as it did so at the sides from resignation, exasperation, or the fact that it was ready to fall apart. And there I was nicely, quietly, and firmly centered on top of the chained ancient prisoner of water. My rowboat intersected the log at mid-point, just as the log intersected my slumped and creaky old boat. Everything remained peaceful and silent, except for the water that was gently sloshing around in the aft of the craft.

The prow pointed upward slightly, due to the extra water weight in the ass end. I moved forward into the bow, hoping my weight would change the dynamics and teeter-totter downward the pointed end; it didn't budge. When I stood up in the bow and used an oar to push against the log, I was able to detect some movement of the boat's bottom on the back of the ancient mariner. Encouraged by this, I shoved harder. I was briefly elated when the bow began to teeter down towards the lake surface. But, I was only briefly elated. When I saw the stern rise up and all the sploshing slop-water suddenly begin to rush toward me, I stopped being elated.

As the icy water that had once been behind me suddenly cascaded over me, swamping the bow and causing it to point straight down toward the lake's bottom, I began to shriek. And then I was swimming, fully clothed. My time-saving shortcut had backfired.

About the same time my boat was settling to the bottom, I had reached the shore. As I sloshed and slogged up to the small store, the elderly storekeeper met me on the gray wood weathered porch, clearly trying his best not to grin.

"What can I getcha?"

"I'm only here for a loaf of bread. I was afraid you would have closed by now."

"I thought I'd stay open a little longer. I got distracted watching you battle with Moby Dick out there," he smiled, pointing out at the stubborn old humpback and then openly beginning to laugh in my face.

He wouldn't allow me in the door, making me stay on the porch in the middle of my puddle until he returned. He was still laughing as he handed me my loaf of Wonder. I paid him and left, heading for the Union Mills Railroad tracks that would eventually take me back to Carpenter Road and the long, heavy, wet, cold walk home.

It's a wonder, the things you have to go through some-times, just to get a damn sandwich.

22

CONVERTIBLE AMPHIBIAN

Being between regular jobs and corresponding pay-checks, without a car and living a third-world exist-ence inside a soot-lined plastic shack, I did what many young men with minimal education do when completely destitute and desperate. I became a roofer.

Although I could go on at great length, telling tons of tragic tales, as well as many mirthful ones, about events that occurred while applying myself to the roofing trade, I won't at this time. Be it sufficient to say for now, the roofing business eventually came to serve me well for many years; at least until my knees gave out.

Working for other roofing contractors at first taught me the ins-and-outs, ups-and-downs, of the occupation. Soon, I was out on my own and doing my own light contracting. And I had saved enough money — $200 — to buy my first convertible, a 1958 Hillman Mynx.

Let me say at the outset, anybody who has ever owned a convertible is basically ruined for life. By that I mean you will always crave another one; no matter how old you get, you'll still be yearning for another convertible. You don't outgrow a relationship with convertibles; it's like sex; you're probably better off if you never take a ride in one, because then you can't know what you're missing. Once owning a convertible and then being deprived of it, is unfinished business, niggling away at you, a feeling of unfulfillment that can linger and drag on for years. Come to think of it, being too easily observed while in a convertible, can in itself lead to other unfinished business and unfulfillment. That, leaks, and consequently mushrooms growing on the backseat floorboards, are the only drawbacks I can think of that come with convertible owner- ship. Getting oneself sunburned in awkward places while driving naked may be another one.

Even the ugliest old convertible is cooler than an average hardtop. My ugly little Hillman Mynx was cute enough to, on rare occasions, snag the odd girl and convince her to climb in. I say *odd* here, because any girl willing to climb into a car with me back in those days had to be odd. Not that things have changed all that much. Even today most of my friends aren't willing to be caught dead with me, let alone get into a car with me behind the wheel.

Sometime at the beginning of my self-employed roofing career and new ownership of my very first convertible, I cajoled a lovely copper-mahogany-red-headed romantic paramour into my Hillman. Her name was Chris Craft. Just like the boat. Her dad, who evidently was a boat lover and perhaps even more odd than I, had indeed named her after the boat. And I can't say as I blamed him.

She was of narrow berth and streamlined. She was en- dowed with a fine upsweep near the bow, had a sleek solid hull and excellent curves; she had a sensational transom and could she purr! She handled nicely and performed well when snug in the harbor. She was fast, firm and beautiful. And, I nearly drowned her in my car. Just like every boat I've ever gotten my hands on, I almost sank the only Chris Craft I've ever taken out — like a stone.

We had parked my Hillman on a slight hill not far from her parents' home overlooking Munn Lake in Tumwater. Purposefully and only momentarily ignoring my genetic proclivity for being sucked into the nearest small pond-like body of water, and also being deeply enthralled in mutually administered tonsil massage, one of us apparently bumped the gearshift into neutral and, unbeknown to us, we started to roll, ever so slightly at first.

Because KGY radio was playing some suitable low-level rock-and-roll, neither of us noticed that the little green Hillman on the hill was slowly rolling quietly over all the little rocks towards the little green lake at the bottom of the hill. Until one of us went, "What the Hell?"

The top was up and the windows were steamed, otherwise we might have earlier noticed that the treetops were sliding past us in the moonlight and I could have stopped my meandering Mynx sooner than I did. Because neither one of us knew we were quietly cruising south for an unanticipated midnight swim, I barely was able to scrunch us to a halt. When I finally did, we were clear down at the bottom of the hill and the front wheels were in the gravelly shallows, half under water. However, I miraculously had no trouble backing out. The ringing in my right ear from my first mate screaming at me to stop didn't cease for some time — and by no means was this to be the only time I would have to listen to my damn dates scream at me to stop. In fact, here I am all these years later, married, and I *still* have to put up with it.

Although over my lifetime I had grown quite used to being swallowed up by small magnetic bodies of water, Chris, in spite of her namesake, wasn't used to underwater near-drowning experiences; she had become frightened by our sudden descent and unscheduled baptism. I understood when she told me to take her home. As we drove, we listened in silence while the newest Sergio Mendez song played on the radio.

In my head, I went over what I would have told her folks — had I not stopped my car in time: "Sorry we're late. Here's your soggy daughter. I've scraped most of the mud and seaweed off of her, but I couldn't get that one leech to turn loose of her left breast. She's breathing better now; I don't think she inhaled as much water as I first thought. I lost track of her bra while I was trying to massage air into her lungs. I loosened all of her clothing so that she could breathe; she hasn't said anything for a while, but I think she can still talk. She still owes me six dollars because we were going dutch. And why on earth did you decide to name her after a boat anyway? She doesn't even float. She sank like a big rock; I was barely able to get her off the bottom, so you're just lucky I'm a good swimmer."

Soon Chris decided she no longer wanted to be caught dead … with the fool on the hill.

23

POOL HUSTLING

From the time I noticed the pool tables at the Lacey Lanes Bowling Alley to when I became a reasonably accomplished pool player, lifetimes passed. I did not become accomplished overnight; no one does. Quite a few coins passed from my hand to someone else's over time. Eventually though, I was able to put an end to that.

Archie Caldwell, the proprietor of "The Bowl" bowling alley on Martin Way on Olympia's Eastside, had watched my progress. Archie's establishment had three well-maintained Brunswick Golden Jubilee 4-1/2' x 9' tables, which were situated directly across from where he sat on his tall stool behind the front counter. From his vantage point and over a period of around three years, he had been able to personally witness my progress. His exact words were, "Alan is by far the most improved pool player I've ever seen."

I was fully aware that this had been little more than a left-handed compliment, but it was still a compliment, so I accepted and appreciated it. Also, his comment was downright accurate. When I had first grabbed a cue stick I probably looked like a blind drunk suffering from a serious head injury trying to push a wet rope through a keyhole from four feet away. After three years of playing almost daily I at least looked as if my head had healed. No longer was I the meal that the average pool players fed on; I now fed on the many levels of less accomplished players below me. There were, of course, still many levels of ability above me; there always are.

By that time my old friend, confidence, had come for a visit. He brought with him his close relative, overconfidence. My ability to play a decent game of 14-1 straight pool or nine ball, gave me the confidence needed to win a few quarters and the occasional dollar. You need *some* confidence in your own abilities if you're going to win at any competitive event of skill.

Overconfidence, curiously enough, can go either way. In some cases, due to self-overvaluation of your own level of skill, you can even appear to onlookers to be a better player than you actually are. Or it can cost you the game. In the more skillful games, such as 14-1, it's almost always the latter.

Outright cockiness, on the other hand, will nearly always cost you money — or at the very least, a healthy dose of pride. A braggadocio pool player will, sooner or later, become relieved of a healthy dose of cash. These types of players are prone to losing more money than, say, an average overconfident contender during a few games of nine-ball. Hustlers enjoy cocky opponents because self-assured players have maneuvered themselves, through their own inflated ego, into the sights of their superior artillery.

I was never in the third category for two reasons. I never had *much* cash to lose in the first place, and I didn't ever allow myself to think I was good enough to get too cocky.

Still, overconfidence, even at the level I maintained, caused me an occasional cash crunch. However, I considered most of the monies I lost as simply lessons — bought-and-paid-for-lessons, mileposts of learning on the way up from bottom fish to slightly higher levels in the food chain. Somewhere in the upper middle of the chain was where my feeding stopped, as well as my being fed on.

My confidence led me into quite a few of the usual billiards room scenarios over the years. Most of them, although remarkable to me at the time, are less than remarkable now, all these years later. But a few stand out and bear telling. At least two of them involve my car; my 1958 Hillman convertible. I'll relate those stories shortly, but for now, I must tell an introductory billiards tale.

This story finds me on foot and has nothing to do with my car because I didn't have one at the time, back in the early part of my billiards career. Rick Bellamy, my pool colleague co-apprentice and I had taken the bus from Olympia up to the big city, Tacoma. We had heard they had real pool halls there, not just bowling alleys with pool tables. Already self-impressed with our own ability to play, we had convinced ourselves that we could feed on some smaller fish. Off we went, country kids, headed up into the big city. We saw ourselves as mini-hustlers on our way up to feed on the unskilled urbanites of downtown Tacoma. Oh-boy!

The Greyhound bus terminal on Pacific Avenue, as handiness would have it, was located right between the two most notorious pool halls of which we had heard. They were separated by a total of maybe six blocks. We hoped to find a couple games of 14-1 straight pool or some three-way nine ball. If we had to, we'd settle for some eight-ball.

We visited briefly the downstairs establishment owned by George "Whitey" Michaels — "Tacoma Whitey" as he was known. We had heard of his exceptional prowess on the green felt rectangles, but that's all; we hadn't actually heard any particulars. Finding the place to be particularly quiet and dull, we left to go feed on the weak at the other parlor.

Passing "Ezmeralda's Dance Club and Tavern," we glanced in and saw a poorly lit establishment with a well-overnourished and underclothed middle-aged lady dancing poorly in front of a well-lit military clientele who were watching, wantonly, the robust dancer wriggle out of what there was left of her remaining underclothing. The wanton watchers appeared to be warm and in want of some form of nourishment, at least from the wistful looks on some of their faces.

Greeted at the second pool parlor — "Max's Eight-Ball" — by the smell of onions and hamburgers frying and having nourishment needs of our own, we seated ourselves at the far end of the lunch-type counter on the round red swivel stools and ordered two cheeseburgers.

A total of maybe eight pool tables occupied the long smoky room. The closest table to us provided a fine visual overview of that table itself, along with the two old geezers who appeared to be almost halfway through their game of eight-ball. We watched them play as our burgers sizzled away nearby. They, the geezers, appeared to be having some difficulty sinking any balls.

Before long our burgers arrived and the two old guys had sunk only one or two balls apiece. As we ate our meal, we continually swiveled around on our stools to follow the game and the painfully pathetic players.

Finally, they appeared to be nearly finished and, as we were waiting for a table to open up, we half expected to get that front table. Eventually, the last ball on the table was the eight ball — game ball. Neither of them seemed qualified to sink it.

Shot after lousy shot.

Several times the winning ball might be only eight inches away from a corner pocket, and each would miss, driving it into the far end bank, only to watch it softly roll all the way back to within six or ten inches of the other corner pocket, back on the same end of the table it had been. Then, same thing again, another pathetic shot, and the eight rolls slowly up-table to lodge on the side rail. Then a missed bank shot. And another. Forever, this went on. It looked as if these two geriatrics were *never* going to get off that table.

About the time I thought I was going to scream or at least jump up and go give one of them a pointer or two to help them out of everyone's misery, one of them eventually sank the eight and the game ended. What a relief!

Then, Rick and I witnessed one of the strangest things. The victorious of the terrible two leaned casually on the corner end closest to us while the lesser skilled of the terrible, the loser, reached into his pocket. The most terrible then pulled out a roll of green big enough to choke a horse. When he flipped them flat, they all appeared to be hundreds!

He started counting them out onto the plush green felt — five, six, seven … hundred! He stacked up seven or eight lush green one-hundred-dollar bills! The best of the terrible casually picked them up, folded them in half around his own horse chokewad, and inserted it into his slacks pocket. *Both* of these guys had giant horserolls; and apparently no ability whatsoever on the billiards green. This was going to be way easier than we had hoped! Although between the two of us, Rick and I hardly had enough money to gag a seahorse, we were sure that before long we would have, now that we had seen what Tacoma had to offer; we had discovered a new source of certain wealth.

Shortly before we were about to make ultra fools of ourselves, the short guy in the dirty apron that had taken our short
order and served us our burgers spoke up, asking from behind
the counter, "So, what is it that you guys think you just saw?"

When we swiveled back around to see who was asking and
why, we could see that he was smiling as if he knew something. He had apparently been watching us watch the old fools
floundering about. He had seen our eyes pop out of our heads
when those hundreds had hit the table. We must have looked
like some of the hungry soldiers next door when the dancer's
undergarments hit the floor, only not as hard.

"Were those hundreds real?" He affirmed they were.

"Are those guys actually that bad and they still play for
that kinda money?" I pressed. That's when he enlightened us.
"One-Pocket." As if that meant anything to us. As if that
answered my question.

"They're playing one-pocket." He acted as if repeating it
would make any more sense to us. Not having enough information in our nearly blank memory banks to service up any
worthwhile reference material pertaining to the words "one-
pocket," we next said the words we knew he was waiting to
hear: "What's one-pocket?"

As the old duffers racked up the full triangle of fifteen
balls I noticed that the eight ball was not in the center where it
should have been. Evidently he was right; they weren't playing eight-ball as we had assumed. They were involved in a
game no one in Olympia had ever played, or had even mentioned, to the best of my knowledge anyway.

Some of the fine points explained to us by our
burgermaster: Each of the two players has *"one pocket"*
designated into which he is to deposit *any* eight out of the
fifteen balls, in order to win. Each player's "pocket" is either

of the two corner pockets at the foot rail closet to the triangle. His opponent "owns" the other pocket.

It is an extremely "safe" game, meaning, one needs to shoot defensively, softly. Giving your opponent "good leave," or position, can cost you several balls into his pocket. Therefore, each player spends considerable effort in leaving the cue ball as *near to the other player's pocket* as possible.

That explained why the two old guys couldn't make simple shots; they weren't shooting for the pocket that seemed obvious to us Olympiads. They were each vying for position while safely leaving the other in a poor position. It also explained why they appeared to be almost too weak to drive the ball more than a couple feet in many cases. They had been playing hyper-defensively; the fact that the eight ball had been the game ball, or the *eighth* ball for each of them was mere coincidence. It was the last ball on the table because each player had pocketed seven balls in his respective single pocket.

We watched through enlightened eyes as the aged, but now skillful, arms swung in perfectly pendulous strokes to deftly push — not hit — the cue ball into the object ball and send the cue ball, in each case, to its desired destination. Hardly a feathery click could be heard. The realization sank in that we were watching not a clumsy choreography of geriatracy but a velvet ballet being performed on a stage of emerald by two very graceful dancers of serious merit as they went about their game, exhibiting what we now knew to be the epitome of finesse. As they did so, they seldom spoke. Their nearly silent articulation was accomplished with sticks. It was also becoming increasingly clear that they were mind readers, at least in regard to what the other player had in mind. Each shooter seemed to know what the other had planned and took an appropriate step to "snooker" him snugly next to his own pocket, thwarting the upcomer's hoped-for position.

Our burgermaster filled us in with more information now that we understood what we had misunderstood.

"The guy with the white hair is George Michaels, "Tacoma Whitey." He's the best one-pocket player in the world; he owns the pool hall up the street, just past the bus station. The other guy, the guy with the thick glasses, is Max Williams; he owns this place. They play like this all the time."

We had already realized that they were indeed accomplished technicians, mechanics of a game we would probably never master. Now we knew not only that we hadn't been watching a bad excursion of two terrible geriatrics on an outing from the local rest home; we had ignorantly witnessed a clash of silent titans. Soon Rick and I skittered off, back to the bus station, tails between our legs. Although our lesson had been free, we felt chagrined that we evidently still had so much to learn. We had come a long way in our pool playing abilities, yet we hadn't even left town, so to speak. I can't speak for my friend Rick, but I certainly had other billiards lessons in store for me. Some were by no means free.

Note: After a few years I got to know "Whitey" Michaels well enough to wangle him out of his "Meucci" custom pool cue with inlaid ivory and ebony dice decorating the shaft. Not through my prowess as a billiards player, mind you. He allowed me to make installment payments on it.

Although I haven't used it for twenty years, I still have it. It's languishing away in a dark closet, similar to my fading memories of when I was a young and confident contender contemplating the clarion's call to cultivate a career on the felted emerald fields of green.

24

GOMER

The first anecdote regarding my small convertible coupled with my love of billiards is only barely worth mentioning. It's just that my obsessive affinity for playing pool is what caused my car to be towed away while I was having my ass kicked in a downtown Seattle pool hall. It was "a serious ass whupping," in the poolroom parlance. But, the worst part was, I knew that if I didn't stop playing and move my car off First Avenue by six o'clock, I would lose my car. The signs on the street said so, and I had heard stories of Seattle's Gestapo parking enforcement techniques; they meant it.

Didn't stop me. Not from playing, that is. A person might understand if I was knee-deep victorious in a billiard blood-bath. That, however, was not at all the case. I *was* knee-deep in a bloodletting, but it was my own poolroom plasma that was gurgling around my ankles, by my own volition nonethe-less. And on top of that, I *knew* my car was being towed, and I *still* would not quit getting my ass stomped by the most back-ward, hillbillyesque, goofy-acting Goober I had ever crossed sticks with! All I had to do was stop playing and leave!

In other words, I had never been truly hustled — not yet. Not until I ran I into … whatever-the-hell-his-name-was. I've always since referred to him, when relating the story, as "Gomer Pyle," because he looked a lot like that guy from Mayberry. Acted just like him. He took all my money. City of Seattle took my car. I had nothing. Nothing but a lesson learned and a story to tell.

At some point in the early afternoon, Gomer and I linked up. As I recall, he was shooting at a table by himself and was stroking way too hard, a sure sign of a not-very-accomplished pool player.

He blasted the balls around the table. The object ball was rattling consistently out of the pockets, the corner pockets especially, because of too much thrust. Once in a while he'd blow a ball off the table and have to chase it down on foot. He was a doofus. I soon set about circling in on my afternoon carrion; he was about to be dead meat, at least in my eyes. How was I to know that he was circling around behind me and was in fact outflanking me? I was about to receive a serious spanking.

We agreed to a few rounds of nine-ball at first, and things went okay for me. I stayed ahead of him by a few bucks; money on the five, and of course the nine. After a couple games, things began to change.

Nine-ball is a game of mini-rotation. You shoot the balls one-through-nine consecutively, and the game ends when the last ball, the nine, is sunk.

Only thing is, if an honest contact is made with the cue ball striking the next object ball in the rotation — say the three-ball — and it or the cue ball somehow careens (caroms) into the nine-ball, sinking it, then it's a pay ball. Then the out-of-rotation money ball is re-spotted on the triangle spot and the game continues.

Repeatedly, Gomer, the lucky bastard that he was, was accidentally sinking money balls on an unnervingly regular basis. He was a sloppy S.O.B.! He seemed to subscribe to what I called the *Triple-H* theory: the *hit-hard-and-hope* belief that if you can make the balls bounce around long enough, something will fall in. He was having a hellacious run of luck; fives and nines were dropping out of order and being re-potted at a scary speed. But that wasn't the worst of it.

Each and every time he slammed the balls around in an erratic fashion, causing a money ball to "accidentally" drop, he *became* Gomer Pyle! Not only did he *resemble* a twenty-something Jim Neighbors/Gomer Pyle character, he repeatedly went into this Gomer-type snickering fit each time the money ball fell out of order. He'd look up at me or his older uninvolved, non-playing uncle who quietly occupied a tall pool hall chair, and put his right hand over his mouth and giggle, silently. Eyes bulging and laughing like an embarrassed high school girl into his cupped hand, he looked amazed and apologetic whenever he clattered a ball of coinage into a corner or a side pocket.

This is getting old. We need to start playing a game that requires a little more skill, one where all sloppiness is eliminated — MY game, fourteen-one straight pool! Plus, I needed to win back my money that this hillbilly had so inadvertently racked up to his column by blindly banging into the pockets whenever he had one of his rattle attacks, a money ball. Gomer agreed to a quick game of straight pool, the backbone billiards game of all time, the game after which all other pocket billiards games rules are patterned —14-1. Now he was mine!

Continuous straight 14-1 is a-point-a-ball, call your pocket, call your shot game. When fourteen are sunk, the last ball remains on the table and the other fourteen are pulled from the pockets and reracked. This continues until one player reaches the designated point mark, fifty or one hundred, possibly one hundred-fifty. (The legendary Willie Mosconi still holds the record for a continuous run in 14-1 pocket billiards — 526!) We had agreed to a quick fifty for starters, at one dollar a point for the difference in our final score.

If I ran three, Gomer would run four. When I pocketed six, he'd run eight. Me twelve, him fifteen. And there was no slop involved. There is no room for erratic behavior in the game of straight pool. And by now, he was all done snickering into his palm; there was no longer a need for it. I lost the first game and we agreed on another, this time to one hundred.

His last run was nineteen and we, *he* reached a hundred on his nineteenth ball of that run, which, coincidentally, was also the first shot on a fresh rack. When he called and pocketed the breaking ball, the odd ball left on the table, he quite profi-ciently scattered the fresh rack of fourteen. In other words, he could have run out the whole rack on top of the nineteen he just pocketed, except the game had ended. With his skill, I knew then that Gomer could probably have continued into the next rack, and possibly the next. *It's a good thing we're not playing to a hundred-fifty.* That's when I called it a day. I couldn't beat him and I knew it. And at a dollar a ball, I was cleaned out.

He had made his point when he effortlessly cleared away a full rack and a half, having another open rack in front of him, which were now easy pickings for someone of his caliber. Not only was my caliber of smaller bore than his, skillfully speak-ing, I had been truly hustled. He had sold me myself. He understood the male ego and had learned how to manipulate it in his favor. His unexpected and unorthodox behavior had sold me the basest human desire: the desire to believe that one's self is superior. It's an easy sell. Especially when conflict of skill is involved.

And, he had done it through his unpredictability. Following an impossible shot he'd act all goofy and surprised, and I had bought into it. My definition of "hustler" changed on that day, which was by then late evening. Up till then I knew what all people assume when the word comes up in conversation, that a hustler is someone who's better than someone else. Which of course is true. But that's only the smaller part of it; the little picture.

A person cannot "hustle" someone else into a game only by being a superior player. The lesser of the two simply will decline when too much skill, bravado, boisterousness, flashiness, strutting, tail fanning, cockiness, bragging, trick shooting or male rutting of any kind is displayed. All any of those things will accomplish is the reinforcement of the intended victim's self-doubt and subsequent departure. Few guys are willing to measure their peckers when there's another guy in the room. Most of us don't want to take the chance; we'd rather save that for later while in the company of someone who doesn't have one. Afterwards, we can hide the measuring device so that she can't check on her own.

Gomer had allowed me to convince myself that I carried a bigger stick, that I could out-gun him. And he fortified my confidence in myself by *slowly* milking me out of my money. He kept his ability shrouded by only out-shooting me in small degrees at first. When he knew I was nearly broke, and we both were quite sure we'd never cross paths again, he pulled out the big guns and blew me off the table; I had been dismissed.

Gomer had my money. City had my car. Gomer's quiet uncle politely offered to give me a ride to Lincoln Towing where I knew my car had been placed in impound by one of the pink "Big Toe" trucks earlier — at about 6:01 as I recall.

As we walked to his car, leaving Gomer and his goofy act to commence carnivorating on some other baby shark, I sheepishly asked the middle-aged uncle just how good Gomer was. When he told me of the countless tournaments his nephew had won — in far away states of course — I, by then, was prepared for what I heard.

Then he began to list off all of the twenty-one cars his nephew had won in pool hall shoot-outs of one type or another: a GTO. A Corvette Stingray. A couple of Hemi's. Twenty-one cars! Mostly ALL muscle cars! And three motorcycles.

And that's how he did it. By appearing to be a stupid-ass hillbilly with a lucky jab and a loose giggle switch, he had taken lamb-fleecing to an art form. No, make that RAM fleecing. He left lambs alone; he went straight for the rams and then he left them hornless, as least as far as their muscle cars — the extension of the American male cue stick — was concerned. Hornless, bumperless, engineless, titleless and carless.

Well, he didn't get my 1958 Hillman muscleless Mynx. The city beat him to it. Gomer's uncle dropped me off at the tow yard; I thanked him for everything and told him to thank Gomer for the lesson and for letting me keep my car.

Back in those days tow yards let you write checks to redeem your wayward vehicle. Which, in my case, was their mistake. They had to run it through three times before it finally cleared. They too have smartened up over the years.

Although I was short of funds for a few days, I was wiser. And I still had my goofy little convertible.

25

ANONYMOUS GAMBLERS

If my diabolical and bloodthirsty old childhood bicycle Sherman had evolved into one of my later cars and reentered my adult life, it wasn't my Hillman convertible. My car had a perfect opportunity to get me killed one day, without even laying a finger on me.

For several months I worked for Bob's Janitorial Service, for a guy named Joe. Joe owned Bob's Janitorial Service — and no, I don't know the answer to that question so don't bother asking.

I was working graveyard hours, like many if not most janitorial personnel. My job was to lock out the bartender and any of his well-lubricated clientele that might be clinging to the floor of "The Spar" restaurant at two a.m. Then I had the place to myself until six a.m. when Kenney the cook showed up to fire up the kitchen. I'd be all done with the cleaning, vacuuming, floor polishing, and, my all-time favorite, the bathrooms, by six. I would then leave "The Spar," on Olympia's downtown Fourth Avenue, to go clean the "Old Oregon Trail" restaurant out in Tumwater next to the Olympia Brewery; two hours more cleaning, max.

Some days, when the sun was rising gloriously on what was promising to be an obviously perfect summer's day, I found it impossible to crawl into my plastic shack to sleep. With the top down on my silly little car, I sometimes wandered north, up to Tacoma.

Occasionally, I found myself down at the Thea Foss Waterway waterfront, hanging out at the run-down marinas and moorage docks, and napping. On a few occasions I'd finalize my morning excursions by stopping at the Bowlero Lanes bowling facility where they had several gold-felt regulation-play pool tables. This is the story of my last visit *ever* to this establishment. I didn't dare go back.

Not that I left them on bad terms. That's not it at all. It's just that I had to leave, rather hurriedly, and I couldn't return for fear of running into others that I had left behind in my haste. But there were no issues between me and the Bowlero people themselves, although they probably were wondering what the hell happened that day and why I was in such a hurry.

Around eight or nine o'clock on any given morning, any pool parlor anywhere in America is probably next to deserted, if it is open for business at all. The billiards area of any given bowling alley is not much different.

There were, however, a couple guys a little older than me, late twenties I'd say, playing nine-ball; they agreed to let me in. Fifty cents on the five; dollar on the nine.

They both were decent shooters, and although I was better than either, I couldn't seem to get ahead of them. I just wasn't getting the "leaves." When my shot came up, I'd be hopelessly snookered behind a cluster of balls, unable to "see" a clear hit on the object ball, the next ball in rotation.

Then, when the one guy would make a couple balls, he'd "choke up" on the money ball or just miss, leaving it right next to the pocket. The other guy would reap the harvest. I, of course, would then wind up with another nasty leave.

Not that I wasn't able to shoot my way out of some of the terrible positions I was handed. My ingenuity under adversity allowed me to triumph in many of these cases, but not enough. As we kept score on the "sliding bean" billiards score-counter that hung on the long wires above our heads, all the dollars seem to be leaning in their direction.

They were by no means hustling me, although in nine-ball and similar games it could be done in this type of situation, basically by causing on purpose the exact scenario I just described, because of the fact there are three people in the game. That's not what was happening though. To be quite honest, they weren't clever enough to be that devious; they were just shooting heads-up pool, and I wasn't doing all that well. Sometimes you get the bear; sometimes the bear gets you.

Not only was I unable to bear it any longer, I knew how much money I had in my black leather tri-fold wallet and that my budget couldn't bear up any longer either. I called it quits. Between the two of them, I owed them about twenty-five bucks, alotta money back in the mid-'60s.

Now it gets interesting.

A couple years earlier I had gotten my hands on an old Olympia Fire Department badge. I kept it in the middle of my tri-fold wallet, pinned to the leather. I was never a fireman. I just thought it was a cool old gold-plated badge and liked it in my wallet. Maybe I had always wanted to be a fireman when I grew up.

When I was in the fourth grade I remember the whole class being asked, one at a time, to name off our preferred occupation when we became adults. Half the girls announced proudly, "nurse!" Half of the boys cheerfully said "fireman!" So I figured I'd be in good hands if I ever caught myself on fire and needed medical attention. But I don't think I said "fireman," although I might have said that I wanted to be a cat burglar. I knew I would enjoy that. Or I may have said that I wanted to burglarize burning hospitals, thereby providing employment opportunities for our whole class!

Not only did my unearned and unwarranted ownership of the small gold badge get me *out of* countless traffic violations over the years, it got me *into* many places that were otherwise restricted. "I'm here to check your fire exits," was a phrase I used more than once. And then I'd waltz right in — no cover charge, nothin'.

Actually, that other part wasn't the interesting part; this is. *This* is when it gets interesting.

The two guys stood next to me, excessively close to me, as if I was gonna get away from them or something. I reached into my jeans back pocket and pulled out my wallet; I was in the process of paying them. We were all standing together between two pool tables; no one else was in the billiards area. The clonking clatter of pins in collision resonated across the entire far end of the bowling area while brightly colored bowling balls barreled down the hard-rock maple lanes. Women's league play had begun.

Time froze for me as I saw, from the corner of my left eye, both of my gambling adversaries slightly seize up as I reluctantly unfolded my wallet — inadvertently exposing the badge. I registered the quick abrupt stiffening in their previously casual stance. As if they were conditioned children who had suffered unexpected face slaps on a regular basis from an abusive and irritated parent, they had flinched, ever so slightly. It didn't take much calculation after observing the change in their body language to know that these two guys either had committed a crime, were on the run, were planning a crime, had previously been pistol-whipped, or had served time, or all of the above. I knew what guilt was. I knew what it could do to you. These guys were guilty of something.

If they hadn't stood practically on top of me when I pulled out my wallet, I wouldn't have noticed. I was already annoyed at the way our billiards marathon had turned out, so I counter-reacted as quickly as they had stiffened. Holding up in front of me, dragnet style, the wallet with gold plated badge attached, I sternly announced, "Washington State Gambling Commission! Walk over to that wall and put your hands on it; spread your feet!"

I knew full well that they hadn't actually *read* the print on the badge. Still they knew it was a *badge;* bad enough, they figured, or at least that's what I figured they'd figure.

"Oooh, nooo! C'mon, man!" Just as I had hoped and expected. Wagering of this type is illegal in Washington State, although I've never heard of anyone actually getting busted in a pool hall. And I doubt if they had either, but everyone knew of the micro-possibility of it.

"C'mon, you're not gonna nail somebody over a pool game, are ya?" They laid their sticks on the gold felt and, moaning in despair, did as I told them.

"Law's the law; I don't write 'em. The Washington State Gambling Commission just sends me out to enforce'em." These two guys were scared, but they weren't as scared as I was. I kept up the act, desperately trying to figure out what to do next. Part of me wanted to just say, "Hey, I was only messin' with ya. Here's your twenty-five bucks." But I knew they might not think my impersonating a fireman-slash-gambling narc was all too humorous. In for a penny, in for a pounding.

"Okay, this is what I'm gonna do," I offered, as I dug into their back pockets and pulled out *their* wallets. "I'm going up to the front counter to call in your I.D.s. If you haven't had any infractions with our department before, we'll see." Remember, this was before global wireless communication and computers and all that bullshit; back then, cops had to make phone calls or, at the very least, get on their car radio.

"I'm calling this in from the front desk," I said, gesturing towards the bowling alley shoe counter near the front door. I held both of their wallets in my other hand as I did so.

"DO NOT MOVE!" I told them forcefully, "Remember, we know who you are and where you live! This is a minor infraction. Don't make it a major one by pulling some chickenshit stunt like ducking out THAT door," I said as I gestured in the other direction from the front counter with my wallet hand, the hand that held both of their wallets, which were a hell of a lot heftier than mine. Mine was back in my back pocket, where it belonged.

"This will only take about three minutes; I'll be RIGHT BACK!" Cautioning the downcast pair as they maintained the position, arms on the wall, legs apart, facing the carpeting and woefully sighing in contrite resignation.

I strolled in pretended confidence, but with every hair up on the back of my neck in what seemed to be the two-mile walk towards the main desk. I stopped and looked back at mid-point to make sure the lowlife gambling ratbastards hadn't bolted for the back door as I hoped they would. Finding them still there, I glared at them as if to say, *just try it, you spineless weasels!*

When I got to within a few steps of the shoe counter service-point and the main entry, I shot ahead like a bad batter trying to make it to first base off of a dribbler hit to the pitcher's mound. And as I went by, I slid the two huge wallets down the long counter, shuffleboard-style, in the general direction of the surprised morning-shift bowling alley manager. I saw him stop both leather satchels with the heel of each hand, just as the heels of both my trembling hands hit the frame of the big glass door; by now I was in full stride.

My faithful little Hillman convertible was parked close to the front door, because when I arrived, as I said, there weren't a lot of people within. My car was also facing away from the establishment's door, out into the parking lot and already aimed in the direction of the street. Because of the beautiful morning weather, the top was down, affording me an opportunity for a running jump onto the trunk lid and a leap into the driver's seat.

I ran is if a bear was after me. *Only a few more steps and I'll be in the car!*

There was only one problem. My faithful little car wasn't always faithful. Sometimes, and for no apparent reason, it wouldn't start. Now I would know! I was about to learn for proof positive whether or not my goofy little car was in any way remotely related to my mean old bike Sherman, and … it … WAS NOT! My faithful companion, my little Mynx, started right up. And away I went.

As I zipped across the spacious parking area, speed-shifting all three of my meager gears powered by a whining little four cylinder, I looked in the rearview mirror expecting to see two pissed off hombres swing open the saloon doors of the bowling alley; but it didn't happen. Maybe it happened after I turned the corner, I don't know.

I was sure that I had looked just like Gene Autry dropping down into the saddle of whatever-his-horse's-name-was from a second-story balcony. Champion, that's it! Champion! And my little Hillman was *my* champion when I dropped down out of the sky that day and into the driver's seat, back when we cleverly made our safe and speedy exit from the hands of nasty outlaws.

Possibly the two ne'er-do-wells had already bolted out the back door at the same time I was going out the front. I'll also never know that. Maybe they just died of old age with their hands stuck on the wall.

Gambling just seems to bring out the worst in everybody.

26
PUGET PIRATES OR
PIRATES OF PENCHANTS

W hen I was a kid, half grown, I had a penchant for being anywhere I wasn't supposed to be. This included closed, as well as possibly locked, buildings. And that even included people's homes on a few occasions — although not often, just every once in a while. Mostly, I kept my harmless burglarizing adventures to old commercial buildings, shacks, and warehouses. And boats.

I never took anything, not once. I never broke anything or vandalized anything. I was, for the most part, like those ghosts in the movies, the ones that can't pick up anything. I would just stand there, wondering. I don't remember what I wondered about. Remember, everything was a wonder to me.

One house a couple of miles from mine had a .22 caliber handgun in the desk drawer. I did pick it up and hold it, realizing full well that that device could alter anyone's future, especially mine. Firm in the knowledge that my future was already dicey enough, I gingerly replaced it next to the coins, dice, decks of cards and dollar bills where it shared space in the mahogany desktop drawer. And then I left, wondering how I would have explained myself had anyone come home while I was there.

A large grimy old warehouse owned by A.G. Homann General Contractor, up near Turner's Grocery and its cold storage facility where we rented a locker and kept our frozen pork, had all sorts of construction related stuff inside, and what appeared to be permanently stationary old trucks. There I also found stacks of boxes of past issue magazines, periodicals from the '20s, '30s, and '40s: *Life, Look, Saturday Evening Post* and others. Hours went by as I read the ads and tried my damnedest to comprehend the archaic and cornball (or way over my head) humor behind the cartoons. And I skimmed over short stories while looking at the pictures of past wars, important events, and apparently famous people I'd never heard of. I'd sit on boxes of musty magazines and read while also watching the rain outside streak down the dirty windows.

Eventually after maybe a couple years, I outgrew it or possibly quit gambling with the inevitability of getting caught. Later I would resume my prowling, although only around and in old buildings that truly were abandoned; that was to be some years distant, however. Then, when I found a nearly empty collapsing structure, I didn't always leave empty-handed. Sometimes, pieces of the building itself left with me, as well as discarded but repairable antique furniture and other odd bits that were left behind — fragmentary pieces of the past tenants' lives.

I cannot say why, as a child, I entered people's houses, not even knowing who lived there. But when I stood there in their space — whoever "they" were — I wondered *why* I was there. There I was, standing where someone else should be standing, and indeed might have been standing had they been home. But they weren't home; I was. Not my home; theirs. I often wondered if I wished I were them and if I would be somehow better off, happier. When I decided I didn't really want to be someone else and that I had my hands full just trying to be me,

I would quietly exit, without leaving a trace to show that I had ever been there.

When I left, I wasn't sadder, nor was I happier. Nor was I wiser. I had learned nothing about the inhabitants because I hadn't wanted to. I've never been one to concern myself very much with other people's affairs. Other than sneaking into some other nice folks' homes once in a while, I've basically minded my own business.

Maybe by my being there, I learned something about myself. And, if I did, I'll be damned if I know what it was.

Once in a while, even today, nearly half a century later, I wonder where I would be had I taken that loaded pistol.

Although my apparent compulsory penchant for covert indoor exploration had not disappeared, it had changed shape by the time I was around twenty, and it was narrowed down to boats. Just boats. Larger boats. Like the boats that were moored for months at a time in slips at the Tacoma or Olympia Marinas. Twenty-five to maybe forty feet in length. The older wooden ones; I wasn't the least bit attracted to fiberglass.

Back in those times, people didn't have to lock up everything, like today. Not that they needed to in my case, because I never harmed or took anything. But because the boat owners seldom had locks on the hatches or cabin doors, I was able to access them and sit around inside, daydreaming. Mostly, I spent my aquatic leisure research time in cruisers. They usually had more than one entrance into the cabins. If the main cabin door was locked, normally the forward hatch was not, so it was easily lifted off. Then I was able to drop down into an uninhabited and largely under-appreciated, I felt, old cabin cruiser.

Most of those languid and lonely lovely ladies of leisure looked as though they hadn't been asked out for many months. Although well maintained, it just seemed to me that they, for the most part, had been denied the warmth of human companionship for far longer than was necessary. So I kindly gave them some. I offered them my companionship. It seemed the least I could do.

Whenever I visited the stately ladies moored in the Thea Foss Waterway in Tacoma, or the Olympia Marina Yacht Club on Budd Bay Inlet in Olympia, I went alone. Except once.

I enjoyed my visits inside the narrow mahogany cramped palaces of aquatic luxury so much I made the mistake of telling a knuckleheaded friend of mine about it. His name was Ron Caparoon. Once I told him about my harmless fetish he wouldn't shut up about it; he wanted a fetish too. However, as near as I could recall, Ron already had several fetishes of his own and I told him there probably wasn't enough room in his head for any more deviated thought than he was presently entertaining. But he was insistent.

So one hot summer evening, after a couple hours of billiards at The Bowl, we went into downtown Olympia to the marina; I had agreed to introduce Ron to one or two of my elderly lady friends.

I parked my car in the almost completely empty parking lot on the far edge of the Yacht Club's property. Parking well away from the closed clubhouse building and the cyclone chain-link fence and gate, I thought, shouldn't attract attention.

We walked across the lot into the shadows past the dark green building on our left, up to the locked gate at the back of the clubhouse. It was very dark at this point because of the height of the large old shingle-sided building; I knew we probably wouldn't be spotted negotiating with the marina's gate. The chain-link fence and gate were eight-feet high, so it only took two agile twenty-year-olds maybe three seconds to

scale; concertina wire was not in wide public use yet, not for
several decades. Dropping down onto the gangway and
dockside, we were through what could be called the main door
of the marina, and officially inside the rest-home's sleepy
saltwater interior. Dark and quiet, except for the peaceful
gurgling noises around the large rocks under the dock at tide
level, the slightly surging tide made slow slurping sounds as
the soft swells swirled among the barnacled boulders below.
We stood there, listening for voices or a possible radio playing, clues that we might not be alone; sometimes people
stayed overnight on their boats while moored in their slip.

And it was quiet, so I optimistically assumed it was safe to
proceed. As I led Ron down the maze of floating docks to
where one or two of the sleeping grand dames of the water lay
in restful quietude, he began talking. I shushed him and told
him about the possibility of someone aboard their boat, asleep,
and how they might not take kindly to boat burglars lurking
around. That quieted him down enough to proceed.

I had already explained to him about how I, on my previous visits, disturbed nothing and took nothing. Had there been
a candy bar of my liking lying on a galley counter I might
have liberated that. But so far, I had never pirated anything,
not even a piece of chocolate, and I told Ron to keep it that
way, and that we were ghost pirates only. I knew Ron was
oddly twisted in some categories, but I was confident that he
wasn't a thief, or I wouldn't have agreed to bring him on
board.

Aided by an overhead light that illuminated the area above
the labyrinth of floating pathways where we stopped, we
climbed onto the bow of one of my favorites. I lifted the two-
by-two hatch cover off and carefully set it down next to the
opening. After placing my feet and legs inside, I lowered

myself into the fore-cabin of the sturdy old wood vessel. I whispered for Ron to do the same. My eyes had adjusted to the dark already, and as Ron's head came down through the hatch opening into the cabin interior I could see him grinning. He had never done anything like this before and it showed; he looked just like that annoying striped cat in Alice in Wonderland.

The summer moon and the Marina's dock light were reflecting off the shimmering water outside through a porthole and onto his grinning teeth. I quietly whispered to him that he was a lousy pirate, that he wasn't stoic enough.

I switched on one of the small electric interior lights, which was enough to barely illuminate something other than the gleam of Ron's toothy crescent. The shiny, heavily varnished mahogany and the brass bright-work accoutrements contributed by reflecting the dim light throughout the interior.

Ron was impressed, not with the boat or the near antiquity of it, but with the fact that he appeared to be getting away with something, the experience of being involved in a clandestine operation that seemed successful in its coversion.

After a short time of sitting there, apart and across from each other on narrow cushioned benches, Ron began showing signs of jittery boredom. No longer grinning, he appeared to be on the edge of anticipatory agitation. He was evidencing by his body language as he sat, all the indications of a kid at the circus waiting for the show to start.

"Can't you just relax and enjoy the solitude?" I whispered loudly.

My question was rhetorical and, of course, a contradiction in terms. The solitude I normally enjoyed had evaporated when I brought with me an apprentice pirate. On top of that, it was becoming increasingly clear: Ron was not a solitary or stoic type of person. He still had that "What's gonna happen

now? *Make* somethin' happen!" look about him. Remember
this was years before they invented ADD.

That's when he reached up to the mahogany panel where
all the toggle switches and buttons were. I watched as I
thought he was about to *pretend* to depress a dark Bakelite
round button marked "Air Horn."

Unfortunately, Ron lost what little self-control he had and
plunged the button in. One long blast! By the time I slapped
his wrist away, every clam, mussel, oyster, boat owner and
police officer in the Puget Sound area was awake! I was sure
of it!

I cursed and hollered at him to climb out as I hit the small
switch on the six-volt night light, turning it off. As he posi-
tioned himself under the open hatch to dive up, I could see that
he was once again grinning. Ron clambered up and out,
noisily, not that it mattered much now. I followed him out and
quickly replaced the canvas-covered hatch lid. Both of us
bounded loudly down the dock, turning at each right angle on
the wooden maze into the direction of the way we had come; I
was calling him names at every turn. Not that he could hear
me; our footsteps on the hollow dock along with his laughter
were drowning out my derisive diatribe.

Fully expecting to see, in the darkness and at any moment,
the flashing lights from the police cars of Olympia's finest, I
kept low and behind Ron, knowing they'd see him first. But I
saw no lights and heard no sirens, and now we had reached the
gate. I was a couple of seconds behind Ron. As I watched him
rattle his way up the chain link gate, from where I was
crouched behind him, I thought I saw something in the dark,
just on the other side of the fence.

In the shadow of the tall clubhouse building, sitting on the
access road maybe twenty feet away from the gate, I saw the
outline of a large shape! A *car* that wasn't there when we had

come through! I stopped and blinked into the large black shadow that faintly held the hinted outline of a shape resembling not just a car, but a *police* car! I could distinguish now the rack of lights on top! I also saw in the blackness, the barest glint of chrome from the grill and rings of headlamp glass. Through the windshield and rear window the faintest ebb of city lights came through, vaguely silhouetting the form behind the wheel! I remained crouched there, long enough to hear Ron land on his feet on the other side of the gate and only a few feet away from the front of the cop car — the cop car that I knew in his haste, he had not seen!

Hoping the cop, or cops, would have enough trouble dealing with Ron, who was very athletic, I thought I had a reasonable chance for escape. Thinking, hoping that I may not have been seen behind Ron and on the wrong side of the fence, I turned off the dock and climbed down onto the large boulders, quickly making my way to water's edge. Expecting at any moment to hear "Stop or I'll shoot!" I dove into the saltwater of Puget Sound. Miraculously, my hands hit no jagged rocks or barnacles, nor did my face, or chest.

Now what? Now what do I do? As I swam out thirty or forty feet, I perceived I probably was doing so unnoticed, but what next? Not hearing any pandemonium around the area of the clubhouse and marina, I assumed Ron's arrest had gone smoothly. I was reasonably sure Ron wasn't the kind of stoolie to give me up, *butcha never know.* I stayed where I was, treading water for several minutes.

Too insecure to go back and look through or climb the fence, especially now, in my soaked clothes and shoes, I chose to swim around the corner to the other side of the marina. I knew I'd be unable to outrun even the slowest, most donut-riddled cop on the force. As I dog-paddled up to the large boulders on the shoreline, I kept low. After waiting and listening among barnacles and seaweed for half an hour or so, I gathered my nerve and slithered up the bank to peer over the edge, level with the asphalt — the warm black asphalt where my car sat, waiting. The two or three-hundred-feet of vacant parking lot between my car and myself looked like a mile-and-a-half.

Although part of me — no, *most* of me — was just *sure* the cops had my car staked out from a distance, I couldn't take it any longer and eventually slogged out onto the blacktop, my wet shoes and pants making loud splattery sploshy sounds with each desperate running stride. I must have sounded like a hydraulic pile driver pounding logs down into the tidal mud for a new wharf. Although it seemed like it took forever to reach my car, and I could be heard for six blocks, no sirens or searchlights came on and no shots rang out; I had made it!

The next day I went down to the bowling alley to see if anyone knew how long Ron would be in prison and, more importantly, to find out if he had squealed on me.

There was Ron! In the corner, passionately but impatiently as always, playing his favorite Bally "Beach Ball" five-cent payout pinball machine. No dangling handcuffs. No visible marks from being recently night-sticked. No Cheshire Cat prison stripes.

He looked up from his nickel machine only briefly and then immediately returned to it, and asked, "Where in hell did you go last night? I thought you were right behind me."

With the heel of his right hand on the corner of the machine, he over-impatiently hammered the ball out of the number twenty-four hole which, had he not hit it so forcefully, would have guaranteed him a win. We both moaned as we watched the shiny steel ball drop into the ball return.

"I *was* right behind you; then I saw the cop car! You almost landed on his hood! I dove in and swam away. What'd they do to you?"

"Nothin'. That cop was sound asleep, maybe dead," he said with his wide Cheshire grin.

Ron was probably right about that; he must have been clinically dead or dead-to-the-world asleep or just dead drunk not to hear that air horn *or* Ron hitting the fence, then practically landing on top of him and running past. I doubt, assuming he wasn't dead, that he ever got promoted to detective.

Now Ron wanted an apology for making him wait for me and then causing him to have to find another way home when I hadn't shown up in what he considered a timely fashion. Then, the wharf rat cheerfully informed me that he most certainly *would have* turned me in had he been caught.

I decided then that I wouldn't introduce Ron to any more of the classy women I knew, wooden or otherwise. He wasn't worthy, even if he probably was a highly devolved descendant from the wrong side of the family of Horatio Hornblower.

27

BULLET IN THE BRAIN

O ne day soon, I shall begin relating stories about how I have nearly died — repeatedly — while in my relentless compulsive pursuit of antiques. But before I do, it seems only fitting to elaborate on my very first antiquities acquisition expedition, and how I also came so very near to acquiring a bullet in my brain at that same exact spot, a forgotten old homestead up near the south end of Kinwood Road. I was almost shot and killed within a few feet of my very first antiques score; although not on the same day, it was only a matter of weeks later.

The largest chunk of my professional life has been in the antiques trade, over thirty-five years now. However, my first "found item" was turned into cash afterwards at the local antique shop on Martin Way at the other end of Kinwood Road and across from where Stone's Candy Cane Company was when I was ten or eleven years old. If my career in antiques officially began then, I've been in antiques for over fifty years now.

The scotch broom and fiddlehead fern, as well as hazelnut bushes and buckbrush, camouflaged all but the most rigid remains of the old cabin. Some remnants of rotting boards were still nailed together at right angles, but they had become soft, black, and silver where exposed to sun and rain. They still protruded defiantly through last year's taller weeds and, as far as the cabin itself, they seemed to be all that was left. At first. But once the eye catches the unexpected anomaly of something artificially made, especially on the edge of a small wilderness, automatically, even instinctively, the eye roves about passively for another visual clue. At least mine does. Though prolific thickets of dense underbrush grow abundantly in the well-watered regions of Western Washington, years of sumac, ivy and scotch broom still have considerable trouble concealing a rusty old "Majestic" iron cookstove. In fact, the presence of ivy itself is an indication of previous human habitation; not an indigenous foliate in this area, it's a telltale sign of a long-gone homestead — not that I knew that back then. I was soon captivated by the thought that I was standing inside the reduced remains of what had once been somebody's kitchen, a kitchen that time and the elements had simmered away to nothing.

The decades had eroded any trace of what I would years later come to know as nickel-plating from the old square stove. Lying behind the back of the rusted hulk were the overhead warming ovens which had collapsed and been hidden for years from the few people who may have wandered by. But there was no trail here, nor were there any houses in the area. So I was certain that I, and I alone, knew of this small and long forgotten old home that belonged to no one, no one living anyway.

After discovering it under the ivy, I thought briefly of the cold and crumbled hearth that time had separated from the once warm heartbeat of its owner and builder. I pondered the callused hands that drove nails into the fresh non-silvered slivery rough-cut and newly sawn rugged boards. At one time they had firmly squared with each other and together had stood upright and marched confidently into the endless winless battle against time. But there they were, nothing more than lifeless soggy fragments of spent and weathered dead lumber. Green ivy and blackberry vines intertwined and trailed up, humping over the clumps of what had been a wall, or the partial floor of another small inner room. Most assuredly this was the outline of a large wooden box that we all would have once called a house, or cabin. And someone had once called it "home."

Just under the tall brown grass that had, the season before, fallen over and blanketed the two-door warming oven as it lay rusting away behind the stove itself, were two emblems, barely visible, one on each oven door. They were two ships similar to and possibly inspired by the "Mayflower," each rusty ship emblem still under full sail yet barely attached to its flimsy, rotted, thin-sheet-steel upper oven door. Two ships, listing to one side and sinking slowly into a silent sea of undergrowth; both ships settling sideways softly into the composting leaves, lumber and sod. Dinner had been served up a long time ago. The once majestic old stove had cooked its last supper and had been forgotten. And like many of us, it was now oxidizing through its senior years and retirement into eventual unrecognizability, its purpose having been served.

Naturally in 1955 or so, and to a boy of ten or eleven, this was unquestionably a cowboy's cabin. Or outlaws. Or some settler who'd been run out by Indians. Or maybe someone who had died of snakebite. It was by all appearances, I thought, a small place suitable for only one — any one cowboy, prospector, outlaw, single homesteader or any lonely old recluse pioneer that my imagination could lay its hands on. Then it was that I saw near my feet a glimmer of glass mostly in and barely peeking out from under the thick mulch of fallen foliage and sodden grasses that time had gathered around the roots of ferns, blackberry and Oregon grape.

Reaching back into the thicket's prickly throat, I extracted a large heavy clear glass bowl. Layers of brown leaves clung to it as if they had been paper-mâchéed on, leaving only the ruffled glass edge of one section of the bowl's rim exposed, the part I had at first barely seen. Even a partially sunny day refracts well the crenellated scallops of a cut glass crystal fruit bowl — not that I knew then what it was; it was a sparkly dish. That is, it sparkled once I peeled the layers of weeds and leaves off and away from it. It also fit nicely over my head.

I began to make the connection between this fancy dish and the feminine world. No longer did I view this place as a lonely cowboy or single sodbuster's cabin of the male gender, unless it had once been his mom's bowl. Even so, I had trouble envisioning a trail-weary saddle-tramp carrying a nineteenth-century fancy-glass heavy lead crystal dish over the plains in his saddlebags while beating back desperadoes and indigenous souvenir-seeking savages. Never had I seen any western movies that had, when bandits were holding up a stagecoach, included the gruff demand, "Hand over all yer purdy plates!"

Or, maybe it had been a parting gift from the buxom schoolmarm who was doomed to spinsterhood when the itchy feet and the heart full of wanderlust lured the handsome cowboy alone into the direction of the setting sun.

After finding below the sod additional fragmentary shards of the types of things more suitable to a china cabinet than a chuck wagon, I made the final concession; this had probably been some old lady's place and not a cowboy's after all. Remnants of ornate picture frames and other more dainty appointments left behind also clued me in to the probability that someone had departed unexpectedly or under the most dire of circumstances.

Never had an item of such shimmering fine quality and caliber as this bowl ever crossed the threshold of our home to grace our mantel or china cabinet. In fact, we owned neither of the latter. If the thought crossed my mind that my mom would have loved this glittering object, it must have made the crossing quickly, because I have no recollection if it. Possibly, I made the snap decision that we didn't deserve anything this good. If so, in thinking so, what I was really saying was that my mom didn't deserve it or possibly that she wouldn't appreciate it. In any case if I didn't want her to get it, I needed to make sure she'd never lay eyes on it.

After unbuttoning the top buttons and tucking my plaid flannel shirt into my jeans, I inserted the big cold bowl between the shirt and my warm skin, resting the toothy edge against my bare stomach. Aware that I appeared like a six-month-pregnant ten-year-old boy, I patted my bowl, climbed on my bike and headed off for the small red-painted antique shop that lay in the other direction from which I had come. Therefore I had to pass our house, our house, devoid of all things glittery, superfluous, ostentatious or unnecessary. I told myself as I pedaled past that if the people at the antique store wouldn't buy it for whatever reason, I'd give it to my mom. That is, if I couldn't *sell* it to her. Knowing that she never ever had any extra money, I was preparing myself for the worst.

Sailing past our house unnoticed, I pedaled my raggedy old bike the rest of the way wondering what I would spend my twenty-five, or hopefully fifty cents on. The notched serration of the bowl's edge was nibbling on my middle each time one of my thighs rose up and bumped the bowl as I pedaled.

Coasting up near the small door of the shop, I saw the gray-haired shop owner sitting inside, next to a side window closest to the highway. And she saw me. By the time I dismounted and leaned my old red crate against the old red wall next to her front step, the old lady had opened her shop door.

I didn't have a kickstand on my bike; I think that may have been one of the first components on my bike to have trickled off and become road shrapnel. Back in those days, kids weren't encouraged to throw their bikes in spinning heaps *right in the doorway* of whatever establishment they're dashing into. That practice started about twenty-five years ago, I think. I also surmise it's directly linked to the advent of video games, much the same as American child obesity and ADD.

She stood in the doorway, possibly to guard it, as if I was going to steal something had I been allowed to enter. Or maybe if I was allowed to enter, I might start reeling about, knocking over showcases and cabinets full of priceless treasures. In her defense I have to say I doubt if I looked as if I was a legitimate peruser, purchaser, or possible collector of antiques of any genre.

Only after unbuttoning the top buttons on my shirt and producing the heavy bowl for her inspection, did she crack a polite smile. I was relieved to remove the jaggedy teeth from my belly. I chattered on about how I found it in the bushes and she got a faraway look on her face while turning the bowl by its rim, as if it were a steering wheel. I pulled my shirt out of my jeans waist and began rubbing my stomach.

"What're ya doin'?" I quizzed, smoothing briskly with the palm of my hand the chomped-on area above my belt line where the glass teeth had lunched on my flesh.

"Checking for chips," matter-of-factly.

"How could'ja even tell the difference?" I asked sarcastically, still massaging the long bite marks across my stomach.

"Three dollars," she announced in a solemn take-it-or-leave-it tone. I slowed my belly-rub and nearly passed out. I'd never had three dollars in my life! And I mean *accumulatively*, not to mention all at one time! Here I was about to receive more money than I had ever had in my whole life altogether. The crystal's munch marks on my midriff immediately stopped receiving attention from my palm, which was now outstretched in greedy anticipation. I nearly jabbed her in the tummy with the upturned fingertips of my hungry hand.

Only a couple of weeks later, while again walking near to where I had for the first time in my life — but not the last — extricated crystal from mossy sod, I heard the loud crack that I recognized as a rifle. I heard the whirring of the bullet coming in my direction before I heard the report of the rifle, but only by a millisecond. When the bullet screamed past, barely above my left ear and very nearly abruptly ending my career in antiques, or anything for that matter, I dove to the ground. Several more shots followed. Although none seemed to send any more lead in my direction, I stayed flat and extremely concerned.

Had someone shot at me? Directly, and on purpose? They had indeed come close enough to certainly make me believe it. But the subsequent rounds seemed to be "thunking" into something solid off in the trees, close to where I, not long before, had mined crystal from someone's depopulated old frontier homestead in the woods. Although I wanted to know who was shooting and why, I crawled away. Even though I wasn't the brightest bulb in the box, I still had enough sense not to charge off into the direction of random gunfire and spinning lead for the purpose of greeting a wild-eyed sniper with a high-powered rifle and an itchy trigger finger.

A couple days later, I cautiously again meandered through the trees and brush to the quiet, old, and forgotten shadow where once had stood somebody's wilderness home, wondering what it would offer me on this visit — cold lead crystal or hot spinning lead?

The rusty ancient cookstove all but covered in ivy and scotch broom had been further insulted. In fact, it had been besieged. Having been the passive victim of someone's target practice, the iron emblem of the third sailing ship that originally adorned the larger, lower oven door had been shot apart, and pieces of it were lying in the weeds. Fresh gray streaks along with corresponding small dents now decorated some of the heavier metal parts of the cold hulk. Elsewhere in the thin timeworn sheet metal there were new holes.

Fifty yards or more away, presumably at the spot where the shooter had stood, judging from the brass casings lying around, I cheerfully retrieved enough freshly emptied Olympia Beer stubbies to score a Hershey's semi-sweet chocolate bar. After trading the bottles for the bar at the back door of the Log Cabin Tavern, I started off for home, knowing that a nice hot dinner was a-waiting. Savoring my chocolate as I walked, I thought about how a deformed, and therefore noisy, lead ricochet deflected from a cold old cookstove had come very, very close to making me miss all my warm meals, forever.

28

DESK JOB

When I was a kid I was always out "finding" stuff with which to build forts, along with things to put in them. Not all of my forts survived the subsequent fires that followed completion, but some did. Because hardly any of my architectural endeavors had actual roofs on them, the endless Northwest rains soon consumed the structures that I hadn't accidentally set fire to while trying to keep warm and read my tattered and moldy comics. I take that back; my *underground* forts actually did have decent roofs on them; they not only didn't burn, they didn't leak. They just got all soggy and then collapsed on top of me.

There wasn't a scrap of lumber or a straight nail within two miles of my house. Small articles of furniture made their way to many of my forts, never to be seen again by the adult world. Hammers and handsaws also had a habit of evaporating within the same radius.

One of my more elaborate and whimsical architectural wonders was nailed to and between four Douglas fir trees and, from ground level, rose to a staggering total of four floors, with separate partitioned rooms on a couple floors. Somehow,

I had located and dragged a heavy old oak four-legged flattop desk into the bottom floor lobby, if you will, of my towering hotel in the woods.

Once, the previous night's rain sifted through the fir boughs above me and permeated the entire three floors overhead and soaked the bottom floor — the lobby — except for the dry patch underneath my sturdy oak desk. The desk, I would learn much later, was actually an Arts and Crafts library table with drawers. It was there that I sought refuge while the melodious dripping leftovers from the night before successfully lured me into slumber. I remained dry and cozy, curled up under the massive slab of quartersawn oak above me.

My otherwise quiet part-time job as day clerk at the Wilderness Hotel, frequented by nobody other than the scolding chipmunk that lived rent-free on the top floor, was interrupted one afternoon by a human scream. I had just hit my head, hard, and it was *I* who screamed; I was screaming quite naturally because I was in pain. *I always knew I never wanted to be a pencil-pushing desk jockey!*

Evidently the noisy little freeloader that occupied floor four had decided that it didn't want me sleeping on the job. After I dove out from under the reception desk in supreme annoyance, to issue an edict of imminent eviction in something less than legal or even printable language, I swung around to crawl back under. But in doing so, my head collided with what I immediately concluded to be a very offensive and unnecessary protrusion from the nearest leg of my hotel desk. One of the mortised-through rectangular knot-like nubbins, a characteristic signature of some of the easily obtained secondhand furniture of the time, had attacked me. So now I was screaming. My screaming further alarmed the chipmunk, which then began screeching louder.

210

Although I was aware of my deep desire to grab the over-stimulated chipmunk and choke it into silent submission or, at the very least, pound a pinecone down its squawky throat, I knew I wouldn't catch it. Through my cloud of pain and rage I also knew that the desk, even though it had four strong legs, was unable to run away.

So, infuriated by pain and deprived of my nap, I proceeded to initiate a retaliatory counter-attack on the desk. This evil desk would just have to suffer the vengeful wrath that was about to be brought upon it, not only because of the nasty upstairs tenant, but because it had sneaked up and kneed me in the head.

Reaching under the damp carpet scrap that adorned the hotel foyer, I extracted my dad's missing and, by now, rusty handsaw. Seething, I slapped the wambly blade up against the side of the leg that had just a second before kicked me when I wasn't looking. As the small crosscut teeth of my dad's favor-ite missing saw began chattering away on the protruding mortised-tenon that had offended me, I felt with my free hand the resulting knot on my temple and made the decision to immediately smooth off all of the oak nubbins, wherever they could be found.

Soon after, each time that an irritating rectangle dropped off and onto the moist floor of the dank lobby, I felt a small degree of relief from my anger. But as soon as the saw stopped, I could once again hear nothing other than the de-monized shrieking from the maniacal scolding chipmunk overhead, which then instantly re-escalated my earlier ebbing enmity back up to where it had been.

Realizing I was quickly running out of rectangles to ream and that my method of self-proscribed mismanagement of indignance and retributeous rage running rampant against small noisy animals and four-legged inanimate objects was turning out to be something less than therapeutic, I momentarily ceased sawing.

Still seething, I continued to kneel in the fresh sawdust, with sweat running over my brow and stinging my eyes. I barely had enough breath left in me to swear out loud. My left hand had several small red ready-to-bleed bite marks on it where the saw had, more than once, jumped its kerf during my rampage and periodically snacked on my flesh. Although I knew I was cursing as loudly as I could, I couldn't hear myself; all I could hear was that damn tree rodent. Immediately the decision was made to amputate the desk legs, just in case one of them might try to kick me again. Or just in case it might try to escape and tell my dad where all of his tools went. In the course of my upward spiraling blind fury it didn't take long for the desk to soon morph into a coffee table.

Semi-aware that the protruding veins in my temples were throbbing painfully in time to the saw's thrusts and recoils, I may have also glimpsed the end of my own dangling, extended, engorged and slathering tongue occasionally flip into view. However, my blinded eyes were too filled with perspiration, sawdust, and vehement rage to tell for sure.

When the desk was shorter, I easily placed my knee upon it and wildly continued to wreak further passionate and irrational havoc on the edges of the top. I quickly notched several deep vee-shaped endorsements from the vicious passion that hovers in residence within the shadows of hostility somewhere on the darker side of my psyche. It was then that I realized the chipmunk had worn itself out and apparently had gone inside for a nap; all my sawing had evidently made it sleepy.

My sustained and frenzied counter-attack on a stationary wooden object had ended, and I put the missing saw, which by then was quite warm to the touch, back under the damp carpet.

Over time, the elements would quietly eliminate any visible trace of the lopsided carved-up coffee table that had originally been a desk that graced the reception area of what had been my homemade hotel in the trees. Time and the elements would also eventually foreclose on the structure itself. The last time I looked in that spot — which was over forty years ago — there were four middle-aged fir trees and, between them, a large mound of chipmunk-discarded fir cones and hazelnut shells. Somewhere beneath the mound, there lay the rotten remains of what had once been a fine Stickley two-drawer quartersawn oak library table. And under that, lay the missing murder weapon — my dad's rusty old handsaw.

Sleeping deep under the sod and only six or eight feet away from that same spot lies what's left of another of my childhood crimes: three decomposed duffel bags full of stolen baseball equipment that were laid to rest immediately after being illegally liberated from nearby St. Martin's College.

29

LAND YACHT

L onnie was sitting in his wheelchair watching the flames in the fireplace of his parent's living room when I asked him for a tow.

Several years had passed since the last time he and I hooked up for a tow job, and it hadn't ended all that well. While being towed on a brakeless bicycle behind Lonnie's Corvair and over the railroad tracks I could have — no, *should have* — been killed or crippled. I had somehow survived without a scratch; although my clothing had suffered, I came through miraculously unscathed.

Lonnie on the other hand had become a paraplegic, al-though there was no connection whatsoever to our last tow adventure together and his recently disconnected spinal cord. He and an XKE Jaguar had abruptly connected with asphalt somewhere in Death Valley. I was not present at the loud high-speed introduction of metal and flesh to tar and gravel. I couldn't be expected to take the blame for that one. For a change.

I had by then tired of living in a plastic Visqueen tent wrapped around and over dogwood trunks and limbs. Winter was again on its way and I needed something more sustainable in the way of shelter. Kitty-corner from the old mushroom farm, nestled in an oak grove, a totally abandoned ancient farm homestead held what was to become my future rambling mansion.

Away from the two-story empty clapboard house, a low but quite long and wide-open, rusty metal-roofed barn held all the usual old junk, and some unusual junk. Steam tractor, huge old grain thresher, and what appeared to me to be the world's very first wooden motor-home.

The emblem on the quite tall and vertically flat radiator said W.K. — which I later came to learn stood for Willys-Knight. The running gear, chassis and front end which included the cab, I would later learn, was vintage 1927.

Situated behind the cab and over the top of it as well was a meticulously crafted large wooden coach. The oversized steel wheels with their hard narrow tires appeared to be the first ones to have been produced after the only slightly more archaic wooden spokes fell out of favor. And if ever there had been a lost silent movie reel entitled "The Keystone Cops Take To The Road," this surely would have been the massive yet graceful old coach the movie would have boasted.

After pulling open the only door, located in the same spot where the door of any typical school bus is placed, I stepped up and in. An oversized wooden steering wheel was the first thing I noticed. Behind the wheel and under it sat an empty and quite stiff ill-padded single seat permanently affixed to the wooden floorboards. The windshield and driver's window, like the radiator, were exactly vertical and flat, everything square and boxy. All the wood joinery and construction was tight and well-engineered. Clearly someone, whether professional coach builder or gifted amateur, knew what they were doing. If crafted by an amateur, this certainly appeared to me to be a labor of love. Some old geezer, I decided, had taken the love of his life, his then young and handsome new bride, on tour; I had no trouble convincing myself they had seen all of North America in this ancient bus.

On the other hand, I suddenly wasn't so sure the old road ship had sailed anywhere. The interior showed no wear. And no clutter. Only the finest dust that somehow, over a period of many years, had sifted in and rested untouched, now covered all the flat horizontal surfaces.

Immediately behind the driver's seat was a thin partition with the carefully executed land yacht's immaculate galley on the other side. Standing room was six feet exactly, but only down the middle, over the length of the aisle, due to the cleverly conceived slight up-curved crown of the roof. I walked the four or five steps down the narrow passageway to where I reached the back of the forgotten craft, passing as I did, small closets, cabinetry, a convertible table for two, and a pair of small windows — one on each side midship of the marooned houseboat on wheels.

In the aft of the rolling box, I located a straw mattress. Only it too was vertical, seemingly hung sideways, and it occupied the entire width of the back wall. Even I knew no one would engineer nor be able to cling to a mattress that stood on edge, no matter how young and in love they were. Not for long anyway; nobody can remain that upstanding forever.

Soon I found, mounted on the corner wall above the bed and connected to a rod, a folding crank that, when turned, began to lay the mattress over and outward at the top. I continued cranking as the bottom of the mattress rose slightly, brushing my knee as I did so. A canvas shroud that had been behind the vertical mattress appeared and lowered, along with the outside edge of the bed. The whole thing operated almost exactly like a medieval drawbridge; the crank operated two chains, one attached to each of the outside corners. One edge of the heavy canvas tent descended with the bed while the top edge was connected to the roof and was tailored at the corners, covering the chains along with the striped mattress and its imagined occupants. Well, they were just gonna hafta move over — I wanted that bed. Bad.

Here was the amalgamated encapsulation of all of my dreams — my love of the outdoors, camping, fishing, aimlessly wandering about. Adventure. No landladies. No rent! Ranging freely the hinterlands of America. Maybe I could even sail my prairie schooner up to British Columbia where I could overturn large boulders of the Canadian badlands in search of my real father's family — all the relatives I had never met, the ones my mom said "were all hatched out from under rocks."

And escape. Escape from our tiny town with its day-to-day drudgery, to the back roads of America and … towns probably even tinier than ours, where the inhabitants would no doubt know what *real* drudgery was and how to cope with it!

And sex! As I sat on the button-tufted stripes of the crunchy old mattress, I slipped quite comfortably into young-man fantasyland. Near-sex in my mildewy old Hillman Mynx convertible was fine … when it wasn't constantly dripping rainwater on us or rolling downhill in the darkness and into a lake. But here! Here was a vehicle with the real thing; a mattress. And if need be I could keep it concealed until just the right moment (the mattress, I mean) so as not to appear too presumptuous or forward. I knew I didn't know much, but I knew women really liked to be surprised like that — spring it on them at the last minute — with one hand reach out in the candlelight and start cranking. When she'd finally realize that the rattling of chains over her head was causing a nice scratchy mattress to materialize from under a moldering musty old canvas tent that had no doubt enshrouded myriad mysteries of other lustful encounters while meandering through Montana, Missouri, Milwaukie or Tenino, she'd surely want me.

As I imagined somebody getting a good toehold on the tuft buttons of the mattress I was dreaming on, I realized that I had nearly worried the round flat mattress-ticking-covered button in my hand from its connection in the tuft. The string was all stretched out and the button was now loose. I put it back in place, patted it twice, wiped my chin and left.

By the time I began tracking down the absentee owner of the property, I had it all figured out. Lonnie's dad had rigged up the gas and brakes of their five- or six-year-old 1960 Chevrolet station wagon to enable Lonnie to operate them with his hands and, therefore, to drive. Although I wasn't positive their wagon had the moxie to pull this massive 1920s road warrior to a new pasture, I knew my Hillman did not.

After I was able to locate the present owner of the acreage, he sold me the coolest thing I've ever seen on wheels for ten dollars. I mailed it to him as he instructed. I then borrowed the heavy-duty fifty-foot length of chain that Lonnie's dad used when pulling out great stumps with his plumbing truck. This was only one of several of Budd's hobbies. He also liked chopping down forests and flattening mountains — things he liked to do in his leisure time.

On a Sunday afternoon sometime near the end of October, amid what seemed like acres of accumulated rust-colored oak leaves that had blown into the barn and covered the wheels up to the hubs, I took possession of my first meaningful home — home of my own anyway.

The tall two-door oak icebox with elaborate brass latches and hinges that sat in the barn, quite near the access door to my new palace, looked at me wistfully, as if to say, "We've shared this barn for all these years; you wouldn't leave me behind, would you?" Looking at the width of the opening of the wood and metal door on the cab of my heavily oxidized new home, I knew the icebox not only had a point, it would fit right in. Although during this period in my life I was still trying to keep my lying and thieving to a minimum, the icebox won; as I said, nobody can remain upstanding forever.

When Lonnie pulled slowly ahead and the chain rose up from under the rustling blanket of crisp brown leaves, I had my doubts. Each time a link in the chain, or the old chassis I sat on, made a tense "bong!" or "clack!" I fully expected the chain to snap and be sent straight back at me, the same way most of my bass plugs had while night fishing with surface lures. Bass plugs can't damage you too much, but a snapped tow chain coming through that old flat windshield could damage me for good. As I gripped tightly the giant wood steering wheel and stared through the dusty glass down the length of the quivering chain, I envisioned myself sitting in a wheelchair alongside Lonnie, staring into the fireplace and still in a young man's fantasyland, but now unable to wipe my own chin.

I still remember how I felt when that big old crate first began to roll out of the barn into the bright but fading light of day. I felt in those first moments when the wheels began to shudder and roll, as if I were flying. Possibly the most victorious I have ever been, I was then. Knowing, of course, in my heart that the ancient relic was never to actually run again, didn't matter. What mattered was … well, in truth I don't know what mattered most. Perhaps in part it was that nobody else had one, and also knowing that nobody else was this crazy; that mattered a lot, to me anyway. Proving to myself and others, through my constantly abstract activities that I must be nuts, has always had a profound effect of validation for me. That's something that's probably true of many people who are somewhat in want of heart in other areas of their life. But knowing that, from the looks of it now that we were moving, I apparently was going to make it home with my prize mattressed dreamboat, mattered for everything — at the time.

As I look back now, as we made the turn at the stinky old mushroom farm and rolled away from the leaf-barren oak grove and its fallow farm, I remember seeing Lonnie's face out the window of the station wagon. Watching Lonnie laughing uncontrollably with the limited lung capacity he still had, made me soar even higher.

If I had asked Budd, Lonnie's dad, to tow my new home to my folk's property, he would have. But I hadn't asked Budd, even though his big truck could have done it with ease; I had asked Lonnie. Lonnie wasn't any longer in much of a position to participate in these types of oddball distractions. Naturally, when Lonnie had paralyzed himself from his nipples down, he had mellowed considerably. Yet, by the time we reached my folks' stand of trees on the north side of their property, Lonnie was appearing even more mellow. In truth, I think he was just flat worn out from laughing.

However, when we first rumbled out of that barn through the crunching leaves and into the coming twilight of a cold sunless October dusk, he became once again the same old Lonnie. And though we were both only in our early twenties, we were suddenly back in *our* "good old days." It was the first time I had seen Lonnie like that in a long time. It would also be the next to the last time. However *this story* isn't exactly over yet. Read on.

30

Fly Low and Slow

Picture: four thick, crackled, nearly petrified rubber tires, half inflated and congealed to their ancient rust-colored rims. A steering mechanism that had neither been pressed into service nor lubricated since the Great Depression. What appeared to be an exhumed circus wagon, a rigorously-mortified motor coach towed by a station wagon with a wheelchair sticking out the back. Both vehicles had single occupants — the drivers, both of them laughing hysterically, maniacally and triumphantly. Lonnie and I were both experiencing a taste of the famous phoenix's rise from ashes, each of us in our own way.

The few witnesses to this flight did not see trailing ashes, but a stream of leaves, cobwebs, birds' nests and the like trickling off and dribbling behind as we shuddered down the road. All four of the stiff old tires that were attempting to separate from their respective wheels and go off in different directions didn't exactly make for a smooth ride.

I watched as, straining under the resistance, the 1960 Chevy wagon occasionally broke into a rumba, the rear-end swaying rhythmically from side to side. Each time my heavy

"Twenty Mule Team Borax" wagon hesitated and issued a defiant tremor, the tremor traveled up the stiff chain, causing the Chevy's axle to stammer and shake. Then the Chevrolet would do its little dance until regaining enough traction to pull me ahead. Lonnie and I celebrated all the way home, about a half hour at two miles-per-hour. But, I knew that Chevy's transmission and differential weren't celebrating.

Although knock-kneed, clubfooted, pigeon-toed and under tow, my clumsy claptrap of a rambling shanty was glad finally to be out of that old barn. I knew. The icebox stood next to me, quietly staring out at the passing October scenery, happy to be along for the ride.

We also made a few people happy along the way. For example, the white haired old-timer who pulled over as we faced him down when he came at us from the other direction; by the time I shambled up to him, he had stopped and was out of his beat-up old Ford pickup, slapping his hat on his thigh and cheering. He didn't appear to own a lot of teeth; as I creaked and squealed past him, I got a nice long look at the few he did have.

By the time Lonnie pulled me to within sight of the Log Cabin Tavern, we had encountered as many irate motorists as we had cheerful ones. I had a good vantage point from which to record the simple fact that not everyone views an event in the same way. We seemed to be the pinnacle of the day's entertainment to many of those we encountered. On the other hand, a few others were more than happy to let us know that we had somehow ruined their day; they referred to my new home in defacatory phraseology that hurt my feelings and nearly upset my icebox.

A couple overly anxious Sunday motorists who we may have caused to miss their Sunday evening service and who needed servicing badly, I might add, sped around me screaming holy expressions and waving single stiff digits. I assumed they were from the church of the middle finger, so I waved at them in similar fashion, pretending to be a member myself.

When Lonnie passed the front windows of the Log Cabin Tavern nothing happened. When the clientele inside caught a glimpse of what he was dragging behind him, the tavern emptied. The front porch filled up with the former occupants in about five seconds. Now, I had seen some of those people move before, and I was unaware of their agility up until then; but then, the circus doesn't come to town every day.

By the time we had passed, they had grown thirsty again, their open mouths all dried out from watching us screech and rattle away; the parched cluster then scrambled back inside as quickly as they had appeared. The show was over.

Only after turning right onto Kinwood Road, the last leg and the last rumba, did Lonnie and I tire of our own open-mouthed self-congratulatory laughter and cheer. Although we couldn't really see or hear each other that well, we both knew we were in the same flight pattern regardless of the severe turbulence, and had enjoyed the flight.

My brand new antique motor-home was then deposited on the slight rise next to my about-to-be previously inhabited plastic shack. I unshackled both wagons and Lonnie left, waving and, once again, laughing.

Soon afterward, I sold the icebox to some hippies who came around looking to buy old furniture and whatnot to fix up and refinish, they said. I got five bucks, half the price of my new house. *What a couple of fools!* I thought, and waved goodbye.

Years later, after I had married and built a home on the other side of the dogwood trees, I winched the old land yacht into the center of the dogwood stand, exactly where my plastic shack had once sheltered me. For some reason, the trees immediately died; something about a blight. Two decades later my marriage did the same thing, possibly for the same reason.

A year or so after building my house, however, a couple old guys who owned Wagon Wheel Antiques up in Federal Way were knocking on my door and asking about the old rustbucket. So I gave it to them. I had lived in it for nearly two years back when single, and was more than happy, now that I had built a real house, to get "the old eyesore," as my wife referred to it, off my property. *What a couple of fools,* I thought, and waved goodbye.

Life, it seems to me as I look back, is not mystical, mysterious or monumental. It is not magnanimous or even hardly worth mentioning, as a whole — one person's life from another. But life *is momentous.* Everybody's life is made of moments. Only moments, small patches and scraps that we save and sew together to form into the crazy-quilt that we call Life.

And at the end of it all maybe we each shall clutch or cling to only a few of those moments as being the meaningful and momentous ones; and those will be our collections, our personal catalog of what was … once. Whether watching a newborn child asleep in its new home for the first night, or when we first … anything … any special moment that chooses to hang forever and for whatever reason as a piece of the fabric of our life — the thinly stitched-together quilted tapestry of what becomes the memory of each of us as an individual.

Rolling out of that old barn and thundering slowly down the road in my 1927 Willys-Knight with Lonnie Woollett at the helm of the tug, and me bringing up the rear in my rumbling hulk, hangs for me.

31

BORDER BANDITS

B

ack again to my late childhood — around age of
fourteen. In telling the previous story I was reminded
of something that crossed my mind as we lumbered
past the porch of the old Log Cabin Tavern. Watching the
shake-roofed, post and pillared, log-style porch fill up with all
the parched people who had previously populated the interior
of the place only seconds before, I suddenly realized this was
not the first time I had emptied the tavern and filled the porch.
Oh no, there had been many other times, years before. But
first, I should tell you about Otto.

If I had to describe Otto (and I guess I have to now that I
said I would), I'd say one would have to picture Orson Welles
in his later roles, after he had filled out a bit. But not as much
as when he had to sit, hiding behind boxes of wine and pro-
claim, "We will sell no wine before its time." Not that filled
out. More like in the film noir classic, "A Touch of Evil," with
Charlton Heston.

In fact, many things were similar between Orson Welles in
that role and Otto, as I look back on it. Although I never saw
the movie until only a few years ago, it's not until just now

that I know who Orson reminded me of. Otto. Orson and Otto. Otto and Orson. I think Orson *was* Otto! Except Otto had a stiff leg.

They both had several chins and did a lot of sweating. They both had big jowls and mumbled. They both represented some bogus form of badge-wielding border authority. They both, in an accusatory fashion, enjoyed hassling handsome young and innocent red-blooded American males. And they both carried guns. In fact, we were told it was *because* Otto packed a .45 caliber pistol on his hip that he *had* a stiff leg. The story was that he shot his kneecap off while trying to practice his quick draw.

Whether it was true or not, we had no trouble whatsoever believing that story. Otto was a clod. Whereas Orson didn't unravel and become profoundly stupid until the end of the movie, Otto had been stupid for a long time. But he was that *scary* kind of stupid, the frightful kind that has a loaded pistol on his hip, who *thinks* he's some kind of sheriff or something, but isn't, and doesn't like fourteen-year-old kids freely wandering about the countryside.

He felt it was his job to patrol the rural back roads of Thurston County in his old Studebaker, looking for kids our age who were trying to make an illegal crossing, I guess. We never did know what it was we were possibly guilty of doing, but his job apparently was to make us *feel* guilty. Even though my friend, Ed, and I were stopped and interrogated at great length many times by Quickdraw McGraw, we were never indicted for anything. And each time he stopped his old gray Studebaker and got out to ascertain what crime we may have recently committed, he never recognized us from any of the other inquests that he had undertaken. Like I said, Otto was a dolt.

Whether or not he regularly rounded up all the other adolescent renegades roundabout, I never heard. But he was diligently perseverant when it came to the two main suspects at large, Alan and Ed. Even though he was vigilant enough to ask us our names each time, he always seemed to make no connection to the last time, so Ed started telling him his name was Bill Hill. I hadn't thought of that. I thought Ed was smart for giving a false name, so I told Otto my name was Ed. Ed didn't think my alias was too clever and glared at me, giving me one of those looks that said, "You're just as dumb as Otto."

After about two weeks from the last inquisition, I eventually came up with a new name. I told him I was Terry something-or-other, the name of Ed's other close friend, of whom I was jealous for taking up too much of Ed's time and causing him to spend less with me. I don't remember his last name now, but I know I didn't like him much because he was funnier than I was and Ed enjoyed his company. His family moved to California after some time and I was glad. But I was sorry they took along with them Terry's sister Janet; they could have left her here. That would've been okay with me. I think their last name was Hall.

"Uuuh-huh," Otto would drawl, looking at us sideways over his pumpkin sized cheeks, acting as if he didn't believe us, which didn't matter to us one iota because no matter what we said, he still reacted the same. We didn't care anyway; we just wanted him to leave us alone.

He'd give us, "Yuh don't saay," or, "Shuure yuh did," or variations thereof when we answered about our destination or recent whereabouts.

He'd lean against his dusty and dented old Studebaker, taking some of the weight of his pear-shaped body off his wooden knee, or whatever the hell he had down there. We'd stand next to him, politely answering his insipid questions while he rested the heel of his corpulent hand on his hogleg. After a while he'd start fondling it. Sometimes he would even extract it from its holster and inspect it. Occasionally he would caress the barrel, flopping it around, this way and that, working himself into a state of mild agitation — and that's what concerned us the most.

Now, I was a healthy fourteen-year-old kid and, although I had a nearly identical problem, I knew I wouldn't cause somebody else to end up with a wooden leg. Or worse. After a bit, Otto would get too sweaty and he'd have to put his gun away so he could pull out his enormous filthy handkerchief and bathe his face.

This was back in the days when kids were polite to adults out of … um … well, now that I think about it, I have absolutely no idea why we were polite to some of those people. Many of them didn't deserve it, so it certainly wasn't out of respect. I guess we were, for the most part, civil and polite because it was required, that's all. Not like kids today. Kids today have it much better. Today's youth get to be rude and mouth off to adults whenever they damn well feel like it. And they hardly ever get shot. At least not often enough to suit me.

But we were polite to Otto not only because he brandished a loaded firearm in our face; we knew that he … did *not* know how to use it. Someone who still played with active armament and who had already deactivated an arm or kneecap or blown off *any* body part was someone who required a degree of some kinda respect.

On top of that, he commanded a small amount of respectful fear, if for no other reason than because he acted as if he was the crooked sheriff out of an old movie. We knew after a while that he had no gendarmely credentials whatsoever. But that didn't stop us from being polite and respectful to his face. As unstable as constable Otto was, he still maintained that air of self-appointed authority of his. So:

When we'd see his Studebaker (which was, by the way, possibly the most visually identifiable car ever produced) coming down the road a mile away, we would have a little fun. I think you could recognize a 1950 Studebaker from ten miles away. And his was the only gray one around.

We'd dart back and forth across the road helter-skelter. Or in the middle of the road we'd pretend to be bludgeoning one another with our fists or a big stick. Then, when Otto's Studebaker was one-fourth of a mile away and disappeared from view down into a dip in the distant road, we would run off and hide. By the time he reached the scene of the crime, we had evaporated.

Hiding in the bushes, we'd giggle and snicker as the portly old pear on a wooden stick stood next to his "Stoody," sweating away and swearing to himself, searching the stickerbushes for some scalawags to shoot. Soon he'd curse out loud and shove himself back into his Studebaker. If we were lucky, we got to see him slam the door on his stiff leg.

We enjoyed it especially when we were able to catch Otto at the Log Cabin Tavern at night. The later the better. After fishing at Long's Lake and on our way out through the woods, the trail came out near the tavern. If we hadn't gotten lucky at the lake, sometimes we'd get lucky at the Log. We were angling for Otto. If his Studebaker was there, so was he. Catching Otto blotto was our game.

.I've heard stories of people fishing with dynamite, although I don't see the charm; may as well blow up a fish market. But we loved to blast Otto off his barstool and onto the front porch of the Log Cabin Tavern with our handful of firecrackers. Of course it wasn't only Otto who came reeling out from the sulfur-filled interior of the tavern in those guerrilla raids. I think he was, however, the only one waving a .45.

After ditching our fishing gear, Ed and I each wound five or six respectable-sized firecrackers together by their fuses. Then we crept between the parked cars up to the corner of the porch where we'd light them — the firecrackers, I mean. By the time we threw them in the open door and they had slid under the barstools, the more alert patronage knew something was happening, but were unsure as to what. The less vigilant of the guzzling cluster, which certainly included Otto, usually took those attacks to mean the communists had arrived, and they were apparently going to accomplish the eventual takeover of the free world by beginning with the local rural taverns. (Come to think of it, had the commies done just that very thing, we'd all be speaking Bolshevik right now: "Grab der beer! Den dey vill do vatefer vee tell dem! Go fort and conquer, comrades! Ant brink me a sex-peck!")

By the time the first cracker had ignited inside the small den of the iniquitous, Ed and I had dived into the ditch on the opposite side of Pacific Highway. We were straight across from the concussive eruptions, the well-lit windows and the half-lit to well-lit clientele, the falling unfortunates, the rolling barstools, the breaking glass, and the porch of pandemonium.

Well after the flashed lights from the explosions had ended and the entire multitude was assembled on the porch, Otto appeared, stomping, swearing and bouncing off either the door jamb, another patron, or a porch post, pistol in one hand and Pilsener beer bottle in the other. The more perceptive of the posse of patrons parted way, pleased to give him most of the porch.

The tall dry weeds of summer shielded us from their sight, but gave us opportunity to see everything perfectly, backlit by the tavern's windows and doorway. As we lay in the ditch peering through the weeds trying to stifle our laughter, we could also hear the talk of retaliation from many of the more courageous porch dwellers. When it had been ascertained by the most astute of the group, which didn't include Otto, that Lacey had not been invaded by the commies, loud threats began to issue forth into the darkness, which of course made us laugh harder. We stopped laughing when one of them hollered, "Them bastards is probl'y layin' right over there in the damn ditch, laffin' at us!"

Remarkably, none of the porch posse nor the sheriff-self-elect wished to cross the road to see. They soon began retreating back into the tavern to tend to the wounded, count the casualties, and bury their dead. The last to abandon porch watch was Otto.

We watched as he grunted defiantly into the night, then wobbled through the doorway, demanding to know why his beer wasn't still on the bar.

"IT'S IN YOUR HAND!" we heard someone yell, "NOT *THAT* HAND! DAMMIT! WILL YOU PUT THAT THING AWAY!"

32

LAKE NIGHT TEENAGE RENDEZVOUS

Night is a hollow thing. Especially so if it's a warm, humid summer night. A cool night or a wet night doesn't have the hollow feel of a warm sultry night — moon or no moon. Still, an extremely cold, frozen or even a snowy night can elicit the same empty hollowness that damp or rainy nights don't. They stifle the emptiness and press down on a person's awareness, stealing away the night, shrinking the experience of full nighthood and blotting out the feeling of being inside a huge hollow metal pipe or culvert of some kind.

Warm night sounds — when whispers are heard from many yards away and you can hear the trees sleeping. The warm hollow nights when a sound seems to be more of an object than a vibration of sound waves. When a whispered word hangs three dimensionally in mid-air in front of the person who spoke it, then slowly dissolves into the darkness. The kind of silent echoey nights when you can hear the little bubbles break inside your own mouth as you whisper to yourself. Or to your lover. The little clicking noises that you would otherwise not notice.

Not that the night itself is silent in its hollowness, just partly empty and hollow sounding, enabling the listener to hear all the small night sounds. Not just the croaking of frogs at the water's edge, but the small blips they and other tiny creatures make in the water as they slip under the surface or as they emerge from the still calm of the warm lake.

Wrapped within the secret hollow inside the culvert of more than one hot summer night was where she agreed to meet me. Down by the lake. These were some of the nights I otherwise would have fished alone, and for catfish rather than bass. I could cast my baited and weighted line out and prop my pole up on shore with a Y-shaped crotch stick, and wait. Catfish feed on the bottom.

Soon I would hear her swish a small branch somewhere on the trail through the woods behind me, then, as she draws closer, her feet in the grass.

Although I never learned her exact age, I knew she was slightly older than I, and also inexperienced. But she was just as eager to learn as was I. The moon illuminated the slope of shore where we sat close together facing the lake and the other moon, the one on the water. Maybe she just seemed older.

I had first seen her at Goldberg's Department Store in downtown Olympia, across from J C Penney on Capitol Way. Weeks later, she had found her way into my night fishing. I made sure not to invite her to meet me on the nights I fished with Ed. Only when I went alone, and not always then did we agree to meet. And only on the warmest nights — the large acoustical nights made for a secret rendezvous.

Whispered kisses. The smell of her neck along with the warm odor of wet mouths, open but not speaking. We had only spoken in our hushed whispers for a short time before we fell under the spell of summer, night, silence, and yearning. My hands on her face, holding her head and searching her lips for a corner I had not yet awakened. Finding none I'd seek elsewhere: her neck, ears, and breasts. Although my adolescent explorations didn't take me too far, we both learned enough in those steamy sultry summer trysts to painfully separate and agree to meet no more. It was much harder for me. Although she was shy and her lovely breasts were small, she was patiently kind and very pretty. She had a wide smile and the moon shone on it, as brightly as it had on her hard white breasts. And even though I was young and clumsy, she had made me feel as if I knew what I was doing. But it was she who had led the way. She had guided me.

The last time I felt her face next to mine and her fragrance on me was the most painful. Because of the parting. I agreed to stay on the summer grass, reclining, and not to call for her or follow her. We had agreed. I watched her leave for the last time, her faded blue jeans easily seen in the moonlight against the darkness of the forest in front of her. She was only a teenager like me, but had the shape of a woman, even in darkness. She was still buttoning the thin white blouse she'd worn many times before.

As I said I would, I remained, propped on one elbow, reclining in the warm grass and listening in the hollow night for the occasional crack of a twig or the rustle of small brush in the trail of darkness. My lips were raw and swollen. A pair of bats flew close to my head, feeding on the mosquitoes that wanted to feed on me. I never saw her again. I landed no catfish that night.

Two or three years later, I landed myself another girlfriend and took her to my secret fishing spot. It was the same kind of night. Everything was identical. Everything was perfect.

Except: she didn't like the dark, and she'd start coughing when she had to whisper. She was allergic to mosquitoes, and the grass made her ass itch. Although she needed to pee, she refused to in the dark, and my kissing her, along with all the pollen that was around, gave her "the hives."

She wouldn't let me touch her because the odor from the small fish I had caught earlier and released was still on my hands. And when she realized the unusual nocturnal "birds" flying around us weren't "nightingales" as I had told her, but bats, she too, hit the trail.

But, she wasn't nearly as quiet in her departure as my imaginary girlfriend had been.

33

GREAT BALLS OF FIRE VS.
THE UNGRATEFUL DEAD

fter living for over a year-and-a-half in my stationary vintage 1927 wooden motor coach, and enjoying the luxurious freedoms it afforded, such as freedom from water, bathroom, heat and electricity, I needed a vacation from my luxury. I was cold and I was tired of peeing out my door.

Periodically, thanks to parental pity, I did enjoy the comfort of a small electric grill-faced space heater, when the 450 feet of frazzled extension cords weren't shorting out at the couplings that lay in snowdrifts or puddles, and when the fuses in my folk's electric panel weren't crackling and fizzing. Which wasn't often. The last straw was when my friend, Rick, and I had come home at two a.m. in January on his motorcycle. It was a starry crisp night — about twenty below, I would have said at the time. Although it was actually around twenty above, it was still damned cold, especially after considering the "windshield" factor.

We made the thirty-mile trip at fifty miles-per-hour. Although we had been all riled up over having our asses kicked in a Tacoma pool hall, the trip home cooled us down considerably. The chill through the wind-exposed thighs of my jeans was closer to one hundred-twenty below.

Rick coasted up to my old motor wagon and pried my dead and stiffened claws off of his shoulders. Once he felt me come loose, he gently popped the clutch and carefully tipped me off the back of his Honda 80, where I landed on the permafrost with the sound of a crashing crystal chandelier contacting the floor of the empty hollow ballroom of night.

"G'mioughmph," I heard him say through frozen jaws just after he popped the clutch and after I had crashed to earth.

"Yauugh, gmioughmph," I managed to muffle through my freezer-burned cheeks and aching teeth. "N'shankkffs."

I crawled up the two tall steps and into my frozen fortress of solitude, where I embraced my small space heater; it wasn't on, but it was warmer than I was. I could hear Rick shifting gears as he turned right onto Pacific Highway about a half-mile away near the Log Cabin Tavern. I barely gathered enough strength to turn my heater switch to the On position. I was a frozen stiff.

Probably about the time Rick was crawling into his folks' nice warm house two miles away, the first inkling of heat was dribbling through the coils of my electrically impeded and amperically challenged heat source. That's about the same time I fell asleep, or possibly died, not just from fatigue, but exposure. I lay on my back on my crunchy cold mattress, still clothed and on top of my sleeping bag, while holding the slow trickling warmth of my heater's grill to the dead flesh of my numbed thigh.

My right thigh. I had been alternating the almost-warm heater between my left and right thighs; when I fell asleep, it remained pressed against the frozen right limb. Soon I was dead to the world while still clutching the central heating device onto my Levi's upper leg, when eventually — lo and behold — the once deadened flesh that lay asleep inside the denim trouser leg boasting a label from the tribe of Levi came roaring back to life. The icy grip of the grave had suddenly given up its dead and the decaying flesh that had lain so long — about ten minutes — in forgotten slumber. Lazarus arose.

Although judgment day had clearly arrived early and Lazarus evidently had been granted an earthly and unexpected sudden resurrection, his apparently sinful appendage obviously had been judged unworthy, or possibly harshly, and had been cast directly into the lake of fire. Lazarus leapt to his feet, and as he did so, casting down towards earth, the fiery serpent, the great dragon that had breathed the flames of misery and hellfire into the mortal flesh of his upper leg. There soon began much wailing and a loud gnashing of teeth. Also, the heater began throwing sparks and flames in every direction as it clattered and bounced around on the floor.

Lazarus had risen; but he had risen too quickly, and an inch or so too far heavenward, surpassing thereby, in his loud exuberance, the six-foot ceiling that until then had restricted his existence to the lower mid-heavens of his small residence and sepulcher. (I hit my head on the ceiling so damn hard I saw sparks everywhere, not just those coming from the bouncing heater.)

And now a great shout was heard throughout the land. The recently exhumed began calling forth the names of many unclean things and a loud clamoring about with noisy exhalation went out for all to hear. Little rejoicing could be found. And the unholy dead with the cursing head and the unworthy leg thundered forth into the darkness, ensnaring his mortal self in the loops and snarls of the extension cord, thereby dragging Sparky, the fiery spitting space heater from hell, with him. More malediction was soon to follow.

So it came to pass that when the sorry stiff with the smoldering limb tripped and pitched forward into the blackness to plant his accursed face flat on the filthy floor of his inner

chamber, the crouching great dragon that he had been dragging whiplashed around and seized the shrieking evildoer by
the ass. And thus it began to devour him.

Continuing to call down damnation and evil on all creation
while at the same time begging for mercy and proclaiming
basic innocence about how he didn't know he had taken up
residence over an ancient chicken burial ground, he loudly
wept and threatened into the chasm of darkness, hoping for a
release and rescue from the pangs of distress and the apparently unquenchable fires of Gehenna. His worthless promises
to abandon all wickedness were evenly mixed with empty
threats to get even with whoever or whatever was causing this
to happen to him. Two voices, one screaming retribution and
the other appealing for merciful benevolence, both voices
spilled forth simultaneously into the otherwise abysmal dead
silent wilderness of the frozen night.

By peeling my pants partway down, I finally untangled
myself from the cords and heater. Using both feet to kick the
heater to the back of my old motor home, I jumped to my feet,
careful not to knot my head again, still howling like hell the
whole time. While I scrambled down the narrow path, the few
feet that were left for me to exit my chamber of torturous
horrors so that I could apply the seared skin of my scorched
leg to the bristling frozen grass outside, my pants, of course,
dropped all the way down to my ankles; whereupon my upper
body continued moving forward towards the narrow door of
salvation, but my feet stopped dead, as if they were two pillars
of salt suddenly anchored somehow to the wood floor. The
door flew open as most of me flew out. My upper torso landed
on the small patch of gravel and dirt that served as my front
porch and door stoop; my legs and feet remained inside, but
not for long. I quickly pried my entire body out of the portal of

pain and crawled onto a cold patch of frosty green. There I lay panting, pants over my shoes while prostrate, grateful to be face down in my own frozen pee. Dogs were barking for miles around.

From across the property, out the dark front door of my folk's house, my dad hollered, "What in *the hell* is all the racket?" Which surprised me, 'cause his hearing wasn't real good.

"I had a small fire. But it's okay; it's just my right thigh."

There was a long pause and I could still hear all the dogs barking in the distance when he hollered again, "I don't give a good god-damn if you *did* have a small tire just the right size! Shut the hell up over there! And how come my lights are all out again?"

The burnt griddle mark on my jeans attracted some degree of attention from a few hippie girls, so I told them I had done it on purpose with a waffle iron. The waffle marks on my thigh healed up by summer so I didn't have to explain anything there.

As I lay under those cold stars in my mixed state of smoldering malediction and annoyed gratitude, I took a vow; I swore I'd find some earthly surroundings more suitable to human habitation … and to relinquish my wicked ways so as to be less likely to become a burnt offering placed on the altar before the great god Stupidity. But I have been eternally thankful for one thing — that I had been alternating the heater from one leg to another when I fell dead asleep, and that I hadn't split the difference and placed the griddle in the middle.

And no matter what, as I've said before, smoking in bed under any circumstances is always a bad idea.

34

INDIAN ATTACK AT LOST LAKE

B y early spring, I had somehow discovered a lost lake
that few people in Thurston County knew existed.
Because so few locals knew of it, it had been named
Lost Lake. Although I wonder to this day who named it — the
people who lost it or the people who found it? The ones who
had lost it couldn't have named it at that location because they
didn't know where it was; they had lost it. The other people,
the ones who don't lose track of things, wouldn't have called it
"lost" because they knew right where they'd left it. I thought
then as I do now that alcohol probably had something to do
with it.

Anyhow, it was and to the best of my knowledge still is
(unless they've gone and lost it again) situated on the eastern
side of Nisqually Valley. Lost Lake was another small inverted
cone, or crater inside a tall hillside, which in this case probably could have been referred to as a misplaced miniature
mountain.

Although it seemed unlikely that I had in my earlier years
overlooked a five- or six-acre body of water within only a few
miles of my home, indeed I had. Soon I would become the

sole resident of the lake's three otherwise empty structures: a small-size house and two cabins — my own little village. Because of the low population count in my small settlement on the shores of a lost lake, I would soon also be referred to as "easy pickin's."

After chasing down the distant owner of the property through the county assessor's tax records, we struck a deal. If I cleaned up and maintained the property, repaired the roof of the main house and cleared the mountains of archival trash out of the voluminous basement, I could move in. After which I would be paying a modest monthly rent. Summer was coming and there I was, about to take up residence on the shores of *yet another* local lake! And I was to have it all to myself. At that point I was one happy guy!

Even though there were still a couple of months left of cold weather, the generous fireplace assured me that I should be warmer in my new digs than I had been the last couple winters. So I saw myself as a soon-to-be *warm* happy guy.

I didn't have a chainsaw. There were trees everywhere, but after all the time I had served planting, processing, packing, and nurturing seedlings into the future, I didn't want to murder any living forestation. I had helped repopulate barren hillsides with baby trees, doing my small part to revitalize our collapsing global ecosystem. I guess I thought I had become an ecology-type guy. But mainly I was just a lazy guy. And I was scared to death of chainsaws; I had nearly dismembered myself a few years earlier with a simple backsaw while back in the high school woodshop.

It wasn't my fault. It was the fault of the beautiful office helper who came around daily to our woodshop class. She was there to collect the role slips from Mr. Bettine, our shop teacher, to see who was and who was not absent. I was hand-sawing an innocent piece of mahogany in half when she came through the door and caused my normally half-present mind to become totally scholastically absent.

I might not have sawn my hand half off if she'd only kept her hands on the small stack of pink papers she was supposed to be collecting. They slipped out of her hand and after they fluttered to the floor and she knelt down to retrieve them, my woodworking abilities faltered. While the more carnal corners of my heart fluttered, I was noticing how neatly stacked she was and that she was nearly spilling out of her plaid jumper. Not having any powers of concentration left over to notice that my saw had wandered off the mahogany and had now jumped onto — and was gnawing away at — my hand, I briefly continued sawing … and concentrating. About the time she stood up and was done quietly spilling out of her jumper, I started silently jumping up and down on my tiptoes while quietly spilling blood on the floor.

Because I had bled on Mr. Bettine's shop floor, I had to serve two hours detention. Bleeding, although not completely discouraged, was only allowable if a student quelled it some-how; it was a cardinal sin to bleed on Bettine's floor. Quickly thrusting a severed finger into your mouth or pocket (or someone else's) was the most common means of concealing woodcraft ineptitude.

I actually completed several rather nice woodshop projects from start to finish with the use of only one hand, the other hand for weeks remaining in my pocket. Eventually I wore a hole through my pocket lining which led to further adolescent distraction and downright moral absenteeism, especially whenever that office girl came around. After some time I grew to be quite fondled of her.

Back to my wood problem.

After depleting my surrounding forest and outbuildings for fallen limbs, old lumber and loose boards, I got lucky. I scored enough firewood to last probably two years, just up the hill and in my own backyard.

Fortuitously, the Burlington Northern Pacific Railway people had decided it was time to replace all the aged railroad ties under the tracks that curved around my little lost lake and mini-misplaced-mountain's rim. A giant yellow diesel dinosaurous monumentous hydraulicus of noise and power that straddled the tracks chopped each tie in half at midpoint between the steel rails. Then, as effortlessly as if they were nothing more than small festering splinters, this monster squirted each half-tie out from under the tracks and down the embankment of each side.

Firewood from heaven!

By the time railroadus enormous and its crew of gandy dancers had pranced, clanged and hammered their way down the line, I had scampered up the wooded slope to claim what was now rightfully mine. My manna from heaven was heavier than hell, but I knew once home it would burn just fine. I "heaved" and I "ho'd" and I dragged and I carried and I stacked and I sweated and I scurried back up to my creosote mine. (My most humble of apologies to Robert W. Service.)

Several hours later I was standing naked, overworked, and sore on my porch verandah, enjoying the final glimmers of a cold early spring sunset overlooking the quiet lake. I was still scrubbing with kerosene the last remaining patches of stubborn tar and creosote from my skin and hair. Kerosene, gasoline, paint thinner — any of these things — have a tendency to cool your skin, except inside the nicks, cuts, and scratches. Those will grow considerably warm, and rather quickly, once petroleum products are introduced into them.

Surprisingly, it didn't rain that night. It should have. By the time the lone naked savage was done dancing his reddened, splotchy, scratched and splinter-riddled skin back and forth across the long porch, hopping up and down, whooping and hollering to high heaven, it should have rained for a week.

By then I was cold, cold enough to start a fire.

Instead of taking a shower first and lighting the large stack of manna in my oversize fireplace afterwards, I decided to kindle my four-foot chunks of wood and tar on fire first. I made that decision largely so that it would be nice and toasty when I left the shower.

Knowing full well that my torso and hair still retained enough kerosene to start, as well as keep, the home fires burning, I knew that I must be careful — and quick.

I wadded up and stuffed some papers — unpaid monthly bills and several threat-laced collection notices of past due payments for my inflatable rubber kayak — under the stack of half ties, and lit the match. And ran.

The hungry fireball, although it immediately located me, no doubt by sniffing me out as soon as it was ignited, only chased me halfway across my living room. I was quite familiar with fire. I knew how it thought. I had years before learned how to dodge and outrun colorful hissing fireballs spewing forth from horizontally aimed roman candles. You must be fast. No dawdling.

As I expected, the flame-thrower had reached for me and my kerosene-saturated hair and face as soon as the match set my unpaid accounts ablaze. And I felt fire nipping at my nude heels as I raced across the wood floor to the open door and porch. So just to be safe, I continued my naked sprint out into the dusky twilight and over to the waist-high porch railing. Because the oily slick that my earlier kerosene bath had left on the porch deck now rendered me unstoppable, I slid, full throttle, into the porch railing and fell over it.

After spending some time scratching around in the leaves and twigs in search of my lungs which I had exhaled when I landed, I thought I'd go in for a nice shower. By that time, the smoke inside the house from the original ignition had cleared somewhat and I was able to locate my bathroom, by crawling on my stomach across my splinter-sprinkled filthy wood floor. Septicemia of the genitalia never entered my mind. My eyes watered from the dark fumes.

I took my shower and crawled back outside, dragging my sleeping bag behind me and slept on the porch.

My very first timber and creosote-fueled fire in my very own misplaced mountain lodge-sized fireplace in my very own house on the shores of my very own mislaid lake raged on for days.

Let it be known: railroad ties not only burn hot, they burn forever. They emit a peculiar odor, much like that of … burning railroad ties. But the most noteworthy thing about flaming creosote-laden trestle-type wood products is the thick oily black smoke that billows about your corner of the state for several weeks after. I don't think it dissipates like normal smoke does. I think it re-congeals into lumps and later falls to earth elsewhere in the form of coal. Or cancer. Or possibly it migrates towards the magnetic poles where it sets about kicking down the doors of the ozone layer so that we white people can enjoy a better suntan — the kind where chunks of past suntans are scalped and carved off our pale faces years later.

I can also tell you this: Lost Lake wasn't lost anymore. Nearby Fort Lewis vigilantly made a couple of helicopter reconnaissance hoverings overhead to check for possible invasive activity, in view of the then ever-present threat of an impending communistic hostile takeover.

Most of the surrounding farmer-settler residents took no notice of the heavy black smoke signals arising from my crater's cone. As acrid billows wafted about the flatlands of

Nisqually Valley, they just assumed Ed Schilter's manure pile had finally erupted in flames. His towering mountain of manure had been smoldering and steaming for several decades by then, so it came as no surprise. Although because of the peculiarity of the putrid petrolianic acridity in the air, some local overly concerned animal rights fanatics wanted to know what Ed was feeding his dairy cows. And some people let Ed know right off the bat that they weren't willing to pay extra for black milk should his cows produce any.

But most exceptional of all the collaterally residual curiosities that arose from carcinogens chuffing out of the top of old smoky was the Indian uprising I inadvertently instigated.

At least I think they were Indians. And I know they were after me. Maybe they were the descendants of whoever had mislaid their lake; now that my copious columns of coal-colored carboned oily coils of creosote had signaled to the Nisqually Nation the location of the previously lost lake, they wanted it back. Indian givers. Within a couple weeks, a late Friday night war party was dispatched. They came over the hill and swarmed down on my creosote ranch. Sneaky bastards attacked when I wasn't home. Thank god. Spears were chucked. Arrows were slung. Sabers rattled.

Except the *spears* were empty Hiedelberg beer bottles chucked into my yard. And the *arrows* were Mad Dog wine bottles slung through the glass of my bedroom window. And the loud rattling of *sabers* was actually the loose fenders of an idling '48 Chrysler with suicide doors and its lights on. I know, because I arrived home late that Friday night after playing roller hockey. While driving my VW Beetle over the crest of the hill, I quickly turned my lights off and stopped. From there I saw that my small settlement in the sagebrush was in the middle of a long and sustained attack from the thirsty savages; I watched. I also heard them slinging stuff around this way and that, terrifying the single villager who could do little more than watch helplessly — albeit safely — from up the hill as they continued their lengthy siege. Finally, I'd had enough.

In a feeble attempt to curb their unprovoked attack on Fort Creosote, Kit Carcinogen stood up and bravely threw a boulder down the hill. It bounced once and then whacked the chattering old Chrysler on one of its flapping fenders, causing it momentarily to stop rattling. It was either that or the initial sound of the loud contact the boulder had made when it smacked the rusty fender that caused the Friday festivities to cease. Or to begin. Depending on your vantage point.

The startled savages turned their attention up the hill in the direction the rock had come. Kit, valiantly hidden behind a tree and in darkness, squealed out in his most defiant high-pitched terrified voice, that they "needed to just go away," hoping to finalize their festivities.

But from where they stood, this was the signal for the *real* games to begin.

While the four doors of the idling Chrysler began slamming shut after being hurriedly loaded up with village pillagers, in total panic I ran over to my VW and started it up. I could see their headlights swinging around and bouncing erratically as the war party negotiated the uphill charge around the road's curves and over its many potholes.

Not turning my headlights on was my defense. Not touching my brakes and consequently keeping the brake lights from illuminating was equally defensive. Running like a scared jackrabbit away from their approaching headlights was also a clever and defensive maneuver. Whimpering like a lost puppy and continually wiping my runny nose with the back of my free hand while my knees shook so uncontrollably I barely could operate the clutch seemed to be my best defense. Half the time I had it in the wrong gear.

The western hillsides of Mount Bighorn were spaghettied with old logging roads. For the better part of an hour, the wild-eyed savages chased the wide-eyed white guy. Finally, the chase ended as they rattled away and down the other side of the hill. They had run low on either gas or beer, not that I cared which; I was just glad I wasn't massacred. My sniveling began to subside. I got out of my car and stood on my violently shaking knees and watched as their headlights traversed down the hill. Shaking my small trembling white-knuckled fist at them in the moonlight, I silently dared them to come back.

So they did. Just not right away. When they did return, they did it repeatedly and regularly. For the next few months I was one scared guy. Eventually almost everything I ever owned disappeared as a result of all those raids; I lost nearly everything, not that I had very much in the first place.

Well … maybe that's why they called it Lost Lake.

35

THE CURIOSITY CHRONICLES: PART 1: TASTE THIS

S ome things that have been relegated to the dustbin of childhood's memory should be left right where they are. They should be left alone where they were laid to rest because they've earned the right to remain there, forever undisturbed. Others need to be, if only for the sake of nostalgia, pulled from the heap of discarded memories, dusted off and taken outside into the sunshine of the present — and caressed. Most fuzzy and intangible memories from our youth are little more than just feelings or episodes or patterns from our early life that we outgrew, forgot, suppressed, denied, or paid therapists and hypnotists to eradicate. This story could be one of those; only I've never had money enough for professional therapy. For most of us, we seem to do just fine leaving these things in the past as we move on in life. Other memories are of things that fall into the classification of being truly missed, missed in the nostalgic sense, begging to be occasionally re-examined.

As in the case of screen doors. Few things can transport me instantaneously into the far distant past horizon of a sweltering summer day like a creaky old wood-framed screen door. If I see one, which is now seldom, or hear one slam, which is even more rare, or maybe if I just picture in my mind's eye an old wood screen door, I am ten again. And it is summer.

The distinctive sound of an extended elongating spring uncoiling while the wire-mesh-over-wood frame is pushed or pulled all the way open is common to many of us, I'm sure. Almost everybody has heard the screeee …..WHACK … Whack … Whack … whack … whk … whk … whk, as the airy sentinel of the back or front porch returns to seal all of the household domesticated flies safely inside. I remember more than once being threatened with physical disablement if I allowed the kitchen screen door to slam which would cause my mom's cake to "fall."

And I'm willing to bet that there are a lot more people out there than would care to admit who have, at some point in their early life, *tasted* a screen door. If they did, I can just about guarantee that they did it once. Only once. No one has done it more than once. No one could be that dumb. I know, because I'm as dumb as they get and I only licked on a screen door one time. That's all it took, and then I was done. I wasn't done spitting though; that went on for quite awhile. I continued spitting, trying to get the iron-oxidized copper-flavored bitter burning acid nasty metallic putrification off my tongue and out of my mouth. And I never did it again. I had been immediately conditioned, like a clever lab rat — and I knew right then and there that I didn't ever want to do that a second time. I never forgot.

I had administered to myself a short and intensely distasteful episode of chemically displeasureable dissatisfaction on a lazy hot afternoon while watching the wild "outside" flies, as I stood inside the doorway along with our homegrown domesticated flies, while both groups clung to either side of the screen. I still can remember with sweet nostalgia those long hot summer days.

And, as I think about it, I realize I'd love to hear the sound of a tired old screen door in full swing right now. The facts that I live in the continuous rain of the Pacific Northwest with small need of a screen door, that it is currently March, that I live in the middle of the city, and that nowadays we all have patio sliding doors anyway, also nourishes the nostalgic absence of a slamming screen. But that sound will always be the auditory symbol of summer for me.

My quick laboratory-rat-like reactions to conditioning against distasteful situations, such as applying my tongue out of plain old curiosity to a screen door, didn't always kick in when they should have. Especially when my craving for *chocolate* overrode my feeble and shallow memory of extreme epicural unpleasantness, which would thereby cause me to spend the rest of an entire afternoon spewing bitter brown spit in every direction.

For instance: After making the unforgettable mistake of licking the patina off our screen door and finding myself soon thereafter rifling through our kitchen cupboards for some stashed away sweet morsel of tastiness that I was hoping my mom might have hidden from me, I found it. The largest chocolate candy bar ever produced by humankind! It was hidden away up on the top shelf where she knew I'd never look, unless I was home alone, bored, too hot to go outside, or needing to purge my taste buds of that horrible and seemingly permanent bitter aftertaste from sampling our front door screen.

So *well* hidden. But now mine. All mine. The biggest candy bar on earth, and I had found it, so it was mine. It was hidden away because of, not only its size, but also obviously because of its superior quality. It wasn't everyday chocolate; it said so right on the giant brown wrapper. This was *professional* chocolate because it read in big silver letters,

BAKER'S CHOCOLATE. Our housecats and houseflies watched bug-eyed in jealous anticipation.

Knowing full well that professional bakers, as well as my mom, knew what they were doing in the baked goods department, after some considerable effort because of its size, I cracked off a three-square-inch, one-inch thick lump of professional chocolate treat and jammed it into my slathery mouth. It didn't fit. Not right away. After pounding on it with the heels of my alternating hands, it slipped in rather nicely and I still had enough of an air passage to breathe. I could only barely feel my tongue, which was quite compressed at that point, due to the size and weight of my prize chocolate monolith. My tongue was also somewhat numbed because of my earlier screen test and the bitter outcome that had followed.

Within only a few seconds that changed.

My warm saliva, along with the grinding abrasions from my teeth at the edges of my choco-prize while I pounded it into place, had chipped away at the corners of it and was now mixing into a fine warm soup inside my stretched-out mouth. About the same time my choco-soup level rose to the level of my airway, my abused taste buds suddenly and rebelliously reactivated.

Never in my life have I tasted anything so repugnantly bitter as that unsweetened chocolate. Compared to the lodged glob of pungent repulsion that I had to contend with, the screen door had tasted like tapioca pudding. My head instantly went into side-to-side spasms at the speed of a commercial paint shaker. I was desperately trying to spew my choco-block of bitter horrification clear back to Hershey, Pennsylvania, where, according to the wrapper, it had been born.

However, a thin brown bitter spray was all that I could expel. The cats quickly left the kitchen along with our pet flies, and both groups sought refuge back at the front screen door, which was still partially clogged with my earlier bitter spittle. All the cats, and the flies as well, began clawing at the screen and yowling, begging to be set free.

After grabbing my oscillating skull with both hands in order to stop its spasms in mid-rattle, the bad block of horrible atrociousness flew into the kitchen sink. I hacked, wheezed, spumed and expectorated for about forty-five minutes. Loudly.

During that period of time, I foggily began to form the faint outline of a memory. Actually, more than one memory, yet it was the same memory, repeated.

Years before, at least two different times, I had discovered a partial chunk of the same ugly dark horror in our cupboard or on the counter. Because it was camouflaged to look like real chocolate, and because of its obviously chocolate odor, I had scarfed it up, only to end up in other earlier fits of unexpected bitter disappointment while spinning around in chowdery puddles of nasty umber-colored spit.

It was then that I realized why my mom had hidden the big bar of blistering bitterness from me, even though she knew that I was able to read the word "unsweetened" on the giant wrapper. She knew what I didn't. When it came to candy, specifically chocolate, I wasn't intelligent enough to apply for the job of a lab rat; I neither had the qualifications nor the diligence for the job. That was painfully obvious now, even to me. My experience with the rusty old screen door could be chalked up to plain old passive curiosity, but my pattern of ignorant behavior regarding chocolate candy, along with my willful disregard of previously and repetitively unpleasant shocking results, would have embarrassed any professionally conditioned laboratory animal.

On top of that, she didn't like the blotchy mess I had, once again, made of the kitchen.

36

THE CURIOSITY CHRONICLES:
PART 2: CURIOUSLY SMOOTH

C uriosity is in and of itself a very curious condition
that to the best of my limited and distorted knowledge
has never been scientifically studied. Just think of the
things we take for granted today because somebody was
curious about something (not counting Adam and Eve and that
one particular year's harvest): electricity, the telephone, peanut
butter, the wheel, and probably drug addiction. Although I
can't think of any of the others right now, I'm sure there are
some.

In my case, curiosity comes in two packages: one package
is the large economy-sized instant-mix kind: just-add stupid-
ness and stir. As in the screen door taste test. It doesn't take
long to realize that type of curiosity will often leave an incredibly bad taste in one's mouth. That's the cheap, empty and
unfulfilling brand of superficial curiosity that we quickly learn
to do without, once we've had a sampling.

Then there is the ongoing and refillable brand of relentless
curiosity, which we eternally find ourselves repeatedly stirring
into the morning mix of our lives. Or as I said, at least in my
case.

Curiosity about sex remains as steadfast and dependably regular as the milkman used to be. Tuesdays and Thursdays — well, maybe not that dependable, but seemingly eternally dependable, the curiosity anyway. I'm sixty years old; don't let me give you the wrong idea; we're addressing the unquenchable nature of my curiosity here, nothing else.

And it's not my fault. That particular brand of constantly recurring curiosity was caused by incorrect input way back in the mid 1950s. I was cruelly and unnecessarily misled by visual misinformation purposefully perpetrated upon a lot of kids my age. Whose idea it was and what they hoped to gain by misleading a whole generation of eager young male prepubescents I do not know. Nor do I need to. The damage is done.

When I was a kid, any kind of an image of female nudity was a quite rare and valuable commodity. Full frontal nudity was nearly unheard of except in "art" magazines of the time or, more truthfully, a few years out of print but still circulating, although quite hard to get your hands on.

Black and white naked art poses of lovely young women frolicking in Elysian fields, sitting in shadowy ancient doorways, windowsills and old barns. *Artplay, Photocade, Art Studio* and other names of thin periodicals to satiate the artistic bent of any budding young student of "art."

The problem was that, although these trickily lit images provided, in most cases, great information on the subject of breasts, they were quite damaging in other areas. Damaging because of the misleading nature (or lack) of the way in which the lower frontal portion of the beauteous human female form was portrayed. Smooth. It took me a long time to find out that they had been fiddling with the evidence. The pictures had been doctored with airbrushes or erasers or something, so that the models were blank and smooth.

And I don't mean smooth only in the hairless definition; I mean smooth as in absolutely no hint of what I shall refer to as, cleavage. Pubic cleavage. And there's the problem. We were lied to. Visually speaking, we had been duped. And why? What incomprehensible purpose could be served by tricking us, the unknowing and curious and what could otherwise have been termed healthy American preteen boys, into believing this anatomical falsehood? And the whole time we were told that's where babies popped out, which was in itself inconceivable and quite impossible, I was sure. (In fact, I still have my doubts.) But this other business was very misleading and unwarranted.

Did Sweden lie to their young boys about this? Had France? Germany? I doubt if even the English distorted the anatomical facts in such a manner as we Americans, and they're the ones who invented Puritanism and Victorian shame. Prudishment is one thing, but covering up the facts, concealing evidence and rearranging reality is not just a crime; it's just plain wrong!

So, for a few years there, I was confused. And overly curious. I just knew there was more to it than met the eye. The naked eye.

Eventually I, along with others my age, found out the truth. Thanks to our own relentless and undying curiosity, we overcame their lies. Their plan no doubt was to keep us misinformed on the subject long enough so that fewer babies would be thrust into this world. Did they think that if they kept it covered up we'd never find it? The truth, I mean. Although, admittedly it took me longer to get to the truth than most, I eventually, through my own unquenchable curiosity, uncovered the naked truth.

When I did, I had to assume that she had hurt herself climbing a fence or in a bad bicycle accident, similar to many of my childhood mishaps, but with a differing scarification. I offered her my sympathy and asked if it still hurt. Only after several patient explanations on her part and excellent lighting did it become sufficiently clear that I had been, once again, victimized.

So I got over the fact that I had been tricked, because of my thirst for truth and my newfound knowledge based in glorious reality. For a short while. Then, my curiosity and doubt reared up again, and I figured I needed to check once more, just to be sure. And that's the way it's continued for about the last half century. Curiosity-doubt-reaffirmation; every couple days, for years and years now. Here I have been all this time wallowing in recurring and unnecessary insecurity — all because I was originally visually lied to. It's just a good thing I'm naturally curious and have been willing to take the time and trouble to regularly resubstantiate the facts.

In my early years, when my indefatigable curiosity had led me into superficial research on the subject, all I could find from which to gather information was store-bought dolls. (Oh, and mannequins; but that's another story by itself.) I didn't like going into department stores for fear that my overpowering curiosity would drag me helplessly over to the doll section where I would uncontrollably snatch them off the displays, turn them upside down and peel back their underwear with a filthy fingernail. The more expensive dolls had panties, the cheaper floozy types exposed raw plastic so they were quicker to research. I soon learned that I not only enjoyed the anticipation involved, I also believed that somehow I was right on the brink of learning something important.

But in every case it was the same. Smooth. Just like in those pictures. Mothers clutched their little girls to their hips and quickly scurried past, covering their children's eyes as, with my furrowed brow and dirty hands, I rooted about the dolls, occasionally grunting in annoyance and jamming them back onto the wrong shelf, upside-down or sideways, arms akimbo and legs askew, violated looks on their small plastic faces. But as always it was I who had been violated. And I don't think the doll manufacturers were doing any favors to my female counterparts at the time either. Those smooth bottomed dolls could have confused girls also, once they took a look for themselves, made their own comparisons, and realized someone was trying to trick them as well.

Well, I'm sure they figured out the truth way before I did, although they did have an unfair advantage. I am not bitter over the [w]hole thing, as I said, I'm just thankful for my own natural perseverant curiosity.

Except for the time I nearly killed myself while trying to examine my own anatomy. My curiosity, that time anyway, nearly killed my cat, me, and certainly dented my flashlight all to hell. My naturally inquisitive obsessive side almost landed me in a wheelchair for life.

37

THE CURIOSITY CHRONICLES:
PART 3: TAFFY PULL

O n a warm summer night after being sent to bed and
after I had, weeks before, memorized my latest
Donald Duck comic book, I set about to do some
top-level research. Top-level, because I was in my bunk bed,
close to the ceiling. My light was off, but I was in possession
of our black metal family flashlight. It contained two new
strong batteries. Although they seemed loose, the flashlight
was quite reliable, even if it did rattle a lot and would only
sometimes fail; usually if I tried to focus on something. Otherwise, the flashlight appeared to have a mind of its own and
would somehow turn itself on and then stay like that, staring
off into daylight, unnoticed, until the batteries died and we
actually needed the flashlight for something. But, that night
the batteries were strong and the light was intensely bright.
My cat was asleep on my pile of clothes which lay on the cool
linoleum applied over the concrete floor of my bedroom.

In school, the subjects of eggs, fertilization, reproduction
and most notably, spermatozoa, had recently been introduced.
Although it had been brief. Apparently they neither wanted us
learning too much nor too fast. Nobody asked any questions at
the time and the teacher appeared relieved.

When it was mentioned that the human male was some-how capable of manufacturing, on his own and without his knowledge or approval, millions of small swimming living organisms with tails, I made a mental note of it — like I could have ignored that.

As if I wasn't already having enough trouble processing all of the information, misinformation, and outright lies that I had been able to gather on these topics, now this. Pollywogs and tadpoles were being produced by me and without my prior permission. Right away I was irritated. And privately embar-rassed. Although seriously doubting the scientific veracity of this latest finding I was also greatly annoyed that this might somehow be going on without my noticing it, and right under my ... nose, at that.

Thus, my curiosity once again awakened and, unable to sleep because of another can of worms being dumped in my lap, I thought I'd better check into the remote possibility of mysterious new life forms multiplying at an alarming rate somewhere in the Netherlands. My "netherlands."

Expecting this to be only more of the kaleidoscope of synchronized incorrect propaganda perpetrated on us innocent young males and me specifically, I dubiously clicked on my flashlight and then placed it between my heels, pointing up at my face and the ceiling. As I sat there, naked, with my legs cocked and my knees up around my ears, I began to wonder.

Listening to the crickets outside my window and feeling much like a crouching cricket myself with my legs jackknifed in such a manner, I wondered how many other ignorant and curious ten and twelve-year-old lads had, or were about to, scrutinize their own scrotums, with a flashlight.

The summer evening heat helped to maximize the pliabil-ity necessary to stretch thin enough the material under inspec-tion; like warm taffy, only not quite nearly as sticky, the crinkles unfolded and the skin stretched enough that soon I could see light — I could actually see light shining through my own living flesh. About the same time I was able to discern veins, the flashlight went dead.

I let go of my living taffy with one hand, grabbed the flashlight, shook it until it rattled, and it came on again. I replaced it between my heels, gripped again my shrinkling pouch of possible pollywogs and pulled it slowly taut once more. Again the flashlight failed. Again I shook, stretched, and again it failed. And again. About the time I was nearly overwhelmed with exasperation, and my stretchy flesh was begging to be left alone and be allowed to sleep, the light not only stayed on, it abruptly became brighter! As I spread for what would be the final time my now feverish human crepe over the brighter light of scientific achievement, I pictured in my imagination sperm — schools of sperm, swimming in unison like fish, randomly changing direction whenever someone slams a door or honks a horn.

Holding carefully now a tender oval of testes over the pinky-flesh-colored light to test for opaque clarity and for my own self-testament regarding tiny testicular tenantry — a giant charley-horse came thundering into the picture. My right thigh, hamstring to be exact, went into one large painful convulsive contraction.

Now, because my right foot was nearest the wall and because my instinctive unconscious reactive impulse was to quickly straighten out my cocked and loaded hair-trigger cricket leg, I was quite suddenly airborne. I had kicked myself out of bed. When I sailed into blackness backwards, the flashlight turned off. But it followed me into the darkness and was soon to join me on the cool hard linoleum floor.

Like an upside-down flying squirrel, I drifted in silence, still clutching in desperation my thinly stretched vestige symbol of the future misery known as fatherhood. I fell soundlessly; I landed soundly. The loud beefy splat when my naked back impacted onto the floor was completely unexpected by our snoring cat, who I had just barely missed flattening into a furry flapjack. She spit and hissed, but she stood her ground on my pile of clothes, if only for a second.

When the flashlight hit the floor, spinning, it came back on. That's when the cat stopped hissing and immediately began leaving. Briefly spinning her wheels on the smooth tile floor, she finally found traction on my heaving airless chest. That's also when my mom arrived.

As my mom entered my bedroom doorway, she was greeted with a shrieking cat clawing its way across my chest and toward the door, a spinning flashlight barely illuminating the darkness with flashes of light on a naked twelve-year-old convulsing on the floor with no air in his lungs, heaving up and down while trying to reactivate his diaphragm, one fist pounding violently on the back of his right thigh and the other hand quite naturally still attached to his scrotum, which was held up in the air and stretched out as tight as a drumskin. She said nothing, then. She just let out a loud guttural baritone moan and left.

The next morning as she drooped one of her signature oversized pancakes onto my plate, she said something, as I was afraid she would. "I didn't like the way things looked last night; I'm not sure what the hell you were doing, but I think I've read about that stuff before. And if I ever catch you doing it again, I'm sending you away, for good."

"Okay." I just wanted her to shut up about it. So I happily agreed to be sent off somewhere. As if I planned on a repeat performance.

"And I don't even want to know what you were doing to that poor cat, but I know it was disgusting."

270

38

CHARLIE'S MANURE FARM

I love it when bugs crawl all over me — most any bugs, even flies and spiders, and especially in warm weather when I am shirtless. Ladybugs incidentally, although most people don't believe it, *do* bite, though not severely. Almost none of the other winged or walking creatures of small wonder, perceived to be evil and carnivorous by the majority of wimps and wussies occupying America's wonderful urban and suburban clusters, will bite. Mosquitoes and the like don't count.

Because of my rural upbringing and practically having been born and reared at the edge of local lakes and streams, deep woods, and tall fields, I became well acquainted early on with the small-multi-legged creatures of insignificant stature. At first and when I was very young, I'm certain I was as startled and squeamish as most suburbanite shopping mall adult squealers today when a spider skitters across their sneakers. They stomp and flail about, shiver and willy, scamper and scream. Then they climb into their SUV and sit, stuck in slow traffic, awaiting their opportunity for the fast lane where they stand a significant chance of speedily becoming a sad statistic on America's highways; yet, they're afraid of spiders.

Serious studies have shown that statistically we stand a twelve-thousand-five-hundred-forty-one percent higher probability of being completely crushed between a late model Ford Explorer and an '85 Oldsmobile Cutlass than any portion of our flesh being crushed in the jaws of a harmless little grasshopper. Although the grasshopper may leave an oily stain on your hand similar to an old Ford, if you're not careful, they *don't* bite.

Our odds of expiring from clogged arteries and malignant growths because of our American diet, along with our refusal to wander — or waddle — a wooded hillside occasionally, is eighteen-million-two-hundred-thousand-six-hundred-five times more likely than dying from a simple spider bite. But still we scream and scamper.

Three-and-a-half-million soft-paunched overweight Americans will die a sedentary death in the jaws of their Barca-loungers in front of their big screen TVs this year, while only four people will die from being chewed on by anything indigenous to our backyards, public parks or forests. Two of those four, time and forensics will show, were simply hacked to pieces by their spouse or a skinny neighbor on the Atkins Diet. Yet the little ones, these harmless insects, the smallest creatures on the earth, will have to suffer unfairly the phobias, therefore shouldering all of the misplaced blame for their unrealistic and unjustifiable fear and angst, usually in the form of a size nine-and-a-half Nike cross-trainer.

Because I grew up in the country and soon realized that nearly all bugs will not bite, and that even bees and wasps will not sting unless they think you're in some way attacking them, I learned to enjoy their small and harmless forays onto my flesh. Now I prefer to look upon them as personal little back-scratchers and massage therapists. I cheerfully share my outdoor meals with yellow-jacket wasps, just to watch the voracious little carnivores of carrion saw a small piece of turkey or sausage off and fly away with it. What's even more entertaining is watching almost all the other picnickers swat and swing and scurry away from the same yellow-jackets, convinced in their own self-importance that the wasps are after them. Nothing could be further from the truth. Just relax and eat. Let them do the same thing and they *will not* bother you. Simply set some food aside for them and make sure you don't try to eat the same piece of meat or whatever they are dining on at that moment. Otherwise you may have difficulty finishing your meal; swallowing wasps whole can leave you breathless and lead to a restrictive dietary intake immediately afterwards due to your esophagus/windpipe swelling shut for the rest of your shortened picnic/life.

On hot summer days when I was a kid on my way to swim or fish in one of the local small lakes near my home, my route to the desired destination of sun-dappled shoreline and cool water would normally involve detouring past Charlie Newkirk's manure farm. At least that's what Dr. Dodge, who lived opposite us on Kinwood Road and who was the local veterinarian, had called it — "Charlie's Manure Farm." And that was indeed an apt and vivid description of what years of hard work on Charlie's part had earned him, by cleverly stockpiling tons of his animals' gross natural product. Towering mountains of manure, taller than the ramshackle barns and biodegrading chicken coops. Manure-covered cows slept in the cool shade of Charlie's lower foothills. Three or four pigs periodically peered out from the dank and sloppy valleys between the mounts of manure. Chickens and ducks waded and paddled in brown rivulets that, in wet weather, meandered throughout the base of the entire range of dark mountainous mounds of moldering muck and mustering methane.

An old lady by the name of Mrs. Marshall may have been the actual landowner and manager of the whole messy menagerie. She rode out to the manure farm twice daily with Charlie in his 1942 International pickup truck. Together they would depart with two 5-gallon milk cans full of what I suspected was supposed to be milk. Although I personally doubted it. Somebody somewhere was actually expected to drink whatever they may have been squeezing out of those mud-caked bovines knee-deep in what appeared to me to be not only cow crap, but also woeful despair. What actually went on inside those buildings behind closed and rotted-off-at-the-bottom barn doors, I never knew for sure. But that's what Charlie always emerged with: two tall milk cans full of something that somebody thought was milk. Charlie did all the milking while Mrs. Marshall wandered around complaining amid the barnyard's blighty, but otherwise and in its own way, bucolic mountains, meadows, slopes and pastures.

That's all she ever did. Complain. Other than open and close the main mud-gate for Charlie's pickup upon their arrivals and departures, mostly all she ever did from what I saw, was yell at Charlie. Yet, because Charlie appeared to do all the work, the farm was known locally as "Charlie's." Old Lady Marshall seemed to be in charge because of all the hollering she did at Charlie and the uncooperative cows, chickens, pigs, and what I think were ducks but may have been a pair of two-legged dogs, and mountainous swarms of egg laying insects. That didn't change the fact that Charlie shoveled and saved all the fecal matter. So Dr. Dodge and everybody else thereabouts (which, by the way, was nearly nobody) gave Charlie credit where credit seemed due. It was forever known, once the good doctor coined the phrase, thereafter as "Charlie's Manure Farm." I guessed that old lady Marshall was little more than a figurehead.

What, if anything, their relationship with each other was beyond that of a landowner and ranch hand, I refuse even today to ponder. Although I didn't want to think about it, I was aware even as a kid, that they must have at some point been involved in some type of a ranch romance and somehow had been in love with each other, impossible as that seemed. Because, as I also believed, that's what people in love always did eventually, yell at each other and complain a lot. Now that I'm the same age as Old Lady Marshall and her cowhand Charlie were then, I'm certain of it.

It could have been called "Charlie's Farm of Flies." At least seasonally — in warm weather when all of the dormant and possibly severely mutated smaller organisms hatched; "all" being all that had somehow survived winter while lying-in-state on and inside the smoldering heaps of slippery shit that Charlie had shoveled to a height of what appeared to be around sixty-feet. Because that's when seventy million or so flies suddenly sprang to life.

Then, unable to cling to the steep and slippery slopes of the mountains of slick manure that they had just hatched from, they hopped onto the nearest cow, or Mrs. Marshall, or whatever other slow-motion host was thereabout, choosing the nostrils, eyes, mouth and interior of the ears as their new place of lodging. Charlie apparently moved too fast for them. Sleeping pigs, milk pails, standing cows and Mrs. Marshall were their preferred migratory stopover in their journey to wherever flies eventually go. They also landed on any idle semi-stationary onlooker, so I tried not to stand still for very long when

passing by and pondering the meaning of life at Charlie's
Manure Farm.

For years I thought Mrs. Marshall always wore the same
heavy black overcoat. One day I happened past when the wind
suddenly blew the half-rotted barn door shut. I then learned
she was sporting a filthy but brightly colored floral print dress,
along with her knee-high black rubber boots which she always
wore — except whenever one of them became stuck in the
muck and subsequently got sucked off her foot while she
struggled and swore a blue streak. The large door had unexpectedly swung shut with a loud CRACK that echoed throughout canyons of fermenting fertilizer and between the bulging
barnsful of cow, chicken, pig and bullshit. Suddenly there was
color everywhere.

The cows, which I previously had thought were black
angus, were now not black but mottled brown and kinda
white. The sleeping pigs were on their feet blinking their eyes
and appearing to be suddenly quite alert; and they were sorta
pink. Not only was I briefly able to discern patches of green
grass and clover blossoms growing on the hillside mounds of
manure, I saw for the first time that Mrs. Marshall simply
wore glasses; before the slamming of the door I had always
thought she wore thick black aviator-type goggles.

Quite soon however, each of the millions of flies that had
only briefly hovered over that small flatulent section of foothills in the northern Cascades re-alighted onto their favorite
spot on whichever pig, cow, Mrs. Marshall, or hillside, they
had just a moment before vacated. The black hills were black
again, as were the cattle, pigs, ponds, posts, pails, Charlie's
pickup, and anything else that didn't fight back. The dark
cloud that had hovered overhead and had only momentarily
blotted out the summer sun quickly dissipated and Charlie's

manure farm was again a fine familiar shade of shimmering anthracite. Mrs. Marshall was once more wearing her heavy coat and flight goggles; also her voice was noticeably muffled.

As I stood at the edge of that scene, swatting and flailing furiously and futilely at the peripheral cluster of flies that were fighting over which of my moist orifices to clog, I listened to Old Lady Marshall yelling to Charlie that Pepper, their main cow, had once again got loose. Evidently Pepper, the perennial escape artist that she was, took advantage of the diversion and had crawled under or through a weak spot in the fence. Indeed, it's entirely possible that it was Pepper herself that had slammed the door, setting up not only the loud distraction, but extrapolating that fifty tons of flies on the wing would momentarily blot out the sun — thereby enabling her to quickly make good her escape; she was a clever cow.

Normally, whenever rounding up the five or six pathetically plastered-with-cowpies pack of plodders from grazing in what they thought was pasture, Mrs. Marshall always hollered "PE-E-E-E-PPERRRRR-PEPPER-PEPPER-PEPPER!" and banged on a bucket until Pepper would give up and come out of hiding from behind some scrabbly scotch broom or mountain of dung and dejectedly head in Mrs. Marshall's direction for milking, experimental crossbreeding with insects, or possibly their evening read of *Washington State Farmer*. The other cows at that point, would dutifully and numbly follow Pepper to whatever it was that went on inside those dismal barns.

More than once, Pepper, in her evening plod homeward, had looked at me with her large brown eyes, pleadingly it seemed, for possible parole from her pestilent imprisonment. Not that she actually needed any help from me. That cow was always loose. Other than not wanting to be fondled by Charlie or ordered around by Old Lady Marshall, escape was the one thing tantamount on Pepper's mind. She spent half her life on Kinwood Road trying to thumb a ride into town, away from all the oppressive crap she had to face on a daily basis.

Little did she know that because the closest actual "city" was Olympia, it was also the State Capitol and was therefore helplessly floundering under mountains of its own self-propagated bureaucratic bullshit and would probably succumb to hopelessness well before any rural and grass-roots nonpartisan anarchistic cow. But anyway, occasionally she would glance at me while she romped around in the ditch of our gravel road and clonked around on its hard-packed shoulders, kicking up her hooves in short-lived freedom until Old Lady Marshall marshaled Charlie's help and together they surrounded poor old Pepper. At which point Pepper would again peer over at me wistfully while I leaned on a post, fanning at flies and looking from a distance into her soft eyes, seeing her plaintive supplication that seemed to simply say, "Just butcher me."

On at least one school morning when I walked to the end of our long dusty road to catch my school bus, I arrived to find Pepper already there, nonchalantly chewing her cud and apparently ready for school. She was planning no doubt to blend in with all of us other dull-eyed dim-witted gum chewers, possibly hoping to make a planned getaway later by becoming chronically truant. Although I admired her plan, I warned her that was also my plan. Then I further explained to her that in my opinion conditions at my school were worse than she knew and told her that she would be better off to go back to the barnyard where she belonged. The reality was, I didn't want to aid and abet a dumb cow that, had she enrolled in my school, doubtlessly would have gotten better grades than I.

I don't know if Pepper ever got away for good or not; to my knowledge she never did. Pepper, along with her faithful followers, and the pigs, chickens, Charlie Newkirk, and Mrs. Marshall just went the way of all flesh, unnoticed by me, a child too wrapped up in his own self-centeredness and preservation to pay much heed. I couldn't help but notice however, as the years went by, that there appeared to be less and less life at Charlie's. The mountains stopped growing, roosters ceased crowing, and no longer were there any cows a-mowing. I had paid little attention to the slow decline of Charlie's empire. By the time I was a teenager in high school, I realized I had also failed to notice the absence of Mrs. Marshall. The flies had even stopped hanging around. Charlie's 1942 International pickup no longer rattled down the dusty road and into the small barnyard.

Within a few more years the ramshackle unpainted barns and coops had oozed completely into the thick lush rich sod that, by then, covered every square inch of Charlie's fertilizer factory, the buildings themselves having become part of the verdant rolling hills of plushness. All traces of it having ever been a farm were gone.

Later, as a young adult, I would drive past and see the tall mounds of broad-blade dark-green sweet grass blowing in the gentle breeze, waving at me as I passed. Nowhere in rural Thurston County — or on God's green earth for that matter — has there ever been a more vibrant patch of fertile green. Charlie's years of hard work shoveling, hoarding and stockpiling his proud peaks of precious ploppings had paid off for nobody. Years later, his mountains were mowed down by bulldozers to be covered by new apartment houses and asphalt. By that time though, few people thereabouts knew why the mounds ever existed in the first place, nor why that acreage was so richly thick with moist heavy black soil.

Looking back, it was possibly then, when I was just a passing kid watching passively the much less than pristine, but in it's own way pastoral, scene of what was soon to become "days gone by," that I learned to be permissive toward what other people describe as pests. It was then, I think, that I accepted an occasional fly, ant, bug or bee walking around on my insignificant flesh, as something tolerable.

Not only will the day come for each of us when we no longer notice the small caressive footsteps of harmless feet on our failed flesh, it will be too late for us to cultivate a tolerance of the tiny creatures; they'll still be here anyway, dancing on our graves.

It's hard to rationalize how it is that I can sit here with a pen in my hand and recollect those smelly steaming scenes of someone else's scroungy barnyard brimming with biblically proportionate swarms of insects with anything close to a sense of nostalgia. But, that's what time does to a person.

EPILOGUE:

Not that you need to know the following. In fact, I'm quite sure you would agree that you were better off not knowing the foregoing. Nevertheless I feel obligated somehow to relate the truth about where I was, geographically, when I wrote it.

I just finished writing the previous story, "Charlie's Manure Farm" near and at Trevi Fountain in ancient Rome — not while visiting some old farm outside Lacey, Washington and not while sitting in my yard, nor while at home with the flu, not even while sitting on the john; I wrote it while visiting Rome. No cows, cowpies, flies, barns, pigs or dirty ducks. No stench and nobody that resembled Charlie Newkirk or Mrs. Marshall.

Ancient Rome and Trevi fountain, here where there are flower carts and swarms of people in love. Beautiful ruins and beautiful women. Young men so handsome *even I* considered we take a couple of them home with us, an idea my wife thought colossal and fell upon with great relish, proclaiming me to be a genius and telling me how I "must have been reading her mind."

After a week of my pretending not to watch most of the men in Italy not pretend to not watch, with monumental interest, my young and lovely wife while I correspondingly exercised a similar lack of self-control pretending not to be watching their young and beautiful Italian women, I decided I'd better sit down and write about what I know — while I could still see.

So, while I was writing about monumental piles of cowpies, my wife was able to wander around Rome and continue distracting the masculine half of Italy from what they were supposed to be doing. I not only *wrote* the earlier story while in Italy visiting its monumental fountains, spires and ruins when *I then immediately lost* the manuscript here. Actually to be specific, I lost my manuscript while visiting Pompeii.

No sooner had I finished writing about colossal mountains of crap, shortly after visiting the Roman Coliseum and after boarding a tour bus and after lingering in the shadow of Mount Vesuvius while crawling around on the slopes of Pompeii with swarms of other bug-eyed tourists, I discovered that I had lost my notebook containing several recently written (hand printed) stories of similar insignificance.

Our twelve hour bus trek there and back had included several hours of meandering through the entire town of

Pompeii itself, trekking wearily along with all the other pic-ture-taking tourists behind Tonio, our tour guide and translator. That was until Tonio, along with my wife and everyone else in our herd, decided to ditch me.

Pompeii incidentally, is huge, and, I'm happy to report, pleasantly pornographic in places. So, while I stared cow-eyed for a little longer than maybe I should have at some of the twenty-five-hundred-year-old porno pictures painted on plaster, while inside the pleasure house owned by one of Pompeii's preferred past prostitutes, of which there seemed to be plenty, my bus-pod of people plodded off.

I think they *ran*. Even the lame ones, the very elderly, and the seriously infirm. As soon as my back was turned they all took off running like Pepper the escape cow, led by Tonio and my wife. When I soon emerged into the bright summer sun and was nearly blinded by it, they were nowhere to be found. So I spent the next couple hours scurrying up and down the ancient stony streets of Pompeii bleating like a lost calf, stopping only briefly whenever I came upon another whore-house where I quickly inspected the frescoes for any fresh input into man's past follies, fantasies, foibles and evidently frequent dalliances of the flesh. Failing as I did so to find my friends, and in a sweaty floundering panic, it was then that I somehow managed to lose my hand-printed manuscript along with my twenty-euro tour book on Pompeii. And my pen. And the top button of my pants.

Three days later, through much difficulty and an under-ground network of concierges, bus drivers, ticket punchers, hotel receptionists, a one-eyed gelato server and an eighty-year-old donkey cart driver, I got everything back, except for my pen and my pants button. It cost me plenty. But that's how it is when dealing with the Italian underworld.

The truth is, I just couldn't bear the thought of archeologists centuries from now unearthing my ring-bound notebook from somewhere in the ruins of Pompeii and reading a story about a farmyard full of dead animals back in Washington State that had essentially smothered to death in their own defecation.

Eventually Tonio and the other handsome young Neapolitan male tour guides also returned Cheryl to me. At no charge. She appeared radiant.

39

STRAINED RELATIONS

Now that I've grown old and my body has caught up with my mind, inasmuch as they are equal in their lack of nimbility, I am relegated to the ranks of millions relying on some forms of medication for survival. My wife helps me in this regard. She doles out my meds. We both know I'd be useless (dead) if such a chore were left to me; I've no idea what any of them are for.

And, as much as I'm ashamed to admit it, according to my wife, I'm apparently already hopelessly addicted to something called "placebos" — whatever the hell *they* are; all I know is, whenever someone nearby opens a package of generic M&M's within my view, I get all jumpy, my face quivers, and my nose runs. But then again, the same thing happens whenever I think about sex. Or car insurance.

I seem to be the only person in our state who gets upset over the fact that we have to pay driver's liability car insurance on *each vehicle* a person owns, even though we, the drivers, are able to pilot only *one car at a time* down the road. In Washington State that's how it is anyhow. No matter which of my medications I misuse, I don't think I've ever driven

more than one car at the same moment. I have lost track of the
whereabouts of a couple vehicles here and there, but driving
two or more cars at the same time remains out of the question,
no matter how hard I try and no matter which meds I take. Yet,
I must pay liability insurance on each vehicle I own. And on
top of that, our state has in place an *Insurance Commissioner
and staff* just to make sure insurance companies don't get
away with that kind of crap.

I never used to take medicines of any kind. Over the years
though, my wife has slowly eased me into a dependency not
unlike many in our society who now receive monthly checks
in the mail over the very fact that they are hopeless addicts. *We
PAY them to be addicts.* Except I don't receive a paycheck for
my disability; I'm not hopeless enough, according to the
people who send out the checks anyhow. According to Cheryl,
I'm not only hopeless, I'm helpless as well. That's why she
helps me with my pharmaceuticals consumption. She pays
careful attention to all my conditions, and from a safe distance
monitors my decline.

And that's just the way I like it, being cared for and tended
to by a member of the opposite sex; I've always bathed in any
attention I have been fortunate enough to receive from women
throughout my life. Although I have ardently sought it, I still
feel as if I have been given very little. In many cases, it has
seemed to me, the more I thought I needed it, the less attention
I got. Many are the times I begged for a kind hand, only to be
sadly ignored and left unattended, seemingly hopeless, helpless, and hapless. And after being subjugated to this level by a
patent lack of interest or generosity from the fair female
gender I have become rigidly conditioned. Because of a lack
of it, I've essentially become sadly addicted to *any* form of
female attention. Therefore, I am more than happy to do

anything they tell me; even strange women. In fact, *especially* strange women.

For instance, when in a restaurant, if a pretty food server puts her hand on my shoulder and tells me to go scrub down the restrooms, I will. On the other hand, if some car salesman or anybody in a striped tie places his hand on my shoulder and extends his other meat-hook for a handshake, I'm most likely to just deck him; I *hate* some fast-talking guy putting his hand on my shoulder! Fast-talking women, or slow talking ones for that matter, have always been encouraged to put their hands wherever they like. For the most part, they have all seemed to like my wallet best. Except for my wife. She normally doesn't mess with my empty wallet, unless she's occasionally going through it looking for unfamiliar and unrecognizable phone numbers with strange feminine names next to them.

It all started with my mom; she was the first woman I allowed to tell me what to do and what not to do. I think the arrangement went somewhat smoothly for the first few years. However, by the time I was around seven years of age, my patient subservience to what I, by then, concluded was nothing more than brutal tyranny, became strained, and I soon began to balk at her unrealistic demands. The breaking point of the natural bond between mother and male child and everything that bond represented, such as it was in our case, came one day while shopping on Capitol Way in downtown Olympia. It was late summer 1952 and we were chasing after school clothes, which had recently risen dramatically in price and I got to hear all about how "it was all those damn Koreans' fault."

I thought at the time my mom and I were getting along just fine. This has been a frequent and unfortunate self-conceived misconception regarding my dealings with women I seem to have inadvertently nurtured, for many decades. Following subordinately along behind her on the sidewalk, after exiting Goldberg's Department store empty-handed and on our way to Woolworth's, she loudly announced to me her sudden displeasure over my ineptitude for walking erect.

It had been, up till then, my personal belief that my natural slouch gave me certain advantages. Being slope-shouldered and slightly hunched over had served me well. I had already found more coins, candy, cool rocks, and countless other small objects of virtue on the ground and sidewalks than any adult on earth. Being slightly tipped forward also came in handy when ducking became a necessary maneuver. Many were the head-blows that faded into thin air because of my quick reactions and my natural slouch. My stooped posture enabled me to keep the sun out of my eyes, although it seldom shone in our state. However, by the end of what around here passed for summer, the backsides of my floppy ears looked like crisp bacon rinds.

"Can't you just *try* to stand up straight?" was her introductory declaration on the subject, followed by, "Throw your shoulders back and keep your back straight; look straight ahead, not down at the sidewalk."

She had, in an instant, taken it upon herself to straighten up my entire slack-shouldered seven-year-old existence. From Goldberg's to Woolworth's this went on. I was glad they were almost next door to the other in the same block, and that it should soon be over.

She had a point when it came to looking ahead. I did suffer somewhat from bruises on my forehead because of parking signs placed indiscriminately but always directly in my path. That's how she knew I was still behind her. The unmistakable "whump" when a warm thick skull hits the cool galvanized metal post of a parking sign, followed by the vibrating "tway-ay-ay-yangg" of the flat metal placard at its top, is a fond though distant auditory memory from the fog of my childhood.

It wasn't until what she said next that I understood why I must suddenly and unrealistically attempt to outwit evolution by quickly scampering ahead to lunge one rung up on Darwin's ladder. "Get up here and walk *next* to me for once, not *behind* me; or else people might think we're with *them.*"

And there they were — *"the goose people."* Although I'd seen the sad single-file family several times before, the possibility of being mistaken for one of their offspring had never occurred to me. They had always been hard to miss and, up till then I thought, easily distinguished from myself. My mom had now scared me.

The goose people, as she had always called them, consisted of eight somewhat unfinished people who individually were sad enough, but as a group — or more like a string — were an epic tragedy of indiscriminatorial and miscalculative copulatory behavior within a too closely confined immediacy, whether geographic or social.

Her exact words were "the whole family had gotten inbred."

All eight of them, from father and mother down to the last stairstep of the six goslings, looked exactly alike. Not similar, *exactly*. Chinless, blank and expressionless, large wet noses and a forward lean over their short stinted walk, each staring somewhat bulgy-eyed at the other's heels, except for the father, the lead goose, who was apparently rather deft at negotiating parking posts, lamp poles and, somehow, intersections. I never saw them converse, break formation, or wait for a streetlight to change. They appeared always to have the right of way and must have lived close to the downtown area because they seemed to know their way around, at least the lead gander did. And none had welts on their foreheads from colliding with misguided street signs. Each had an identical overbite to accentuate the lack of a chin. Always, at least up till then, whenever I'd seen them I had felt quite sorry for them. Now, the very sight of them irritated me, thanks to my mom and the remote possibility that I could be mistaken for one of their family.

I stood up straighter, pulled my shoulders back and, with my fingers, felt my lips, nose and chin to see if they might appear vertically arranged in their appearance to a profiling observer. It was hard to discern, so I leaned back even further, just in case. When we stopped unexpectedly, I nearly fell over backwards.

"Stop playing with your mouth like that, and *why* do you always have to act like an idiot whenever we come to town?" I knew it was nothing more than a rhetorical accusation, so I didn't answer and I did as she said. My nose started running.

"Whose fault is it they all got 'in bread' anyway?" I asked, thinking they'd eaten some bad sandwiches and that's how they all turned out that way. Remember, I was seven. She ignored my question and pushed the heavy Woolworth's door open.

As I crossed the threshold to enter behind her, I heard a car's tires softly squeak to an unanticipated stop behind me as the goose family evidently took control of the intersection. I exhaled heavily, slumped forward slightly and immediately spotted two pieces of hard speckled brown candy on the floor near the Woolworth's expansive candy showcases. My mom saw me see them and glared at me is if to say, "Just try it." By now it had become clear to me that she was looking for a fight, so I averted my eyes from the free candy; it was grossly against my nature and therefore quite difficult, but I followed the advice of her instructive and threatening glare.

I continued doing as she said for the rest of our shopping spree at Woolworth's, knowing it would soon be to no avail. There was going to be a fight of some kind; her mind was made up. The Koreans, and the somehow related subsequent overpricing of school clothes, especially the ones in my size, had ticked her off. She was festering. And I could feel it as only a child can; nothing's worse than feeling your mom fester when you're that small. The ominous helplessness is magnified if one is raised as an only child and you know you'll get to suffer her wrath alone.

By the time we were finishing a shared cheeseburger at the lunch counter, the bickering had begun; she had wanted a tuna sandwich, but I told her I was off regular bread for recent health reasons. I watched the clear condensation drops form into driplets on the stainless steel milkshake canister next to my emptying tall heavy glass of cherry milkshake. She was going on about something; I think it was something about how I had "no respect" for my clothes and how I "seemed to wear them out from the inside." I was savoring every last drop of my smooth cherry shake. A two-hundred-year-old waitress across the counter was hollering "ham-and-cheese-on-rye-extra-pickle-hold-the-mayo," loudly after taking a long pull from her cigarette and replacing it in the ashtray next to the toaster on the back counter. That's when my straw pulled up the last of my shake from the tall empty glass. It was my third loud "sssnaaarrrrkkkk" that set her off. Not the waitress, my mom.

"If you do that one more time with that damn straw, I'm gonna jam it in your eye socket and knock you offa' that bar stool, then I'm gonna kick your ass all the way over to the candy counter." Which was nearly on the other end of the store. Briefly, I wondered if those two pieces of speckled candy were still there. They'd be easily retrieved if I was prone and sliding past, assuming I was still conscious and the straw sticking out of my eye socket didn't interfere with my ability to snatch at the candy as I passed. But I was seven now and growing tired of the dictatorial and tyrannical methods of her stewardship in the case of my upbringing. So, although I stopped snarking on my depleted milkshake and had done as she said in that regard, I began to argue back; clothing and school being the issues. I reasoned with her not to send me to school and how I hated it anyway and how much money she'd save not buying school clothes and that's how we'd beat the Koreans and how I never was going to eat bread again and how she'd save money there too and how ... "Will you just shut up!" was her interruptive reply.

The two-hundred-year-old waitress rammed another tall tapered chrome-colored container cup under the twirler blade of the nearby green Hamilton Beach milkshake-making machine, making the machine automatically start to make another milkshake. I wished it was mine. The loud grinding whine nearly drowned out my mom's grinding whine. I wanted to drown my misery in somebody else's creamy milkshake. It was chocolate; I had watched her make it while mom ranted on. The two-hundred-year-old waitress took a long pull from yet another cigarette and looked at mom and me; then she rolled her eyes to a hundred-year-old waitress down the counter. I'd had enough. I decided to take a stand.

"I got another idea how to save money," I began to threaten loudly. Barely able to hear myself over the shrill whirl of the milkshake mixer, the heavy clatter of thick china, the bustle and stomp of shoppers behind us, and the yelling of the short order cooks in the kitchen, I raised my voice. "How's about I GO LIVE WITH THE GOOSE PEOPLE WHERE I BELONG?" That's when I realized the milkshake maker had been turned off just a moment before, while I was right in the middle of my empty ultimatum.

In that instant, time stopped at the downtown Olympia Woolworth's store — the whole store. Both floors and maybe the basement. There was no sound anywhere in the building. All conversation and movement ceased. Everywhere there were eyeballs. Out the corner of my bulging left eye I saw cigarette ashes noiselessly fall from the large and thickly red and wrinkled lips of the eldest soda fountain maiden, into the chocolate shake I once coveted for my own. Far behind me and to my right, near the front entrance and candy counter, I heard a malted milk ball fall to the floor, bounce twice and roll. I wanted to look.

Instead, I threw my shoulders back stiffly and maintained the defiant gaze between mother and son. Although she had been silent during the meltaway of the milkshake machine, she arched one eyebrow when the maltball beckoned to me; I knew that if I so much as twitched in the direction of the candy counter, I'd belong to the goose people. I tried again to sit up straighter as I felt my upper lip slip out past and droop over the lower one. I could feel my chin recede and my right ear flop forward.

It also became abundantly clear, in that moment of silence, that it wasn't just my mom who had nicknamed my tragic new family, "the goose people," as I had earlier assumed. All people in the greater Olympia area apparently referred to them in the same terms. Everyone in Woolworth's knew them by that name; that was obvious.

293

And now, the goose family was about to receive a nice new stoop-shouldered runny-nosed addition to their fine little gaggle; I wondered where they'd place me in line. I wiped my nose on the back of my hand and up my entire arm to where I spotted a glob of catsup near the inside of my elbow, which I licked off. I decided they'd probably put me in the middle, unless of course, I had to pass an I.Q. test. The familiar thrum of Woolworth's began to return and I detected some movement. Then, it quickly got back to normal, with archival waitresses yelling for pea soups, tuna salads, and french fries. Noisy cash registers, pots, pans and silverware. Feet shuffling, bags rustling, people talking. My mom, however, remained silent and motionless. From this, I knew she was still trying to figure out exactly where the goose family lived so that I could be delivered there — properly and promptly. Involuntarily, my narrow shoulders curled forward. Never breaking her granite gaze from my face, she shook her head slowly, paid the bill, and we slipped away to catch the bus for home.

The goose people didn't get me, lucky for them, or so my mom would remind me as the years went by. And I don't know if anyone at Woolworth's that day had told them I was headed there or not. It may be that somebody forewarned them I was on my way, because I never saw the goose family again, not that I was actively seeking them. Whether they packed up and escaped the unfair responsibility of getting stuck with another beak to feed by sneaking off, single file, in the middle of the night, or if they all got run over by an out-of-town rogue driver who didn't know the regional rules of right-of-way, or whether they all got jobs in the Washington State Insurance Commissioner's office, I'll never know.

Alan Gooseboy. Ya know, it's really not all that much different from the name I wound up with anyhow.

40

DOG AND PONY SHOW

T he last adventure I shared with Lonnie Woollett was when I was twenty-two or so. Lonnie, although by then relegated to a wheelchair for the rest of his life, still nursed not just a permanent case of paraplegia, but seemingly a permanent death wish as well.

I, however, still nursed illusions of becoming a stunt man in the movies someday. That's all behind me now. Now I'm too old and feeble to even think about it. Although, once in a while I fondle the remote notion of applying for the job of stunt man in the porn movie industry. At my advanced age I don't know what I'd be any good at though — faking a heart attack probably. Except under those circumstances, I'd no doubt have a real heart attack induced by visual overload from witnessing the "actors" ply their trade; so maybe I should just stop thinking about it altogether.

Lonnie's self-contempt and careless approach to what was left of his life nicely coalesced with my proclivity for seeing how close I could come to my own permanent self-mutilation. We conjoined on a hot lazy Sunday afternoon for an enjoyable intermissive display of theatrics — free theatrics for a theater load of theatergoers standing outside the downtown Tacoma "Roxy" theater, smoking.

It's called the Pantages Theater now, or I should say, again. In the first part of the last century, Alexander Pantages built a string of lavish vaudeville theaters up and down the West Coast. Downtown Tacoma boasts one of the finest restored examples to yet exist of his theatrical accomplishments. Nowadays it's a performing arts theater, a proud part of the downtown Tacoma Theater District's Broadway Center Complex — a shimmering group of nicely restored older theaters and some fancy new ones as well. Today, I live a block away.

But in 1967 it didn't shimmer. Like so many American towns, shopping malls had been springing up outside the downtown core, in the sub-urban regions, effectively emptying almost all of the economic energy from every affected American urban center — over the issue of parking. Everybody left the city to shop at the malls because of their vast new asphalt parking lots.

Even today most Americans will whine if they can't park *directly* in front of their desired *downtown* destination. Because that's not likely to happen, they still prefer parking and shopping at the mall. *Going to the mall* is the all-time great American pastime. They manage to ignore the fact that they have to walk an average of eight blocks — four each way — once they park and get to their preferred cookie cutter chain store or favorite fast fat vast chain restaurant inside the mall; where everything shimmers. I consider them a great waste of land. Still they build them. Still the demand for them grows. Exactly like the great American waistband.

Back then it was a movie theater called the Roxy, fifteen years before the local forward/backward-thinking preservationists saved it and returned to it its original name, Pantages.

And like much of downtown Tacoma, it shimmers once again. Not in the tinselly-plasticized oversized, supersized American mall mentality description, however. Like many culturally revived downtown American City cores, it shimmers from civic pride, historic preservation and elbow grease.

They hadn't yet invented the other all-time great American pastime: going to the local movie theater multiplex and *talking* through the whole damn film! That's because multiplexes hadn't been invented yet. Or maybe they had; apparently a few years had to pass for America to breed enough loose-tongued, empty-headed idiots with enough jugheaded ignorance to converse with each other while everybody else strains in polite silence to concentrate on the movie. It's because of those few idiots who can't keep their mouths shut during a film that I suffer from movie rage. Therefore, I no longer waste my money going to movies where I stand a good chance of ending up in jail because I may become motivated to assault the movie murmurers. I do, however, frequent the Tacoma Grand small-screen theater. There, the screening rooms are small enough I can reach back and slap someone if they are stupid enough to start blathering during the movie; or at least I can threaten to, which so far has been effective enough to afford silence for the rest of the flick.

Because people used to be considerate enough to shut up during the movie, the movie people used to provide two movies for the same price! And a cartoon! And sometimes a news item or two! And an intermission between the two main attractions! It was during one of those intermissions and on that particular Sunday afternoon when most of the theater patronage went outside to talk and smoke that Lonnie and I gave them some real entertainment and something to talk about. For years. For free.

The Ninth Avenue hill, which is quite steep — comparable to any that San Francisco has to offer — runs past the Pantages/Roxy Theater. Although not as long as some in the "City by the Bay," it can, if you are careening wildly down it in a wheelchair, take your breath away — along with your kneecaps, teeth, face, elbows, ability to form thought, speak during movies, blow smoke rings, and most everything else. And your life.

But that's what we had decided to do — both of us, in and on Lonnie's wheelchair. We would careen down the long steep Ninth Avenue hill. I've always been a good careener; I've made a career of careening. Decision made — Lonnie in his wheelchair seat with me standing behind him on the two protruding lower chrome extensions underneath and behind Lonnie. My hands were on the handgrips behind his shoulders. No brakes. No brains. No reason to be doing this in the first place.

"No problem! Let's start way up at the top!"

"Yeah, the top! Let's start clear up on Yakima Avenue," four or five blocks uphill from the Roxy corner of Ninth and Broadway.

This was one of the very few times I actually knew better and would not have hurled my young life directly at the reaper's scythe. But somehow I felt I had to do it for Lonnie's sake. He wanted once again to experience the thrill of trying to kill himself; with the bonus thrill of taking someone with him. And if you don't think Lonnie had a self-destructive end goal, let me let you in on something.

A couple years previous to this, after he had been physically rehabilitated to the best of the medical community's ability and had resigned himself to the fact he would never walk again, one night he up and threw his paralyzed leg and foot into the roaring fireplace. And he left it there until it was done. The University of Washington Hospital in Seattle spent the next year and a half rebuilding his severely barbecued lower leg. I think he did it partly for the dark satisfaction or reverse-narcissistic self-indulgence he felt; or *something*. I actually have no idea why he or anyone would throw their leg on the fire as if it was a soggy wet log, unless it was for all of the attention he might later derive from the pretty nurses at the University of Washington Hospital. Definitely not reason enough for me, nor for most any other female-attention-deficient young male, I'd say. But that was Lonnie. And no matter what, it can be safely said, Lonnie was *not* into taking care of himself.

Anyway, off we went. We began to coast down the long hill with several traffic lights, one at each block's intersection between us and ... what? A story to later tell? A massive scar to show off? Lonnie did it for self-something. I did it for Lonnie ... and ... okay, I did it just for the hell of it and I guess so that someday I could write this stupid story. Or this story of stupidity.

When we first started to roll, we were in complete control — control being an extremely relative term in this case. We were, in reality, in control of nothing. Not even our bladders. Lonnie's bladder was already out of control and was attached to a leg bag through a catheter. My bladder was attached directly to my confidence, both of which I visualized would soon be splattered all over Pacific Avenue down at the far bottom of the hill. I suddenly felt the need to pee, but it was by then too late. We quietly rolled on, the soft overburdened rubber tires of Lonnie's rear wheels barely heard on the gritty hot concrete.

The first couple of blocks went so smoothly I actually wondered why we had never thought of this before. It occurred to me that this may be one of the best ideas we'd ever had. We sailed along nicely and, for some reason, weren't killed or even honked at by cross traffic. I don't recall if we hit any green traffic lights that we intersected; I believe there just wasn't as much traffic then. As I mentioned, Tacoma wasn't the shimmering hub of activity it had once been or is now. The downtown area then barely had a detectable pulse, especially on lazy Sunday afternoons. So we weren't too concerned about intersecting cars.

Laughing and hollering like the pair of lunatics we were, we sailed down the hill and over the flat cross street and through the intersection at Tacoma Avenue, past the courthouse and jail. The interior of which, decades later, I would become quite familiar with through nationally and internationally infamous judicial miscarriages. As we crossed Tacoma Avenue, it crossed my mind that, although we knew there was nobody waiting at the bottom of the Ninth Avenue hill with a nice shiny trophy for our mantels, we might come across a cross cop waiting with some nice shiny handcuffs. Or somebody with straightjackets and a free ride to the nearby Steilacoom Mental Hospital.

After crossing Tacoma Avenue, the grade steepened considerably. As we picked up more speed, I shed my thin mantle of composure, stopped laughing and mentally prepared myself to shed blood, skin, and tears.

The front wheels of Lonnie's chair began to chatter and rattle like a kid running with a stick down a picket fence. My knees and teeth started doing the same thing. We quickly went into a horrible speed wobble and no longer did we sizzle in a straight line down the hill. Our erratically chattering front wheels took control of the remainder of our ride, traversing us in zigzag fashion back and forth across Ninth Avenue, which was becoming steeper yet. I had, by then, decided this whole thing was a bad idea; possibly our worst idea ever. Lonnie held on, leaned forward and laughed even harder.

The only time the violent wobbling stopped, and then only momentarily, was when we hit an irregularity in the roadway or when we careened all the way over to the sidewalk and grazed the curb, which would then send us back towards the other side of Ninth. How it is we never tipped over when we clipped the concrete curbs on those criss-crossings, causing thereby a crashing calamity, causes me to wonder, even now.

Somehow, by leaning this way and that, I had kept us upright and screaming towards our imaginary finish line. By the time we rattled, squealed and screamed past the old Rialto Theater just one block up the hill from the Roxy, we had grazed the sidewalk on our left and were now traversing down and across Ninth to our right, and we were headed right for the front lobby windows and box office of the fine old theater itself.

Although we had put together one hell of an act and could prove to be entertaining, we would never make it into the theater of course. Not that day anyway. Because, in order to bring down the house and literally "shatter the box office," we would have to pass through six inches of concrete curbing that we were now headed dead straight into. That's not to mention the fact that there was also a smoking, talking, surprised and puzzled crowd of around seventy-five theater patrons enjoying their outside Sunday matinee intermission on that same side-walk. Their clustered, smoky presence filled the sidewalk space between the looming curb and the theater's glass and tile facade behind them.

So, I knew we wouldn't be breaking into the movie business that day — the six o'clock news maybe, but not the movies. All the smoking movie talkies stopped talking, sucked in what could have been their final breaths of smoky air, and stood there, watching us coming straight for them. They were silent movie stills. They looked to me as if they were watching a 3D movie, transfixed, yet safe, appearing as if they were somehow insulated from the violent make-believe carnage they seemed to think they were viewing on a screen. A couple of them lit up fresh cigarettes. I was hoping that once we collided into the curb that we would fly into a few of the big soft ones. Our wheelchair sounded like a runaway freight train.

Watching the rigid curb growing closer, I knew it was going to have the final word on our outcome — or overthrow. I say *overthrow* because I knew exactly what was going to happen when Lonnie's front footrests hit that curb: he and I both would be thrown off the train. The crowd stuck around, mesmerized by their opportunity to witness a train wreck, obviously previously desensitized by too much violence in the movies. Lonnie was impersonating Slim Pickens who, at the end of the movie, "Dr. Strangelove," rode the bomb down, rodeo style, hollering like hell and waving his cowboy hat. I was impersonating Lucille Ball, whenever she inevitably came to the end of her rope, crying and yelling "RICK-EEEE."

Visualizing our runaway chair coming to the end of its line when it impacted the immovable curb, I knew that Lonnie, who was also handicapped by the fact he was in control of none of the muscles below his chest, would fly out first. I felt it was my responsibility to curb the damage to Lonnie. I visualized also the slim possibility that if I applied my rusty gymnastic-tumbling abilities to the situation, I could maybe reduce the gratuitous and needless bloodshed at the Sunday matinee. Knowing we both would be ejected, him out and me over, I prepared for the inevitable.

I timed it correctly — believe it or not — so that precisely when we smashed into the curb, I pushed myself up and off by jumping, hoping to go over Lonnie and maybe into space alone. As I said, it was clear that's what was going to happen anyhow. I was hoping to minimize the damage by trying to take control of an out-of-control situation. I was thinking that, by pushing downward with my legs and jumping up at the exact moment of impact, I might somewhat offset the inertia of Lonnie's forward moving body weight. That might prevent him from becoming a projectile mass ejected into the now silent Sunday mass and avoid causing a huge mess. I launched.

I'm happy to relate that, as bad as I am at thinking quickly and even worse at thinking quickly correctly, that day I was "on the money," and the show was able to go on. I don't mean the second feature inside the movie house; I'm talking here about the street performers.

The show's not over, folks.

ACT II

I perceived, as I sailed over Lonnie's head and shoulders, that I had been at least half right in my momentum and inertia-moving mass-transference calculations, because I went *up* as well as over, while holding onto the handgrips. Only my lower body and legs left the wheelchair. Like a gymnast on the parallel bars, I *swung* over Lonnie, upside down.

I was acting only by instinct, because there was no time for actual clear thought — as there seldom ever seems to be, in my case — intending to keep Lonnie in the chair and the chair upright. Somehow I then *turned in midair* to face him, and was thereby able to stop the chair from tipping forward by next planting my feet firmly on the sidewalk.

It worked. I had, as nearly as I can figure out, turned

completely around while I was directly over Lonnie — when my legs were pointing straight up at twelve o'clock, while we were in mid-crash, so to speak. Next, both my feet slapped flat backwards onto the Sunday sidewalk. I held onto the handgrips and came face to face with a hysterically laughing madman. Show over.

At this point, let me just say that the sidewalk full of people behind me who had watched our cheap theatrics was the *most receptive* crowd I have ever encountered in my life! Cigarettes were thrown in every direction and the roar of applause was deafening. They all agreed that the free entertainment outside was far better than what they had already seen inside, and they further agreed that it was probably better than what they expected from the second feature advertised overhead on the marquee. People in Tacoma do love good theater. Especially if it's cheap.

How I managed to *subconsciously* switch my hands as I turned to face Lonnie so that my arms weren't crossed when I came down, still keeps me awake at night. When my feet hit the sidewalk to stabilize the runaway locomotive with its loco cargo, my arms were locked straight ahead on each handgrip. Not only am I with no recollection of doing a handgrip switch, I have no idea *how* I did it.

Of course, we both acted nonchalant, as if we did this every Sunday when, in truth, I was just glad to be alive; Lonnie didn't care one way or the other.

Pulling lard-ass laughing Lonnie back up the Ninth Avenue hill — backwards to where we had left his station wagon — damned near killed me.

Very soon thereafter, someone invented wheelchair curbs. Not that that would have helped either one of us. We were each a different kind of handicapped.

41

THE BEGINNING

M y sole residency as the single populant of my very own lake — Lost Lake — down in the Nisqually Valley and inside a comfortable old house right on the water was fortuitous indeed.

I had gotten lucky — that is, until I later was besieged by rampaging, thieving savages. The terms of my tenancy had included completely cleaning the canyonous cellar of the decades of outdated clutter and ancient crap it had accumulated. Although the volume of junk seemed to be more than the cavernous Thurston County landfill could handle, it was still a good deal. A good deal for me. It took me only one full day and two over-heaped one-and-a-half-ton flatbed truckloads. Plus, I've always loved visiting the local dump; never know watcha' might find.

It wasn't my truck. It was a borrowed brand-new International Harvester, "Cornbinders," the old-timers used to call them, and this one had recently been purchased by Milt Willie, the iron-fisted sole proprietor of the Olympia Shingle Company in the Port of Olympia. Milt, over the years had done well for himself. He owned Olympia Tug, Olympia Sand and

Gravel, and way more commercial land, various other properties, money, and semi-ungrateful children and grandchildren
than most other people should ever have the privilege of
calling their own.

And Milt Willie had earned all of it. One way or another.

When I first came to know old man Willie, through his
Shingle Company and Roofing Supply business, he was
around eighty-years-old, cankerous, cancerous and as cantankerous as a three-month-old festering open wound under
saltwater in a swirling tide. He scared the hell outta me. And
he knew it. I kept any conversations with him brief; he was a
mean old codger, I thought. He had a nasty mouth. In fact, his
grandson was extra proud of him because he, Grandpa, had
years before been kicked out of the Elk's Club for profanity.
The Elk's club, mind you, one of the very fraternities begun
for the sole purpose of men gathering together to drink,
smoke, raise general hell and, at the very least, think and
speak profanely. Of course, over the years, that's all changed.

Any of the indigenous business owners that I knew in the
Olympia locale, knew all about Milt and how he apparently
also had written the original exhaustive Encyclopedic Concor-
dance on treachery. He was therefore admired by, if no one
else, his family and especially so by his grandson, Jim Willie,
who was my age, in his early twenties.

When I came to know him, Jim had been working part-
time at the Olympia Shingle Company roofing supply for his
grandpa, and he related to me some scary stories. About how
his grandpa, during the depression, started out penniless and,
through his own hard work, clever business chicanery, and a
natural aptitude for devious misdealing, had appropriated for
himself his empire as it was then. Apparently, according to
Jim, his grandfather's methods weren't the least bit questionable — they were *downright outrageous.*

When Milt in his younger years had worked for the long-since-gone original owners of the large Olympia Cedar Shake and Shingle Mill, before asphalt/asbestos shingles appeared on the market, he had a shot at becoming the mill's manager. So did another guy. Milt won.

He didn't have to actually shoot the other guy to become the new manager, but he may as well have. He damned near killed him.

The deal had been made, at Milt's suggestion — the smaller and less physical of the two contenders for manager — that they fight for it. As in … fight … physical hand-to-hand combat, and with no one else around. The deal was struck between the two eager young and anxious feisty cocks that they would secretly fight it out after work one day.

So they did. One night after shift at the designated place and on their agreed upon date, winner take all. No rules. No judges. No witnesses. No way was Milt planning on losing. He had made sure of it.

The fight raged on, on the waterfront, in and around the large wood buildings of the shingle mill, in the log yard area, among the machinery and between tall stacks of pallets of finished bundles of waterlogged western red cedar shingles. The fight also involved a lot of running.

The underdog, of course, was the smaller Milt, so he did all the running. The big guy did all the chasing. Whenever the big guy caught the little guy, he gave him a beating, all part of Milt's plan. Milt planned on getting beat a lot, so that after he'd led the big guy to the area where he had a gun stashed and where he planned to shoot him, it could be easily shown that it had been done in self-defense.

"Just look at me," Milt could say. "I knew he was gonna kill me if I didn't protect myself. He just went crazy! What else could I do? He was twice my size and there was no one else around to help me." In other words, no witnesses to the execution.

But they never got to that point, because somewhere in one of the huge warehouse drying sheds, among the maze of tall stacks of bundled shingles, Milt's earlier plan worked … well. Dodging and running around all the corners and aisles between tall mountains of cedar, Milt led his large quarry into the less questionable of the clever contingencies in his quest for mill managerial position. Outrunning and dodging around corners, Milt was able to conceal himself. And while in position and hidden behind and high-up between towers of cedar bundles, he then was able to tip the taller part of the stack, maybe forty or fifty chunky bundled blocks of heavy "pond dried" shingles onto his pursuer.

Milt had made it to mill manager; the other guy was laid up in the hospital for a few months.

Somehow, within a few years Milt actually acquired ownership of Olympia Shingle Company. Details were quite sketchy on how that came about, but I guess there weren't a lot of questions asked. More years went by and he somehow acquired Olympia Tug and Barge Company. Having never heard any stories regarding his acquisition of that, I had to assume that chances were it was also a smooth but colorful transition — knowing Milt.

And, as the story was related to me by his grandson, *this* is how he procured Olympia Sand and Gravel:

His tug and barge operation was the principal means of transporting eighty-foot-long ocean-going barges of fine sand, pea gravel and commercial gravel in the Puget Sound area. The sand and gravel were mined one place and brought into port, then stocked and sold by the long-established Olympia Sand and Gravel Company. Every month, scores and scores, maybe hundreds of loaded barges that were by then owned by Milt, freighted gravel and sand for the then-owners. For years.

Every month over a period of several years, Milt would hold back a few invoices. Every month there were a few unaccounted for and *uncharged* barge loads, that had in fact been delivered by Milt. Milt had the logbooks, dates, invoices and proof that his tugs and barges had made the deliveries. He just didn't produce all of the bills for payment. He was purposefully saving them up, letting the unpaid and unnoticed accounts payable to him accumulate. Not too many each month, just two or three.

During the next inevitable economic downturn — whether it was only a local recession or broader, I don't remember my having being told — Milt walked into the Olympia Sand and Gravel office with a box. Only after Milt dumped the contents of unpaid and overdue freight invoices like a box of rocks onto their sales counter, did the owners realize they were seriously in arrears. They suddenly and unexpectedly owed Milt a lot of money. His timing couldn't have been worse for them; nor better for Milt. The friendly and, till then, warm business climate that existed between the two companies and that had been enjoyed by both for so long was suddenly over. Milt had waited until the long-standing sand and gravel business was already struggling, and then capitalized on their economic misery by putting them out of it. Claiming loudly that he wasn't going to wait any longer for his money, he took legal action for satisfaction, was granted receivership, and soon owned Olympia Sand and Gravel Company — another smooth transition.

If all these and other stories were true, or any versions of them that bore a remote similarity, Milt was indeed a business barracuda. He extended credit to no one in his roofing supply trade, a policy which he often proudly announced, something his middle-aged sons also verified to me on more than one occasion.

"So why does he let *you* take so long to pay?" They would ask. "The old man doesn't carry *anybody — period.* He doesn't trust roofing contractors any farther than he can throw them, so you're the only one on the books. *Why is that?*" they asked, looking at me distrustfully.

"... I dunno," was my truthful reply.

Cash on the barrelhead. That's how old man Willie operated. And everybody knew it. However, over a period of some time I slowly became even more deeply in debt because of being in arrears on my materials bill. His sons studied me with sideways glares, befuddled. But they were no less befuddled than was I. At the time I was trying to build a small home, out of pocket; because my pockets were nearly empty, I was sort of "borrowing" from my materials account at Olympia Shingle Company.

"*Now* the old man tells me he's gonna let you borrow our new flatbed. He doesn't let *anybody* borrow equipment. Hell, *I get yelled at* when I drive it and I'm fifty-years-old, so why's he lettin' some kid like you use it? What're you holdin' over him?"

"... Nothin'. I just asked him if I could use it to go to the dump, and after he hollered and complained for a while, he said, 'arright.'"

"Buncha' bullshit! But I guess you got him buffaloed somehow." They always attempted by their gruff demeanor to be as barracuda-like in their positions as their father's sons as others expected of them.

"No, really, I don't know either. But did'ja know he's lettin' me tear down that old empty warehouse over there, for the huge beams?"

"What! Now he's gonna letcha tear the whole damned place down around our ears? What's next? You gonna be in his *will* too?"

"I'm not tearing the whole place down, just that one old warehouse, the one that's gettin' ready to fall down anyway."

"… Yeah, it should come down anyhow, I s'pose, before some waterfront wino sets fire to it and they all go up in flames." He was speaking about the other warehouses, empty and full, and the large silent antiquated shingle mill building itself. Shingles hadn't actually been milled in the tired old mill for a couple decades. They were now brought in from other small mills, mostly from the Olympic Peninsula and Aberdeen-Hoquiam area. I had seen some tags from a few places way up north around Darrington, Marysville, Everett, and sometimes Canada. But even though the sleepy old mill was out of work and the structure's roof and walls sagged in places, I could feel the hum.

More than once I wandered through the unemployed or more accurately, retired, sawmill's industrial innards, usually with Milt's grandson. Looking up at the motionless and outdated overhead lap-belt friction-driven wheelwork with its heavy canvas swags and rusted linkage, I could hear all the racket: the thunder and whine of belts and wheels, pulleys and the many saw blades. Large whirling circular saw blades. Swing saws, cutoff saws and ripsaws. Conveyers, strappers, banders and bandsaws. And, I could easily imagine the occasional finger landing softly in the sawdust under the screaming blades of the treacherous bandsaws. Along with the howling that would follow. Back then it was easy to tell how long someone had worked in one of the many shingle mills of the Pacific Northwest — by counting the spaces where once he had fingers. One missing finger for every five years was roughly the common formula. If you asked an old shingle cutter how long he had worked in the shingle and shake mills, he would just hold up his hand for tally. If there were two fingers missing you knew he'd put in at least ten years on the bandsaw or bolt splitter. He had worked there for around two fingers.

But much time had passed and it was all quiet then. As even more time passed, my materials bill quietly edged up while I squirreled away other building materials for a house I would begin building a couple years later. And quite naturally, when I did begin building, I had even less money to pay off my back due bill to Milt and the Olympia Shingle Company; so it continued to slide. Once in a great while I'd bring or send in a token payment so that maybe he wouldn't send his boys around to lop off one or two of my fingers. But not much; I wouldn't send in too much. I just didn't have it. The universal constant in every formula where money is owed is this: the person that is owed the money will begin to see *less and less* of the person that owes the money. *That* is a guarantee.

So, after a couple years, I still owed Olympia Shingle about twenty-eight hundred dollars; jumping ahead to 1970 or so. For some reason, it had been interest free, although I had been receiving dreaded, however polite, monthly bills for the unpaid balance. By that time, because of my embarrassing debt at Olympia Shingle Company, I was buying — cash only — most of my materials at other wholesale roofing supply places in the area.

Then someone told me they had read in the paper that old man Willie had died a couple weeks back.

I could almost hear the barracuda — wolf-boys — howling at my door. Eventually unable to bear up under the newly concentrated dread any longer, I decided to go in to face the issue and beg not only for my fingers, but for more time as well. I thought maybe if I approached the sons, empty-handed but with every intention, they might not devour me as they had been taught to do by Milt's example.

"Yah, well … you don't owe us any money. Not anymore," I was told with the same look of scorn and curious mistrust as always.

Thinking they were inferring that because I hadn't been around or paid, that I appeared to them as if I had been *acting* as though I wasn't in their debt, and that therefore I had been greeted with more of their sarcasm, I asked; "Whadya' mean I don't owe you? I get a bill every month for around twenty eight-hundred." A fortune to me at the time.

"Not anymore you won't," he said, holding his breath with the last drag from his cigarette, at the same time squashing it out in the heaping ashtray that overflowed onto his desk situated behind the sales counter. He then placed his open hands up on either side of his head in resignation, as if to say, *"I give up. It's out of my hands; I've tried everything. There's just nothing more I can do about it."*

Unable to comprehend, although I deeply wanted to, I stood there in silence waiting for an explanation. He was Milt's son, a chip off the old cedar block; he was up to something. Finally, he added, "The old man left instructions that when he died to erase your bill. So you don't owe us *anything*; understand?" He was disgusted.

Of course I didn't, so I didn't agree or even nod my head as if I might. But, I wasn't going to press the issue. I didn't ask *why* the old man had done it, because it was clear that his sons not only didn't *like* it, they didn't know either. I sheepishly thanked him.

"Don't *thank* ME! I had nothin' to do with it; neither did anyone else in the family! We'll never know why the old man did it either. He never did anything like it in his whole life; he never gave anybody anything EVER!" he yelled, slamming stuff around on the counter. "One hell of a way to run a business, that's all I can say. I guess the old man musta' seen *somethin'* in you."

And that was the end of it. My debts were lifted. I *had,* in effect, been in old man Willie's will! But I have no idea why. This just wasn't the way he did things.

Possibly he had devised other plans for me that were never fulfilled, but I don't think so. I think maybe he just wanted to cause some discord in his own family for the hell of it. As cantankerous as he was, that *was* the way he liked to do things. Maybe it was his way of annoying his less than grateful progeny. If so, I think he succeeded. But, as near as I can tell, the moral or whatever it might be called, of his message/ story was probably lost on everybody, including me. Although, don't get me wrong I was, and still am, very grateful for his generosity.

But back to my first story. On my second overflowing truckload of musty unidentifiable basement rubble from an arcane house on a "lost" lake, I didn't examine too much the contents for its future candidacy for the landfill; I was throwing it *all* away. As I had agreed to.

However, on my first trip, I remember pondering, if only briefly, about the origin and identification of a very few of the items that eventually found their way onto the truck and which were consequently sentenced to eternal sleep under the sand, gravel, and garbage of the county's landfill canyon.

On my second trip, I had even less patience or time to cater to my curious nature. As I furiously peeled back the layers of time to reveal many odd things that were way outside my frame of reference, things far before my time, I just threw them onto the heaping truckload; one glance and onto the flatbed it went. It was hot. I was tired. I needed to finish up and return Milt's truck, clean and before dark. There were a couple insignificant smaller items that caught my eye and those I saved from the dump and kept for many years. But they're all gone now. Most of the stuff from that cleanout was to be unceremoniously kicked off the truck, without fanfare, into the big hole of the Thurston County dump.

As frenzied as I was in my desire to finish loading and to quickly deposit the second run of nondescript old junk, my attention was somehow drawn to this cool brown bottle that sat among all the crap on top of a grimy workbench. I noticed that the quart-sized bottle had a fragile appearing glass handle attached to it. After glancing at its peculiarities and holding it up to the light for brief examination, I made the quick decision that it too was trash. Three separate times, one after the other, I had my arm cranked all the way back, ready to toss the amber-glass junior-football-sized cylinder onto the flatbed. I had earlier backed the truck up to where it was, nearly touching the cellar door, so it was a tempting throw. By now, I had burrowed a clear path to the back wall of the cellar and was, at that point, the farthest away from the narrow open cellar doorway that I could be, there, at that spot where the cluttered greasy workbench was. And if my forward pass didn't clear the doorway, so what? If it broke on the back of the truck bed or smashed on the door jamb, what's the difference? It's only a bottle and I still had a lot of sweeping to do anyhow. There was plenty of old broken window glass and other shattered jars, bottles, and jugs all over the place anyway; what would one more be?

But, it just wouldn't release itself from my hand. Three times I faked a forward toss. Three times I pumped the little brown jug overhand as if to complete a quick ten yard pass for a simple first down. But all three times, at the last split second, I simply could not release it. Each time my right arm went past my head, I seemed to involuntarily clutch that little brown glass bottle with its thin loop handle. Or maybe it was clutching me. Each time my arm dropped slowly in mid-throw and each time, I again examined the old root beer-colored bottle to see why it was refusing to become refuse.

Although I couldn't see the attraction, there seemed to be some kind of a cosmic connection that this bottle had with my right hand. This would by no means be the only time in my life that my right hand would refuse to become disconnected from an object within its grip, especially an occasional brown bottle; it would though be one of the most remarkable times; because, other than its obvious age, it was after all just an empty old bottle.

Apparently, because of its curiously crude appearance, along with the odd little handle on it, and because it managed to retain its grasp on life through an odd ability to cling to my hand and somehow maintain a strange hold on me, I set it aside. I sidelined it, pulled it from the game and benched it. It had been released, pardoned or at least reprieved, from permanent retirement at the landfill.

That was four decades ago.

And I still have it. My A.M. BININGER No.19 BROAD ST. NEW YORK cylinder jug with applied glass handle sits proudly in the sometimes sun of Western Washington on a series of shelves built just for it and my collection of other Bininger bottles, upstairs in our roof garden greenhouse. For nearly forty years I have periodically — no, religiously — picked up that nicely whittled and crisply embossed circa 1860's empty spirits jug and examined it. But, for the first three years, I had no idea why. Just as I have never figured out to this day what old man Willie saw in me during the several years I knew him, I couldn't figure out for sure what I saw in that old bottle.

Then, one day in 1970, while working in construction near Wallkill, New York, my wife of two years and I were vacationing and camping at the Rocky Neck Campground, close to Mystic and Niantic, Connecticut. On my way back from a grocery store to the campground, I stopped in at a local yard sale.

And there was this guy with, among all the usual stuff, tables full of old bottles. Why anybody would be selling old bottles was a mystery to me, so I asked him. Whereupon he proudly announced to me that he was a bottle digger and collector. He continued ranting about the life-enhancing benefits of empty old bottles for quite a time while I pretended to show some tactile interest. He was quite obviously nuts.

Then, I remembered my glass jug and told him about it. At first, he showed less interest in my feeble story and single bottle than I had in all of his, although he also politely pretended to listen. I proudly told him that I had memorized the "embossing" on it, a technical term he had only a moment before explained to me. I told him the raised lettering in the glass was "A.M. BININGER NO 19 BROAD ST NEW YORK" and that it also had a handle on it. His eyes lit up and he went quickly into his house.

Shortly, he reappeared with a thick hardbound book and laid it on the table, open to pictures of bottles. Right there was my bottle! Suddenly, he had my full attention; I actually appeared to own something with pedigree, a real-life documented historical artifact!

When he offered to give me fifty-dollars on the spot, for my little brown jug, I'd have to say that's when I probably became — in that very instant — a bottle collector. It was also

317

then that I wondered, and still do, *what else* I may have held in my hands and threw away on that hot summer day three years earlier.

He began ranting again, about how the most important bottle collector *ever* lived right next door. Some other crazy guy, named Charlie Gardner, and how Charlie's passion for old bottles had contagiously infected this guy.

Unaware at the time that he had passed their damn disease on to me, I eventually returned home to Washington State. Months later I sought out other similarly diseased people and quickly found some. When Wynn and Patti Smith, local bottle collector-dealers, saw my Bininger, they offered me *two hundred*-dollars for it! When they did that, I decided in that instant, to become not just a bottle collector, but a dealer as well!

And that's how it all started. Within four years of digging for bottles as a hobby, selling them at bottle shows and also through the *Antique Trader*, I opened my first small antique shop which I named "Sanford & Son" — stolen right from *"We buy junk and sell antiques"* Redd Fox, himself.

Soon, all of the whirlwind antique-buying cross-country road trips would start, along with all the stories they would spawn. All because of a bottle in my basement and a chance encounter with the next-door neighbor to the most famous bottle collector in history.

Soon also, the front-page color picture news stories of my antique slot machines being confiscated and sledge-hammered into rubble would appear. As well as stories of large trucks afire several times and in several states, along with trailer loads of antiques either on fire or disconnected and rolling aimlessly through the Wyoming, Montana and South Dakota sagebrush. People with guns. Murder and mayhem. Being jailed for stealing my own antiques. Being attacked by big guys with blackjacks, and being chased by packs of wild dogs.

And, stories of how I was able to procure for myself the enviable position of record holder for — so some thought at the time — *perpetrating* the largest counterfeit antiquities scam endeavor *ever* in history, except for canvases. [For an excellent preview into that story please obtain for yourself a copy of the highly insightful book by Leigh and Leslie Keno, *Hidden Treasures* published by Warner Books.] I'm sure you have seen the very knowledgeable and highly accredited Keno brothers if you have ever watched "The Antiques Road Show." In their book you will please note that the Keno brothers *also* started out as bottle diggers. So we have a lot in common. Except, I just can't visualize Leigh or Leslie running down runaway trailers in the sagebrush, extinguishing burning trucks with cartons of milk, being jailed for stealing their own stuff, or being chased around by people with guns or big knives. Or by wild dogs. Or having, while they slept, their shoes stolen from them in the middle of the night in the middle of a church lawn in the middle of Jamestown, New York — the same night that two other campers, sleeping peacefully and legitimately in the real campground nearby, and where my friend Jim and I nearly checked into, were stabbed to death as they slept.

Other stories stemming from me include trusting more than one elderly man in his seventies, and winding up, more than once, on the national news, international news, and ABC's Primetime Television. All because *some* elderly people lie.

Stories of buying, then building a market through the international media, and subsequently auctioning off the only known complete *ticket* from the Titanic, setting as I did so other world records — only to be sued for doing too good a job of it immediately thereafter and *losing* because of *one juror* who just *happened* to be a judge's wife.

And "junking" in Brimfield, Shipshewana and Nappanee. Deadwood, South Dakota and Mexico, New York, both Buffalos (New York and Wyoming); "Where the Virginian got his man." Stories of crossing paths with crazy people at Kane County flea markets in St. Charles, Illinois to buying huge stacks of cool rusty old "nineteenth century" cast-iron wood-handled waffle irons at a dust devil of a tiny flea market — somewhere in two-dot Nebraska — only to find out when I got home that they were all Teflon coated reproductions made in China.

Details of these and other stories — from childhood to old age — from humor to outrage — are soon to be available in Volume III.

About The Author

Soon to appear at a freeway exit near you!

Living the life of an aged milktoast antiques dealer, Alan Gorsuch could hardly get arrested anymore, until he began writing — and what he calls "marketing" — a couple years back. Now he gets picked up, somewhere, just about as often as his books: around twice a week. No, that's not true at all; sales of his first volume have gone rather well, and that's not counting the ones that were simply snatched off the shelves and burned by: protestants, scandinavians, optimists, coin collectors, school teachers, pentecostals, winos, catholics, crack dealers, agnostics, apathetics, metaphorphisists, volkswagen mechanics, pessimists, oystershuckers, nudists, stray cats, cops, poultry farmers, civil war survivors, state employees, mental health professionals, former classmates (both alive and deceased), nearsighted clairvoyants, and almost every living humorist here and abroad. And dentists. And loggers.

When he's not out by the roadside or standing in a ditch somewhere "promoting" *Volume One*, he can be found at home or in their downtown Tacoma, Washington, antique shop, Sanford & Son, with his very patient and somewhat understanding wife Cheryl and Peanut, their cat. There Alan sits around and whines about how unfairly life has treated him, all the while hoping someone will bring him candy.*

* He does NOT consider horehound to be candy.